WRESTLE BLACK BART

BLACK BART
VINNY BERRY

CREDITS:
Written by Vinny Berry
Photography by Rick Harris, Jon-Paul Le Blanc & 4 Corners, Peter Lederberg, Greg Bowle Collection, M. Roof Photography, Duane Long, Ric Davies, & James Beard
Produced by Wrestleville
Layouts - Wrestleville
Cover Art & Graphics – Alyssa Berry
Website – www.wrestleville.com

All the people in this book were important to Bart's life from one time to another. We have tried to best recreate events, locations and conversations from their memories. In order to maintain anonymity, some names have been changed or omitted of a few individuals, places, identifying characteristics, and details - such as physical properties, occupations and locations. Although the author and publisher have made every effort to ensure that the information in this book was correct at press time, the author and publisher do not assume and hereby disclaim any liability to any party for any loss, damage, or disruption caused by errors or omissions, whether such errors or omissions result from negligence, accident, or any other cause. The stories contained in this book are the way Bart remembered that they occurred. All stories are property of Wrestleville.com.

WRESTLE BLACK BART

ISBN: 979-8-9856684-5-2

Third Printing

www.wrestleville.com

TABLE OF CONTENTS

PROLOGUE

My friends and family know me as Rick Jones. Since the late 1970s, wrestling fans have seen me in action under such names as the Arkansas Strangler, Hangman Rick Harris, El Lobo, Mountain Man Harris, and a few others. My notoriety grew tremendously in December of 1983 after Dusty Rhodes put the Black Bart gimmick on me. Working in the Florida territory was a special time in my career. I had a decent spot on the roster and the money was exceptional. It felt as if all the years of hard work that I had invested into my profession up until that point had paid off.

I felt as if I had found my place in professional wrestling. However, some more triumphs and disappointments awaited me. The world would never see me wrestle as The Undertaker, an idea that Dusty had presented to me in the fall of 1990. However, Vince McMahon Jr. thought that the ominous character was a far better fit for Mark Calloway. You'd probably think that I would be bitter over something like that, but I'm not. Vince was right. Mark was, is, and always will be The Undertaker. It's how situations sometimes work out in the trade of professional wrestling. I've learned not to take things too personal because pro wrestling is a business. The wind may sway your way and sometimes it blows in a different direction. You can only hope for not too much shit to be in that passing gust.

Over the years, there have been a lot of negative things said about professional wrestling, but it has been very good to me. I think that has a lot to do with me being good to the sport. In my nearly three decades of in-ring activity, I am proud to say that I have never hurt one of my many opponents. I can't say that for everyone who has laced up a pair of wrestling boots, but that's on them.

During my time in the sport, I saw my share of

drugs and there was a ton of alcohol consumption. I have no problem saying that a majority of the boys medicated themselves with something when I was active in wrestling. From time to time, I did drugs, but it wasn't my thing. I drank a lot of alcohol, and it's safe to say that I consumed a minimum of 12 beers before I ever stepped into the ring for a match. If you worked as intensely as I, and my colleagues, did back then; you would understand. Today, that sort of practice might not be accepted. However, at the time we deemed it necessary.

If I were to create a Mount Rushmore to honor four professional wrestlers who were my all-time favorites, I would include John Shaw (Ivan the Terrible), Dusty Rhodes, Fritz Von Erich, and Skandor Akbar. These were the men who earned my respect and impressed upon me what wrestling truly is. I would never place Black Bart at that same level. I will say this about myself with full confidence when it comes to my career in pro wrestling, I am and have always been the real deal!

Black Bart

FOREWARD BY JOHN BRADSHAW LAYFIELD

To me, Bart is a guy that we can call a mechanic. You have to have guys that can work and guys that can do anything. A mechanic is completely different than a jobber. A mechanic can work in the main event, he can carry the title, and he can also put somebody over. Bart could do anything. He could be in the main event and if you needed a champion, he could be a good champion. If you needed him in the first match to put over a young guy and make him look good, he could do that too. Bart was a tremendous worker. You need guys like Bart in every territory because they're indispensable. Bart's a good guy to be in a locker room with, because he's a good guy. Plus, he's very entertaining and a lot of fun, because he hated being bored. Bart had the gift of banter and he could bicker with the best of them. He was extremely intelligent because someone couldn't cut promos like he did if he wasn't. Bart loved being a part of professional wrestling and being around the boys. He was truly good at everything he did.

John Bradshaw Layfield (JBL) - WWE

AKA - Johnny Hawk

Photo courtesy of James Beard

James Beard & Johnny Hawk (JBL) - Dallas, Texas

CONTRIBUTION FROM JAMES BEARD

Looking back on almost 40 years of being in the wrestling business, I have been very fortunate to have worked with many of the very best wrestlers from all over the world. When I'm asked who I enjoyed being in the ring with most, one of those names I always mention is Rick Harris, AKA Black Bart.

The simple reason for my love of working with Bart has to do with the fact I always knew his matches would be both entertaining and sound in psychology. Plus, he was one of those who understood how to interact with me in order to get the best out of the wrestler/referee relationship, which if done correctly, always enhances the way a wrestling match is perceived by fans. In short, he was a joy to be in the ring with, regardless if he was the guy fans loved or hated. He always knew how to get the most out of any situation and that made it fun and utterly satisfying for me to be involved.

I tell folks that some might have thought my nose and Bart's were joined together due to the times we would get into rather intense and visually demonstrative discussions in the ring about one thing or another…usually something he had done to get under my skin…or vice versa. Regardless of the reason, our interactions were often loud and obviously a result of some degree of conflict that enhanced the goings on in the ring.

The truth is, in real life outside the ring, we have been close friends for many years. My love and respect for Bart is just as real as the in- ring disagreements appeared to be to fans. Bart is one of those guys you could always count on and believe in when it came to being a true friend and someone who stood up for what was right in life or in wrestling. In the dressing room, he was a leader and one of those who made sure respect and decorum was in order. In short, Black Bart was always one of those guys you wanted and needed if you had anything to do with running a wrestling program or business. But, most of all, he has always been a true friend and someone my love for is honest and long lasting.

This is his story, told his way. Trust me, Bart's way is always unique, entertaining, and true to his character. He might step on a few toes. You can take it from me, if you get nose to nose with him, you will believe in everything he says being exactly how he sees it.

James Beard - Pro Wrestling Referee

Photo by Jon Paul LeBlanc & Four Corners Photography

James Beard

WORDS FROM SAM HOUSTON

I first met Bart in New Orleans, Louisianna. He was wrestling as "The Hangman" Rick Harris. I was 17 and at a crossroads in my life. I had just been released from the hospital after complications from a tonsillectomy that nearly ended my life. My father tried to take away my childhood dream of being a wrestler. That night I met Bart; we talked about the business. I asked him if it was worth it? He told me, "Look at me, I'm rasslin in the Superdome, living the dream, yeah, it's worth it kid." Hangman wasn't there long but he gave me the inspiration to keep trying. I got my chance, took it, and a couple of years later I stepped in the ring with a familiar face but a new name, "Black Bart". We had epic battles to say the least. Some of the absolute best matches of my career were with him. Bart was the first guy that I had a program with and I learned so much. Bart, you are Aces to me. We've faced each other, tagged together, and set the bar high, thank you for it all.

Sam Houston

Photo by Jon Paul LeBlanc & Four Corners Photography

Black Bart & Sam Houston

Photo courtesty by Sam Houston

Sam Houston - 1985

CHAPTER 1 - GROWING UP IN NORTH TEXAS

I had the great fortune of being reared in North Texas during the 1950s and 60s. My family lived in a small town on the outskirts of the northeast side of Fort Worth. Back then, we felt a strong sense of community that bonded the people together in our area. Our town was Haltom City. It was kind, friendly, and supportive. I was the fifth child born out of six to my parents. Leon and Mary Ellen were the oldest, then there was John and Linda, and after myself, Judy arrived. Judy might have thought that she was my parents' favorite, and my siblings and I lovingly joked that Judy was their pet. Anytime that we saw either my mother or my father, Judy was there. The three of them were tight, but my entire family was close. I am blessed to say that I grew up in a family that was loving and caring. We might have had our differences from time to time, but nothing that we couldn't work through. Despite some of the challenges we faced as a family, we were determined to persevere and overcome our difficulties no matter what.

Most Texans refer to the Lone Star State as God's country, and it is! However, professional wrestling fans of specific eras will tell you that it is Von Erich's country, and that couldn't be truer. The Von Erich name was, is, and probably always will be synonymous with professional wrestling in Texas. My father's favorite wrestler was Fritz Von Erich. I thought that the master of the Iron Claw hung the moon until I ended up working for him in the 80s. Fritz had a larger-than-life personality and when he said he was going to kick somebody's ass, he did it! That might have been one of the reasons why my dad liked pro wrestling so much. I think he respected the fact if people had issues with each other, they solved it right then and there. I liked wrestling because I found it so captivating and exciting.

The athletes and characters inside the ring drew me in with their personalities and theatrics. Pro wrestling was an interest my father and I shared. It provided something for us to talk about and it allowed us to spend time together when we watched it on television. However, I had to find out the hard way what happens if I got too excited while watching the action on our set. Within seconds of standing in front of our black and white T.V. screen, I felt something hit me in the back of my head. I didn't know what it was, but I saw stars. I thought Johnny Valentine reached out of the television set and hit me! As I came to my senses, I realized it was my dad's work boot that made contact with my melon.

"Ricky, sit down. I can't see what's happening when you do that!" my father shouted.

"That hurt," I replied as I rubbed my hand on my head.

"It's going to hurt worse if you do it again!" he said with a stern tone.

"I'm not going to do it again, I promise," I persuaded.

"Don't make promises you can't keep Ricky," my dad said to me with a smile on his face.

"You know how I get when I'm excited Dad," I grinned.

Quickly I returned to my place on the living room floor and refocused on the match in progress. Wrestling was an escape for me.

My father was a foreman of a spray-painting crew at the Molly Trailer Company in Fort Worth. He worked from the break of dawn until sunset. He went to work day after day and if he could pick up side jobs on the weekend, he did that too. I thought it was cool that my father knew how to properly paint cars. When I got older, if I ever wanted to change the color of any of my vehicles, I could go to him and he always helped me with that task. The paint job was professional at a fraction of the normal cost. My dad was a hell of a mechanic too. He always worked on our cars, and taught me and my brothers how to do that too. When my father wasn't working, he liked to hunt and fish. I can still remember the smile on my dad's face when he was out in the woods enjoying nature.

As far back as my earliest memory, my mother had always been bound to a wheelchair. She suffered from rheumatoid arthritis and it caused her a great deal of pain. The only time I didn't see my mom in a wheelchair, was when I came across some old photos of her from when she was younger. She didn't work and she rarely left the house. Rheumatoid arthritis affected her joints and her knuckles, and because of the affliction her fingers were knotted up. The image of her crooked fingers are something I wish I could forget. It was hard to watch my mother struggle with her affliction. Since my father worked all the time, as soon as my siblings and I were old enough to walk, we were responsible for all the cooking, cleaning, and taking care of my mother.

When I wasn't helping my mother, I hung out with my friends. We were typical kids. We rode bikes, went fishing, threw the football around, and we wrestled. Back then, one of my best friends was Rick Miller. We were close in age and we both liked wrestling. I can't tell you how many times Rick and I laid a piece of old discarded carpet down in one of our front yards to wrestle on. Having matches with the other kids in our neighborhood took up a lot of our time. I loved stepping on that old dirty mat. When I faced my opponent, I always pretended that I was in a real wrestling ring in front of a cheering crowd. I don't know if my friends imagined the same things that I did or even if they felt the same way about wrestling as I did. None of that mattered to me. In my mind, I was bad to the bone, and in reality, I was. I had an advantage over the other kids, I was bigger. I had always been a good size boy. I wasn't chubby, I was just taller than my friends and I had a little more meat on my bones. Everyone always thought

I was a couple of years older than my peers, but actually, we were all the same age. Each time that it was my turn to wrestle, I morphed into my favorite in-ring performer.

"I'm going to get you with the Iron Claw," I snarled as I lunged toward a smaller kid who stood across from me on our mat.

"You better not hurt me, Ricky," my opponent whimpered.

"My name isn't Ricky, it's Fritz Von Erich. I'm the master of the Iron Claw," I declared as I closed in on the boy.

"If you hurt me, I will tell my daddy," The kid said.

"Go ahead and tell your daddy. I will put the claw on him too, you big baby!" I returned.

My size, confidence, and my ability to get physical was the main reasons I had one of the better wrestling records on my street. If the kids that I was wrestling with were smaller than me, I never lost. From time to time, I got challenged by someone my size, but even if their strength was equivalent to mine, they never outlasted me. My determination to come out on top always prevailed. It felt at times as if I was unstoppable!

Growing up in the Dallas – Fort Worth area had its perks. For a kid who loved professional wrestling, having the events just miles from where we lived was convenient. Back then, the matches in Fort Worth took place on Monday nights at the Northside Coliseum. Eventually, they moved to the Will Rogers Coliseum. My dad couldn't afford to take me to the events. Having five other siblings and knowing how hard he worked to provide for us, I never wanted to ask him to take me. I knew that he didn't have the money for that sort of thing. Sitting with my father and watching our favorite wrestlers resolve their issues in the ring through television brought me great pleasure. However, that didn't stop me from trying to figure out a way to get to events so I could watch the matches in person.

I think I was about eight years old when my friend Rick got a job selling sodas at the Northside Coliseum. In that day and age, a person who was willing to work didn't need to be 16 years old, they just needed to have a note signed by their parents. The cool thing about Rick working at the wrestling matches was that he could always bring one guest, and I was ever so grateful when he brought me. Watching such great wrestlers as Johnny Valentine, Pepper Gomez, Killer Karl Kox, and Duke Keomuka had me pinching myself to make sure I wasn't dreaming. Professional wrestling was cool to me because when I was watching it, I wasn't thinking about anything else.

By the time I was 13, I was flipping hamburgers in Fort Worth at the Riverside Drive-in. I can still remember how hot it could get standing in front of that flat stainless-steel grill. The sizzling sound of the hamburger patties frying to perfection has always stayed with me. One of my favorite memories of the drive-in was eating a hamburger that I cooked myself when my shift was over. Life didn't get any better than that for me back then. My parents instilled a strong work ethic in me and my siblings. All of my brothers and sisters worked outside of the home, except for Judy at that time. She was busy keeping up with Mama and all the chores at home. The money that my siblings and I made at our jobs went to my parents to help support the family. If we didn't work throughout the entire year, we all especially worked in the months leading up to Christmas. The extra money helped my dad with the additional expenses during the holiday season. I have fond memories of working at a Christmas tree lot that belonged to the family of one of Leon's friends. I did every job that was associated with the tree business and I worked there seasonally for years.

Growing up, I was always athletic. From the time I was in elementary school, I participated in a variety of sports.

Each year, I consistently signed up for basketball, track and field, and football. I excelled in those sports mostly because I enjoyed being a part of them. I had so many ribbons, medals, and trophies collectively, that I couldn't remember when I received some of those awards. The trophies found their home on top of my dresser, and any open space on my bookshelves. I also had a small pile that accumulated in my closet. I played baseball for a short period, but I couldn't get into it. Baseball was just not my thing. I wanted to focus on the sports that I enjoyed. I loved playing football. I was damn good at it too! As far back as I can remember, I wanted to play professional football. Playing in the National Football League was something I had always hoped I could do.

By the time I entered Haltom City Junior High School, I had a reputation for being one of their top athletes. Sports seemed to be easy for me. Don't get me wrong, I had to work out and I had to practice, but it was fun! I was blessed with good genes and my body continued to grow. By the time I was 15, I was the same size or even bigger than some of my male teachers. Junior High was an exciting time for the Haltom City Tigers. From 1969 until 1971 our team was undefeated. I always played on the field. I played on the offensive side, I played on the defensive side, I played on the punting and kicking teams, and I was NEVER on the bench! The reason why the Tigers were so good, was because every kid that played on that team put in the effort. We all wanted to be a part of a winning organization. Walking on my campus and going to the weekly football pep rallies while wearing my team jersey gave me a great sense of belonging. Knowing that my dad and other family members were in the stands watching me play, made me want to leave all my strength and energy out on the field.

The football team was a lot different when I made my way over to the Haltom City High School. The coach for the Buffalos then was the late Joe Bob Tyler. Then Tyler had a winning track record, and today his legacy is honored in the Texas High School Coaches Hall of Fame. Despite having a strong leader in Coach Tyler, WE SUCKED! In my junior and senior years, the team was lucky if we finished with a four and six record. A lot of my teammates looked baffled walking off the field after a loss. I wasn't puzzled at all. I knew what was happening! The same guys that I played with in junior high were no longer interested in giving all their efforts on the gridiron. All my buddies decided that it was more important to chase girls and to get high. Their lack of effort didn't detour me from achieving the goals that I had set for myself. I was determined to play professional football.

My senior year in high school was memorable, even though the Haltom City Buffalos didn't make the playoffs. It brought me great honor when I was presented with a couple of prestigious awards. In 1974, I was recognized for my accomplishments with an honorable mention from the All-American team and the Texas Blue Chippers Association. That same year brought me another surprise when I was presented with the Christian Athlete of the Year Award. The man who handed me that plaque was Dallas Cowboys legend, Tom Landry. To say that my family was proud, was an understatement! When it came to sharing his feelings, my dad was a man of few words. However, no number of words could equal the love and approval I received from the smile that was on his face that day. It is something I will cherish for the rest of my life.

A specific memory stands out in my mind from my senior year in high school football. My team traveled in the northwest direction of the state in Texas. The team on the schedule for that night was the Raiders from Wichita Falls Rider. It was sort of a homecoming for Coach Tyler, who left Rider in 1969 to coach for Haltom City. Understanding the competitive nature of sports, I knew he wanted us to go up there and whoop his former team's ass. We didn't! I think the final score was 74 to 10, but when the score is like that, who cares what the final tally of the game is?

At some point in the fourth quarter, somewhere about the time that I had accepted the fact that we were not going to win the game, I was blindsided and sent to the ground by a member of the opposing team. As I attempted to get myself up from the field, I realized that the kid was on my back and unknowingly he had his fingers in the ear holes of my football helmet. As I broke free from his grasp, this particular player pulled my helmet off my head and I watched him throw it down the field. At that moment, I had a split second to decide to make one of two choices. One, return to the sideline, or two, kick my opposition's ass. I chose option number two. Knowing that I wasn't going to hurt him with my fists since he was all padded up and still wearing his helmet, I picked the player up and slammed him onto the field as hard as I could. At that moment every player from each team stormed the field. The adults in charge lost all control and the kids went crazy. As I recall, that was my very first battle royal, but it wouldn't be my last! When our fight was broken up and the referees restored some kind of order, I knew that Coach Tyler had some words waiting for me. He let me have his fury as I returned to the bench with the rest of my team.

"What are you doing out there, Rick?" Coach Tyler shouted.

"Did you see what he did to me out there?" I asked.

"I saw what you did and that is unacceptable! Sit Down!" He demanded. "You will never play another down of football!

"You're right Coach, the season is over," I replied.

"No! Your football days are over Jones! You got it?" Coach Tyler yelled with a commanding tone.

"We will see about that!" I added as I turned my attention back to the game.

Our season ended unfavorably; the same group of guys that played lights-out football during junior high couldn't keep it together. I know this might sound like an exaggeration, but my teammates lost their focus, but I didn't. The highly publicized award banquets I attended and the scholarship I received to play football at Howard Payne University in Brownwood, Texas proved everything to me. I truly believed in my heart, that I was on my way to achieving my lifelong dream of playing in the NFL. Unfortunately, after I arrived at college and went to my first practice with the Yellowjackets, was when reality sunk in. Football at Howard Payne University was taken very seriously. When I was there, Dean Slayton was the head coach. The coaching staff lived, breathed, and ate football. There were so many coaches assigned to that team, that it was impossible to meet them all. I can tell you that I never met the head coach. I have no idea where Coach Slayton learned his coaching methods, but his approach toward football was grueling and torturous.

The preparation for the football season took place in the Summer. The Summers in Texas can easily see the temperatures rise well past 100 degrees. Imagine running around with the sun bearing down on you all day long while wearing a football helmet and pads. It was scorching! We had to be on the field and ready for practice by 4:30 in the morning. It was common to run drills and different formations until midnight. Now, when I was in high school, we did what we called two-a-days. In college, we did three-a-days and because of it, those who were expecting to make the team were only getting 4 hours of sleep every night, if they were lucky. I put up with Coach Slayton's system for five days. On the fifth day, I decided to quit football and leave Howard Payne University. So, I packed up my Ford Mustang, gave the campus one last single-middle finger salute, and I headed back home to Haltom City. I left without telling Coach Slayton or anyone else on his staff about the decision that I had made.

A few days later after being back home, the telephone rang. It was Coach Joe Bob Tyler. He asked me to come to his office at the high school so he could talk to me. He told me over the phone that he received a call from Coach Slayton about my departure. I agreed to meet with Coach Tyler. When I arrived at Coach Tyler's office he was sitting with Nolan Ryan. At the time Ryan was the pitcher for the California Angels and I was a bit shocked to see him. I had no idea that Nolan Ryan and Coach Tyler were friends. He stayed in the office as my former coach attempted to talk some sense into me about the decision that I made for leaving Howard Payne.

"Rick, what did you do?" Coach Tyler asked.

"I left. I came back home," I spoke.

"I see that, but why did you leave? You walked out on a great opportunity," he said to me with a puzzled look on his face.

"I'm done with football and I'm done with Howard Payne." I returned.

"Rick, it has only been five days. Don't you think that you owe it to yourself to give it more time than just five days?" the coach challenged.

"Coach Tyler, if I wanted to be in the Army, then I would have joined the Army. I went to Brownwood to play football and that sucked! I'm done!" I responded with a strong tone.

"We might be able to talk to Coach Slayton and get you back on the team," he mentioned.

"I don't want to be back on the team! I'm done!" I replied.

"Rick, what are you going to do?" he asked.

"I'm going to become a professional wrestler," I stated.

"Rick, go pack your stuff in your car and get back down

to Brownwood," Coach Tyler demanded.

"I can't go back to Howard Payne, Coach. I have to see if I can make it in professional wrestling," I exclaimed.

Nothing else was said about me returning to play football. I looked Coach Tyler straight in the eye and stuck my hand out to shake his. He lifted his arm and grabbed my hand and he gave it a firm shake.

"Thank you for everything Coach," I said.

"You're welcome, Rick. Thank you for all of your hard work," Coach Tyler returned.

I turned to Nolan who was sitting there quietly the whole time. I put my hand out in front of him and we shook hands.

"It was a pleasure meeting you, Mr. Ryan," I smiled.

"Good luck Rick," Nolan replied.

As I walked out of Coach Tyler's office, I had a strong feeling of confidence that I was doing the right thing. I needed to see if I could make a career for myself in pro wrestling. Now, I just needed someone to train me in the sport. As for Coach Tyler, that was the last time that I ever saw him alive. Sadly, the next time that I saw him was at his funeral in 2010.

CHAPTER 2 - MY WRESTLING TRAINING

In the Fall of 1974 and into the Spring of 1975, the pro wrestling scene in North Texas was at its best. Superstars such as Red Bastien, Blackjack Lanza, Jose Lothario, Mad Dog Vachon, Roddy Piper, Don Muraco, and many others made their presence known inside the ring during that period. I went to the matches as often as I could and I watched wrestling every time that it was on television. Becoming a pro wrestler was all that I could think about and it was something that I had to do. I don't know how to explain it, but to say that I was driven to pursue pro wrestling was an understatement. As soon as I returned home from Brownwood, Texas, I reconnected with my friend, Rick Miller. He immediately informed me that there was a wrestling school in the area that had opened up. Rick said that he met with the trainer and mentioned my name to him. That school was located in a gym in downtown Dallas across the street from the Sheriff's Department. It was about five miles away from the Sportatorium.

The training facility was an old red brick building and it was right next to Doug's Gym. Doug's Gym was a weightlifting facility and it was always full of wrestlers, serious weightlifters, and bodybuilders. In the wrestling facility, there was a bathroom in the back where the students could change into their workout clothes when they arrived. The ring that was used for training, was in the middle of the main room. It was an old boxing ring and I can still remember how hard it felt when my body landed on it. Some rings are 16 feet by 16 feet and some are smaller. Some stand shorter and some are taller than others too. I found out as time passed how important it was to understand the different characteristics of each ring that I stepped into before the match even started.

It was there that I met Jim Wehba. Jim was from Texas and was a professional wrestler with an old-school style, which was common for guys of that era. Jim loved Texas football. He followed all the college teams, but what was so impressive to me was his knowledge of high school football in the Lone Star State. He knew all kinds of information about teams in Houston, San Antonio, Waco, and just about any other city. Jim knew the coaches' names, the players, their accomplishments and the team's records. I don't know how he did it, because this was before the age of the internet. The thing that I found most interesting about Jim, was that he knew of my high school football career like the back of his hand. He knew of all my accomplishments, who my coaches were, and even the guys that I played with. There was almost nothing that he didn't know about the topic of football. Eventually, I found out Jim's wrestling name was Skandor Akbar, and he went on to become a villainous wrestling manager of the heel stable called Devastation Inc.

The wrestling school was run by John Shaw. In the world of professional wrestling, John was known as Ivan the Terrible or Ivan Bulba. I always called him Ivan and he was a good person. I believe he had his last match sometime in the 1950s. It seemed if he liked someone, he took a genuine interest in them, or at least it was that way with me. Over time, the friendship I had with Ivan grew into something like him being a second father to me. At the time that I met Ivan, he was in his sixties. He was almost six feet tall, heavy set, and barrel-chested. Ivan was mostly bald, but he did have a subtle ring of silver hair that went around his head from ear to ear. If Ivan ever wanted to hide in the desert, he could do it easily because of his fondness for khaki clothing. From head to toe, all his apparel was made of tan-colored material. From time to time, Ivan had a rough beard, more like a five o'clock shadow, but most of the time he was cleanly-shaved. Ivan's kindness and ability to communicate made him a special person. I remember the first conversation that had I with Ivan as if it was just yesterday.

"So, you want to be a pro wrestler?" Ivan asked as he eyeballed me up and down.

"I sure do. My football career didn't go anywhere," I told him.

"That's what your friend told me. A lot of people want to wrestle, but not everyone has the talent for it," he confirmed.

"If I start training, I'm not going to quit," I responded.

"If I train you, you will have to take what I teach you to the next level, and you'll have to take it to the next level after that," he stated.

I think the main thing that I received from my talk with Ivan, was that the training was going to be challenging. I knew I had to bring my best effort. I started learning from Ivan right away and he immediately taught me the basics. At first, the sessions were on Saturday and Sunday. During the week, I worked full-time. I was working with my dad at the Molly Trailer Company spray painting horse trailers. After that, usually around seven o'clock, I'd start welding a variety of parts for the travel units. The money that I earned from the welding, went toward the gas for my vehicle. The extra earnings helped since Haltom City is 30 miles away from Dallas.

With Ivan being up there at his age, he had a couple of retired wrestlers help him do the physical part of the training. Helping pass the wrestling skills on to me and the others, were Irish Jack Kennedy, and Buddy Farmer. They just weren't tough; they were mean too. Thank God for Ivan, because he knew how to reel those two in. Some of their tactics were questionable. However, as my wrestling career progressed, I could see how and what they taught me was beneficial. No matter what they put me through, I did it with no questions asked. Jack had a 20-year career and he had been in the ring with many great performers. Some of his opponents were Lou Thesz, Ed Lewis, Warren Bockwinkle, Antonio Rocca, and Bill Longson to name just a few. I didn't know much about Buddy's career, but I was told that he had been in the ring with Fritz Von Erich, Primo Camera, and Arnold Skaaland. The names of Jack's and Buddy's opponents earned them points with me.

In our training sessions, Buddy liked to walk around the ring with a nine-foot-long, three-quarter-inch water hose. Anytime that I touched the ropes with any part of my body, he whipped the crap out of me with it. Several months passed before the trainers ever allowed the new students to use the ropes in any way. Jack and Buddy had their ways of teaching the sport of wrestling. Training to become a professional wrestler was grueling. At the same time, I was confident that Ivan, Jack, and Buddy were teaching me what I needed to know so that I could succeed. I recall a particular time during my training when well over 50 people were wanting to be trained, the next day only 10 remained. That should give you some idea of how difficult it is to become a pro wrestler. A few of the guys that stuck it out right beside me were Mike Hudspeth, Johnny McBrown, and Jerry Caldwell. Ivan wanted to make sure that everything that he put me through while I was being trained, was going to sustain me for a long and rewarding career.

At some point during this time of my training, I felt as if the process for me was taking longer than it needed to. That was when I decided to find someone else to help me. I met a man named Red; he helped with setting up the ring at the Sportatorium. One night, I happened to be in the venue with him after the matches ended. I was told that he had some wrestling experience so, I asked him if he could help me. He was more than happy to step into the ring with me. Within seconds, he easily took me to the mat and put a Boston Crab hold on me. That particular move is applied when the person who is taking the punishment is lying face down. That person in this story was me. The person in the offensive role is standing over my back, facing my feet, and pulling up on my legs as his body is leaning toward my head. It didn't take long to realize that this crazy fool was trying to hurt me. I let out an agonizing scream.

"Stop!" I exclaimed.

"Come on, it can't hurt that bad," he laughed.

"I need you to stop," I insisted.

"And you want to be a wrestler?" he asked with a sarcastic tone.

"If you don't stop, you're going to break my back!" I yelled out in pain.

Suddenly, I heard a voice from outside the ring command my adversary to cease.

"Damnit Red, let him go!" Red's wife shouted.

Red was demonstrating a common practice in pro wrestling that is known as "stretching." Stretching is a way to torture someone and get away with it. One might think after experiencing an incident such as that, I would have learned my lesson. I didn't. I tracked down Rocky Johnson who at the time was wrestling in Dallas. If his name sounds familiar, he is the father of the Rock, superstar wrestler, and movie actor. Rocky's method was a little different than Red's way of doing things, however, they both had the same concept and it wasn't to help me. For three days Rocky had a guy who was a trained Navy SEAL slam me around on a concrete slab. Yep! I said a concrete slab! Back then, if you went to someone and told them that you wanted to train to become a wrestler, they tried to break your spirit. After three days of literal torture, I could barely walk. I felt like one gigantic bruise! Rocky told me if I wanted to continue with him training me, it was going to cost me $6,000. I turned down his offer and I returned to Ivan. I never forgot the conversation that I had with Ivan when I told him about what happened to me with Red and Rocky.

"Rick, what were you thinking?" Ivan questioned.

"I have to do this. I have to be a wrestler," I pleaded.

"You are going to be a wrestler, but everything takes time Rick," he returned."

"I feel as if it is not happening fast enough," I confided.

"Rick, if these people hurt you and it is obvious that is what they are trying to do, you won't be a wrestler at all. I'm not trying to hurt you. I'm trying to help you." Ivan shared.

After I had that conversation with Ivan, I was convinced that he wanted the best for me. It was time for me to continue with him no matter how long it took me to start my wrestling career. My training was a series of repetitive drills. I must have performed a million wrist locks and hammer locks. The trainers had us do front bumps and back bumps over and over again. I was tossed, thrown, and dropped so many times, that I started to enjoy it. Over time, working at that type of pace increased my stamina. However, until it improved, I was constantly out of breath. If I messed up a maneuver and if my coaches thought my execution of a certain move could have been better, they made me stay in the ring until I got it right. I was taught to work stiff, which means that when the action is taking place in the ring, the wrestlers are using a certain amount of force against each other. If it ever came down to needing to defend ourselves, Ivan wanted us to know how to do that. I'd arrive at the gym at eight in the morning, we took a lunch break, and then the session continued until four in the afternoon. At the end of the day, I drove back to Haltom City, and by the time I got home, I was worn out. I had enough energy to get something to eat and then I went straight to bed.

The payoff came when my trainer thought I was ready

to wrestle on a show. Ivan and his crew went out to the small towns in North Texas and put on wrestling events. In wrestling, especially in the era when I started doing it, there were certain unwritten rules for promoters. One practice was that a promoter didn't put on events in the same town as another promoter did. I don't know if Fritz and Ivan had an agreement with each other, but as far as I knew there never seemed to be any issues between the two men. We put shows on in cities that Fritz's promotion never went to. The main difference between Ivan's company and Fritz's is that Fritz had the stars. Most importantly he had his sons, Kevin, David, and Kerry. Several years after I started, Fritz's two youngest boys, Mike and Chris, came into the picture. Ivan's wrestlers were his students. There was no person on his roster with a notable name. Wrestling on the road for us meant getting experience working in front of a live crowd. Despite having unfamiliar names on the event card, the shows that we put on drew large crowds. I think one of the main reasons for that was the style of wrestling that Ivan had passed on to us. It was the old-school wrestling that the fans seemed to love.

I wanted desperately to stay in the Dallas-Fort Worth area and wrestle for Fritz. Fritz was familiar with me and knew that I was being trained by Ivan. To me it made sense because I lived there and I knew the shows at the Sportatorium were drawing in big crowds. So, I went to talk to him when I finished going through my initial training.

"Hello Fritz, I'm ready to come wrestle for your promotion," I explained.

"What makes you think that you are ready to do something like that," Fritz asked.

"I went through Ivan's training. He said I was ready to work," I returned.

"It doesn't quite work like that," he answered.

"What do you mean?" I wanted to know.

"You need to leave Texas and go make a name for yourself. After you do that, you can come back here and I will have a job for you," Fritz said.

I'm not going to lie, I was pretty disappointed, but what Fritz told me lit a fire under me. I knew I was going to get a job wrestling somewhere. I knew that I was going to make a name for myself and I knew one day I was going to wrestle for Fritz Von Erich.

Ivan wanted me to wrestle as his son, bearing the name Ivan the Terrible Junior. Instead, I wrestled as the Arkansas Strangler. You guessed it! I was the bad guy. One particular night in Marshall, Texas, we put on a show in the city's convention center. I was on the outside of the ring with my opponent and I had him bent over a table. I was beating the piss out of my competitor when I noticed a man in the front row get out of his seat to walk in my direction. I didn't think too much about it until he pulled a buck knife from its holder that he had attached to his belt. At that moment I thought I was going to be stabbed. The officers working the show apprehended him and he was put into police custody. Throughout the years, I have found out the hard way that fans like to get involved in the action. In the wrestling business, we call these types of fans, "marks." I loved working in front of a crowd. I didn't like the idea that there were people in the audience who could hurt me or my peers, but it confirmed one thing, I was doing my job of being a good heel! Over time, my ability to play that role in wrestling got better and better.

After being there for quite some time, Ivan had me assist in the training process when the newer students came in. His trust in me to assist in the teaching process increased the confidence that I had in myself. I mainly got into the ring with the newer students to teach them the basics of pro wrestling. Mike Hudspeth, Johnny McBrown, and Jerry Caldwell were guys that did the sort of thing too. One day as the four of us were running some drills in the ring, eight biker looking dudes came into the facility. Most of the guys were 200 pounds or more, they either had beards or long hair, and they all had tattoos. They all were wearing black leather or jean jackets and vests. Their apparel had all kinds of patches which included emblems such as skulls, the devil, and the Iron Cross which was a German military decoration. They wanted to become wrestlers. After having a conversation with Ivan, it was time for each one of them to get into the ring with me or one of my three friends.

"Those are some tough looking guys," Johnny said.

"They can't be tougher than us, we all have been training for a while and Buddy has been kicking our asses," I returned.

"Johnny is right, they look pretty scary," Jerry chimed in.

"Some of those guys look like they just got out of prison," Mike continued. "I just remembered that I have to take off early today.

"I'll do it. I will work with these dudes," I replied.

For the next two days, I got in the ring with every single one of the biker dudes. They all must have been slammed, dropped and thrown into the ropes and corner posts several hundred times. On the third day only one returned and that was a guy who went by the name of Preacher. Preacher wanted to be a wrestler just as bad I wanted to. I later found out that he and I had a lot in common and we became pretty good friends. I have to say that Preacher might be one of the very first people that I trained to be a wrestler. He had the will, desire, and the toughness to be a wrestler. Preacher went on to wrestle under name General Von Hessler, a German character and during that time in the sport, that kind of persona drew heat. He had the ability to work in front of an audience and to draw their emotions out of the fans without saying a word. His look and mannerisms were enough to have the entire crowd hate him in seconds. Preacher fit into Ivan's group of guys quite well.

The trainees were also responsible for setting up the shows. One of the biggest challenges of taking shows on the road was getting the ring out of the building that we trained in. Our gym was on the second floor and the narrow halls and stairway did not allow us to take it out that way. The ring had to be dissembled and lowered out the window piece by piece to the ground below with ropes. Then it was loaded onto the trailer, tied down, and taken to where the event was going to be held. That job was difficult to do, but when several people helped, it was easier. One time I had to do this task all by myself. I also set up the ring and took it down three other times that same weekend. When it was all said and done, I was paid nine dollars. I was paying my dues in professional wrestling and I was happy to do it. I was shocked that I could make money by doing this type of work.

Teaching me the inside workings of the business was to be expected. Ivan also shared some of the office practices that happen behind the scenes. He was willing to share advice and stories from his personal experiences that took him years to learn. I appreciated the fact that he did that with me. It helped me be on the lookout for people who didn't always have pure motives.

"Rick, never turn your back on your opponent. Keep your eyes on him all the time," Ivan said with conviction in his voice.

"Yes Sir, Ivan," I returned.

"If your opponent is in the ring or on the street, do not turn your back on him," Ivan said again.

"I hear what you're saying Ivan," I replied.

"Keep your opponent close to you at all times. The more space you create between each other, the more dangerous the situation can get," he mentioned.

"Tell me what you mean by that." I wanted to know.

"If you keep your opponent close, he can't spin around and kick you or pull back and knock your block off. If you keep your opponent close to you at all times, you can rip his ear, tear his mouth, or gauge his eyes if you ever feel that you need to defend yourself," Ivan explained.

Ivan impressed upon me that the wrestling business wasn't always as glamorous as it might have looked on the surface. Not everyone in the wrestling business had good intentions. He told me to be on the lookout for promoters who didn't pay what they promised. He told me to pull my head from my ass and to use my eyeballs. He said it was professional wrestling, not Disneyland! He told me the story of the Sportatorium being set ablaze by arsonists on May 1st, 1953. Many rumors were tossed around about why and how that fire happened. Ivan seemed to believe it occurred because a few wrestlers retaliated by burning the building after not being paid for a show that they wrestled on. When the case went to trial, it was revealed that the blaze was intentionally set by a third party. That person was hired by a rival promoter of Ed McLemore. Ed promoted wrestling and put on shows at the Sportatorium. The purpose of the fire came out in the court, and it was set to destroy all the films that contained the matches that Ed kept stored in his office. That story and others that Ivan shared didn't always glorify our sport, but I know he felt obligated to let me know what kind of a business I could be walking into. Ivan described pro wrestling as a cutthroat business. He also warned me that if a booker didn't like a wrestler, that wrestler wouldn't be pushed to the top of the rankings. Not getting a push in pro wrestling could make a big difference in one's finances.

Ivan had connections with other trainers and promoters from all over the United States. Back then, to become a wrestler you had to know somebody that knew somebody. That was just the way it was. Two of the people that I knew he kept in contact with often were brothers, George and Sandy Scott. They worked in the office of the Mid-Atlantic territory based out of Charlotte, North Carolina. A lot of the time when George and Sandy needed a new wrestler, they turned to Ivan. Ivan sent the wrestler who he thought was ready to start working full-time in pro wrestling. I have to admit that I was pretty disappointed when Ivan sent Jerry Caldwell instead of me. I was becoming impatient, I wanted it to be my turn. Jerry went to work in the Carolinas, but there was one aspect of the sport that he struggled with, and that was the ribbing! Ribbing is easily summed up as practical jokes, which lean to the side of harassment. Many of the boys find humor in doing an array of jokes or pranks on one another. Over the years I have seen many wrestlers spend a lot of time thinking about how to pull off such hijinks. Jerry lasted three months before he made his return to Texas. The Sheepherders, Luke Williams, and Butch Miller were constantly doing pranks to him that nearly pushed Jerry over the edge. One of the things that the Sheepherders told Jerry to do so he could preserve his Patent leather wrestling boots, that he needed to keep them in the freezer. That particular style of boot cost $500 back then. When Patent leather stays in the freezer long enough and then comes out, it breaks like glass. After Jerry ruined a couple of pairs he gave up on his dream. He had enough!

CHAPTER 3 - WRESTLING FOR THE CROCKETTS

In 1981, the Scotts called Ivan again. This time they wanted a wrestler who had a German gimmick. That wasn't me. In our group at that time, that was Johnny McBrown. Ivan went to Johnny and told him that he had a spot in the Mid-Atlantic territory with the Crocketts. Disappointment set in for me once again. I had been paying my dues in pro wrestling for five years at this point. I was starting to think my dream of becoming a wrestler was not going to happen after all. I thought for sure that Ivan was going to send me this time. I started to second-guess myself. "When was my time ever going to come?" I thought. I felt as if I was going to lose my ever-loving mind!

A day or two passed after Ivan had spoken to Johnny. I was upset because I didn't get the call to work in the Mid-Atlantic territory. I was determined that my time was going to eventually come. There was nothing else that I wanted to do than to become a professional wrestler. To me, it felt like it was what I was supposed to do. I went back to the gym and continued with my training. I was in the ring, and I was running the ropes when Ivan walked into the facility. He noticed me and came my way. I stopped what I was doing, and I met him by the side of the ring that he was on.

"Hello Rick, how are you today?" Ivan asked.

"I'm doing good Ivan," I returned.

"Come on down from there Rick, I have some news for you," he said as I went to meet him where he stood on the floor.

"I received a call from Johnny last night," Ivan continued.

"Johnny decided not to go and wrestle for the Crocketts. I spoke with George this morning. The spot is yours if you want it."

"I want it!" I exclaimed!

"Okay, get your things together, they will want you there by the end of the week," he told me.

I immediately went home to work on a plan. I made a list of all the items I had accumulated over the years that I knew I could sell for some quick cash. I had been working since I was 15 years old, and my mother had done a particularly good job of showing me how to manage my money. I had a brand-new Dodge pickup truck, a bass boat, rods, reels, and rifles, and I sold it all. With the money I had gotten from all those items, I bought a light blue Delta 88 Oldsmobile. Ivan suggested that I get a vehicle that could carry several of the boys from one town to the other in it, so that was what I did. Most of my family was happy for me. They all knew how hard I had been pursuing my dream of becoming a professional wrestler, and now the time had finally come. My brother Leon didn't like that I was leaving. He wanted me to stay and help the family and go into the welding business full-time with him. Out of spite, he had his son burn all my wrestling memorabilia, my cowboy hat, and other items that I kept in my room at my parent's house. Despite his animosity, I never thought twice about leaving for the Carolinas to go wrestle. Nothing was going to keep me from wrestling. I knew that I could always go out and buy more stuff, but I didn't think that my dream was going to wait for me if I didn't jump on the opportunity that was offered to me. I have to admit I was pretty disappointed with Leon by his actions.

I packed up what I was going to take with me, and I stuck my belongings into the trunk of my car. I said goodbye to every one of my family members. I waited until the day I left to do that. It was hard for me to leave my loved ones behind, and my home state of Texas. I had lived there my whole life. My parents were proud and happy for me. Though my mother didn't verbalize it, I knew that she was feeling sad.

I hugged her one more time and I kissed her on the cheek before I got into my car to drive away on my journey.

"I love you, Mama," I said in a soft voice."

"You be good, Ricky," Mama returned.

"I will Mama," I told her.

"I love you, son," she wept.

"I love you too, Mama," I replied.

At that moment, the smile that appeared on my mother's face was what told me I was doing the right thing. That was all I needed to be okay with getting in my vehicle and driving away. I drove non-stop to the Carolinas. I only stopped for gas, food, and to go to the restroom. I stopped at a rest area or two for a nap, but I didn't stay the night anywhere. I was too excited to do that. When I arrived in North Carolina, I went to the address that Ivan had given me. I walked into the building, and I was sent down the hallway to a small office. Inside was Gene Anderson. Gene booked the guys that were under the main event, co-main event, and mid-card status of the roster. To put it nicely, Gene was an asshole, but I don't think he cared about what people thought of him. He was moody and a bit unpredictable, and I think everyone came to expect and to accept that side of him. When I walked into his office, he stared at me with a hard look. I just came from Texas, and I was dressed in blue jeans, a t-shirt, and my cowboy boots and hat.

"You don't look like no German to me," Gene complained.

"That's because I'm not German. The German didn't come," I returned.

"Why not?" He asked.

"I guess he changed his mind," I stated.

"He changed his mind?" Gene questioned.

"Did you have a chance to talk to Ivan?" I returned.

"Yes. He said that he was sending me a German.

You're about as German as Charlie Chan," he snapped.

"I don't think Charlie Chan is German either," I grinned.

"That's my point," He growled. "Come in and have a seat."

"My name is Rick," I stretched out my arm to shake his hand before I sat down.

"I guess we won't be able to call you Baron Von, whatever the hell your name was supposed to be," Gene fumed.

I could tell that Gene was upset, but after I had been in the territory a while and I got to know him better, he always acted the same way. He never needed an excuse to be an asshole. That was the way he always behaved.

"Well, since you are a cowboy and not a German, we'll call you Rick Harris," he affirmed.

Gene's office was small and there wasn't much in there. Besides the desk that he sat at, there was a brown cardboard box that rested on the floor near the door. Gene made it a point to draw my attention to it as if he were baiting me with it.

"Do you see that box over there, Harris?" Gene asked.

"Yes, I do," I answered back.

"Whatever you do, don't you dare touch that box," he told me.

"Why not?" I asked.

"It's not a good idea, plus because I said not to," he returned.

Gene continued to talk to me about the schedule and everything that was expected of me. However, I kept looking over at the box that he brought to my attention and now that was the only thing I could focus on. Suddenly, I saw something from the corner of my eye shoot out from behind Gene's desk, it was furry and brown. The object flew right past my head, and I bolted out of the chair that I was sitting in. I tried to run out of the office, and I nearly pulled the door off its hinges as I tried to leave the room.

"What are you running from?" Gene laughed.

"What the hell was that?" I asked in a panic.

"You scare just a little too easy, Harris," he grinned.

That might have been the first practical joke that Gene played on me, but I can assure you that it wasn't the last. There were plenty more ribs to come and not just from Gene.

The schedule in the Carolinas kept us on our toes. Every Wednesday was the television tapings in Winston-Salem. I could wrestle in four or five matches there because they were taping programs for different channels and cable networks. The talent that was on the roster during that time was incredible. Some of the wrestlers were Mr. Fuji, Greg Valentine, Roddy Piper, Jimmy Valiant, Genichiro Tenryu, Ricky Steamboat, Ken Timbs, Gene & Ole Anderson, Jay Youngblood, Johnny Weaver, The Iron Sheik, and Sgt. Slaughter. Honestly, that was a short list, guys were coming in and going out of there all the time. My job was to make all those wrestlers look good when they beat me in the ring. I took my job very seriously. There were a handful of wrestlers that spent a lot of time helping me adapt my in-ring style to their style of wrestling. I knew how to wrestle when I arrived in the Carolinas, but I had been trained by a man that hadn't wrestled in nearly 30 years, and his in-ring techniques were a little outdated. I give guys like Jimmy Snuka, and Charlie Fulton, a ton of credit for spending extra time inside the ring to share different move sets with me so, I felt more comfortable when I wrestled.

One of the closest friends that I have ever made in my life was Mike Davis. In wrestling he used the nickname the Maniac, and that fit him perfectly. I met Mike there while I worked in the Mid-Atlantic territory. I think we hit it off from the first day we met each other. As our careers continued, they paralleled each other's very closely. His career was like mine, he too, had his time of being the low man on the totem pole. However, the two of us also experienced what it was like to be in the spotlight by wrestling on the mid-card and main event matches. In 1984, Mike held the National Wrestling Alliance Jr. Heavyweight Title. That was an era in his career that meant just as much to me, as it did to him. Mike and I were like brothers, and he worked with me in almost every territory that I wrestled in.

In the days when there were wrestling territories, it was common for wrestlers to stay in a place anywhere from six months to a year. Then it was time to move on to the next territory. At that time, in the Mid-Atlantic area, pro wrestling was an extremely hot commodity. The Crocketts had an A-Team, a B-Team, and a C-Team. Which usually meant that they were running three shows a night, with each team in different cities and towns. How somebody in the office was able to keep up with a schedule like that was beyond me. This should help give some kind of perspective on how big of a business professional wrestling was back then, in that area of the country. The A-Team went to the larger cities and the more well-known guys were on that roster. That team traveled on a Leer Jet and a twin-engine Cessna. Everybody wanted to be on the A- Team because that it is where a wrestler made the most money. The B-Team had a certain set of guys, there were always good names on that team, but they weren't getting pushed like the A-Team was. The C-Team was a smaller group of guys with a good main event and then the other matches had mid or lower-tier wrestlers slated on that one.

I always had to pay attention to the booking sheet because no wrestler wanted to miss his spot. However, sometimes I noticed that the office screwed with me.

Sometimes, I was booked for a solid two or three weeks, and then I had no matches for two or three weeks. Some of the time I got a couple hundred dollars a match, and sometimes I only got paid 50 bucks. At first, I thought I was getting paid based on what the promoter was making off the gate. Over time, other wrestlers told me that bookers and promoters messed with the wrestler's schedule and pay just to see how loyal they were. That made more sense to me when it was explained to me like that. I worked with a lot of promoters over the years that didn't appreciate that I sacrificed my body every night. Then again, no one held a gun up to my head telling me to do it, so I took the good with the bad! Even with the hectic itinerary that I kept up with in North and South Carolina, I could also fly to Atlanta, Georgia, and do plenty of shots there too.

Sometime in 1981, the Crocketts made some kind of a business deal with Jim Barnett. At the time, Jim owned Georgia Championship Wrestling. I don't know if the Crocketts bought a portion of the company or if they bought the television time slot. The Georgia territory later morphed into World Championship Wrestling or better known as WCW. At some point, I started making shots there. Back in the Carolinas, getting booked in Greensboro or Charlotte was what I hoped for. The cards there were always good, and because the crowds were always large, the money I made when I wrestled there was decent. In the other direction were places like Greenville, Blue Ridge, Roanoke, Lynchburg, and Richmond. There were times when I felt as if I was still being tested by the office. I wasn't leaving no matter what I had to put up with. Dynamite wasn't going to get my fat ass out of that place. I guess the Crocketts were testing me.

Sending the boys to Canada to wrestle was another way that the Crocketts tested their wrestlers. Most of the time, it was cold when we were sent up there. I remember it being as cold as 20 degrees and ice covered the sidewalks and the roads. The biggest turn-off to working there was that we didn't get paid until we went back to the country to work there on the following trip. So, not being able to get my pay right away wasn't easy for me to accept. It was especially hard because there were times when I didn't return to Canada for six months. However, when that money finally came it was always at the right time.

Some of the worst plane travel I ever experienced was when I went to the Great White North. We always flew on a commercial airline going to the neighboring country, however, when we had to fly into the smaller towns, we piled into a single-engine plane. Traveling on smaller planes was ideal for an out-of-the-way show. Some of the small isolated places we wrestled in didn't have major airports. On some of those flights, I thought I was going to die! On a particular trip to Winnipeg, I traveled with Ron Bass, Leo Burke, and Don Kernodle, along with the pilot. Inside the aircraft, the mood was cordial and lighthearted. Leo sat in the co-pilot's seat. Since he was in the cockpit, he could see everything that the pilot was doing. It was loud in the cabin. I knew that we had to be low on fuel by this time and I'm sure that was a great concern for the man flying the plane. Leo could see the pilot better than anyone. I watched the pilot struggle with visibility as he appeared to look through the bottom part of the window that was fogged over. Without our knowledge, the front windshield had accumulated ice and our pilot was flying blind. Leo gained an understanding of the seriousness of the problem and turned back to look at me, Bass, and Don. Leo didn't have to speak, his face said everything.

"We're going to die!" I thought.

I looked forward to see if I could make sense of the situation in the front of the plane. I then turned my head to look at Bass. Ron didn't say anything, but when I looked at him, I read his facial expressions to be a lot calmer than Leo's. To compare Leo and Ron at that moment, Leo was probably close to just jumping out of the plane and I think Ron wanted to shake some sense into the pilot. I just happened to look over at Don, I could tell that he was concerned as well. I think everyone on the plane had come to terms that we might not land safely. Don raised his arms and he made a praying gesture with his hands. I nodded my head back to him in agreement. Instantly, Don grabbed my hand, and I gripped Ron's. I knew Ron to be an ordained Deacon in his church, so, I wanted to have him involved in our prayer session. Though it was loud inside the cabin of the aircraft, all three of us were saying the Lord's Prayer on cue. We were about halfway through our conversation with God when Leo interrupted us, and I heard him speak as clearly as day!

"I see lights on my right!" Leo exclaimed.

My eyes opened and Leo was the first person I saw. His face was lit up, but we hadn't landed yet.

"Wait until we are on the ground to celebrate, Dummy," were the words that ran through my mind.

"Confirmed, I see the runway," the pilot spoke.

Our pilot landed the plane safely on the ground and we couldn't have been happier. We stayed the night in that town until we got more fuel for the plane. The next day we got to our event, and we worked against the wrestlers that were assigned to us. I think all of them were local Canadian wrestlers. When the trip was over, I was glad to return to Charlotte. I never liked the snow or being up in the air, so, those trips to the Canada were never too much fun for me.

Getting thrown back into my routine meant that I'd be working and hanging out with my friends again. There seemed to be an unspoken motto among the wrestlers, "work hard and play hard." When I moved to Charlotte, I rented a room at the Days Inn Motel. It was only $300 a month, it was fully furnished, and all bills were paid. It was the best deal in town. Most of the wrestlers in the territory at the time lived there. There were a few guys that had homes in the area, and they had no intentions of taking off to another promotion. The boys that stayed at the Days Inn, were willing to move for the next best opportunity. I lived right below Roddy Piper. Roddy had a huge influence on my career. He shared his wisdom and his psychology of wrestling with me. Roddy was a lot like me, he always knew that he wanted to be a pro wrestler and he was determined to follow his dream, despite the naysayers. Roddy was funny, he spoke his mind, but he was as genuine as a man could be.

When we had a day off or some downtime, all of the wrestlers living at the Days Inn got together. We had huge cookouts when we were not on the road. Most of the time the party was at my place. I had a small area in the back of my apartment, somewhat like a little backyard. That was the space where I kept my grill, and I cooked all the meats on it. I cooked sausage, brisket, steaks, ribs, and chicken. The other guys brought the beer and whiskey. The girls that hung out with us cooked all the sides. The women cooked corn, baked beans, macaroni and cheese, coleslaw, potato salad, and whatever else they could think of. Even several of the neighbors that weren't wrestlers who we made friends with living at the motel came to eat and drink with us too.

Nearly the entire roster showed up to the parties. Bobby Duncum Sr., Sgt. Slaughter, The Grappler, Ken Timbs, Greg Valentine, Scott Irwin, Jimmy Snuka, Ray Stevens, Charlie Fulton, Gene Anderson, even Tommy Young the referee was there, and so many others. I can't tell you how many times I had to threaten to smack one of the boys that picked at the meat before I could pull it off the grill.

"Piper, I'm watching you," I warned.

"We're hungry Harris, how much longer is it going to

take?" Roddy asked.

"I'm sure it's dead by now," Scott grinned.

"You can't rush perfection," I returned.

Tommy always held off as long as he could, but he was usually one of the first guys to grab a quick treat before I finished cooking.

"Tommy, stay away from my grill," I snapped.

"One little piece isn't going to hurt anything," Tommy said as he grabbed a chicken leg.

"You better hope that one is cooked all the through, Tommy," I told him as I shook my head.

"You're going to overcook it if you're not careful," Tommy declared.

"Get away from my grill, all of you. Tommy, I hope you get diarrhea," I said with a half-joking laugh.

The boys loved my grilling, and I got a lot of compliments on my chicken. Tommy always ate so well when he came over, that I thought he was going to bust his gut.

There were always women hanging around us at the Days Inn. I don't remember if they knew other women who lived in the motel, or if they were friends of one the wrestler's girlfriends. Whatever the reason, they were always with us at our cookouts and parties. One day, I was in my car with Roddy Piper, and we were waiting for Greg Valentine to come downstairs and meet us. I was just sitting in the driver's seat when I noticed a lady in her 20s. She just walked out of the motel restaurant. I knew her name was Bonnie. I knew that she was one of the girls that hung out with us all the time, but I never really spoke with her. I never saw Bonnie looking quite like the angel that she appeared to me at that moment. Her hair wasn't combed, and honestly, it looked like she just woke up and threw on some clothes quickly. Bonnie had flip-flops on her feet and she was wearing an exceptionally large t-shirt. It was so big, that I couldn't even tell if she was wearing any shorts underneath it. I turned to Roddy, and I looked him dead in the eye.

"Piper, do you see that girl right there?" I asked with a serious tone.

"That girl? Are you talking about Bonnie?" he returned.

"Yes, Bonnie," I replied.

"What about her?" Roddy questioned.

"I'm going to marry her, Piper," I said.

"Have you ever spoken to her Harris?" he inquired.

"No, but she looks like an angel, Piper," I declared.

"I assure you that Bonnie is no angel," Roddy grinned.

"Don't talk about the mother of my children that way," I snapped.

"Take it easy, Lover Boy," Piper said with a laugh.

Over the next couple of weeks, I saw Bonnie often. I thought about her all the time. When I saw Bonnie at our weekly get-togethers, I tried to talk to her, but I could never really find the right time or words. She had her friends and she was outgoing, so it was not uncommon for her to be hanging out or talking to someone when I saw her. One day Piper came to me with an idea that he had, which he thought was a surefire way for Bonnie to fall in love with me. I was open to his idea, and I was eager to hear all about it.

"So, what to do you got, Piper?" I inquired.

"I'll play the heel and you'll play the babyface," Piper told me while smiling from ear to ear.

"Okay, I'm listening," I returned.

"That's the plan," he stated.

"Yes, but what am I supposed to do," I asked.

"Whenever the three of us are together, I will act like an obnoxious jerk, and since you're such a nice guy, you'll defend her honor," he said smiling.

"Do you think that's going to work?" I questioned Piper with a puzzled look on my face.

"Yes, I think it's going to work, Harris. If anyone can be an obnoxious jerk it's me," he said with a smile.

So, just like Roddy said, every time that the three of us were around each other, he came through and he acted like a real jerk. It wasn't hard for him at all, because Roddy played a good heel on television when he had to. If Bonnie made something for everyone to eat, Roddy criticized it, and just like we planned I was always the good guy.

"Who made the potato salad?" Roddy asked.

"I did. Do you like it?" Bonnie wondered.

"I have had better. Is this the first time that you have ever made potato salad?" he questioned.

"Excuse me! What did you just say, Roddy?" Bonnie asked sternly.

"The potato salad isn't very good. It tastes like you put rotten eggs in it," Roddy suggested.

"Alright! That's enough Piper! You're being rude," I declared.

"Obviously you haven't tried it yet, Harris. Can I get you some?" He inquired.

"I think you need to apologize and leave, Piper" I demanded.

"If it means I don't have to eat another bite of that crap, then I will gladly leave," Roddy said as he walked out of my apartment.

Just like Roddy predicted, after he left the party, Bonnie started talking to me and she seemed to take a genuine interest in me. Piper's plan continued to work as time went by. Bonnie paid more attention to me and it didn't take long for us to strike up a friendship. I guess I had always been a little shy when it came to talking to girls. With Piper's help, I got over that. My nervousness went away when Piper put me on the spot.

Bonnie had a small Chihuahua dog named Buddy, and she loved that little animal. She had it with her all the time. When a lot of people showed up to our parties, Bonnie usually held Buddy to keep him calm and from being stepped on due to his size. Piper knew that he could upset Bonnie if he complained about or said negative things about her dog. I remember one day when he came over to hang out. Several of the boys and girls were drinking beer when he walked in. Piper noticed Bonnie and he knew Buddy must be in the apartment too.

"Harris, I think you need to make a complaint to the front office of the motel," he spoke in my direction.

"Why do you say that?" I asked.

"Don't you smell that foul odor?" Roddy questioned.

"I smell the meat that is cooking on the grill," I returned.

"It's coming from that corner. It smells like a rat," he said as he pointed to a small blanket folded on the floor that Buddy was sleeping on.

"Piper, if you are going to be rude again, you can get your ass out of here, "I shouted.

"I will gladly leave. I don't want to get rabies from that rat," Roddy replied with a subtle wink that he sent my way right before he turned around and walked out of my apartment.

I must admit it, Roddy's scheme was pretty sneaky. However, I was right all along, I married Bonnie and she became the mother of my children. I don't think I could have done that without Roddy's help.

CHAPTER 4 - SGT. SLAUGHTER & DON KERNODLE

If you are looking for a colorful character in pro wrestling, look no further than Sgt. Slaughter. The sergeant's real name is Bob Remus, but I always called him Sarge. The six-and-a-half-foot and 300-pound wrestler who wore camouflaged fatigues, sunglasses, and a Drill Instructor's hat, began his career in 1972, under the tutelage of Verne Gagne. Sgt. Slaughter could either make the fans love him or hate him as easily as turning on a light switch. To have that kind of control over a large wrestling audience is rare, yet essential if you want to be a successful wrestler, and the Sarge was!

If he was the babyface, he made the fans love him the most. If the Sarge was the heel, he made the people hate him the most. I've seen wrestlers throughout my career switch roles from good guy to bad guy, but nobody did it better than Sgt. Slaughter. He worked his way to the top spot in nearly every promotion that he worked for. The Crocketts pushed Sgt. Slaughter and he had quite the run in the Carolinas. He held the National Wrestling Alliance United States Championship on two separate occasions, and he also held the NWA World Tag Team Titles along with Don Kernodle.

For some time, I had always questioned why Don Kernodle and Sgt. Slaughter were in a tag team. To me, they didn't fit each other. The Sarge had a military look to him and Don just looked like an old-school wrestler. However, when the two of them were in a match together, it all made sense. Very few teams had the chemistry that those two men had. When they were in a match with Jay Youngblood and Ricky Steamboat, it was like watching a well-oiled machine go to work. It was very difficult to take your eyes off the action when those four men were in the ring.

Being in the opening matches at those events offered me the opportunity to watch all the matches after mine and to see how the entire show progressed. Watching Sgt. Slaughter wrestle was always enjoyable because I knew that I was watching a special performer work his magic. I got to know the Sarge on a more personal level when he came by the Days Inn. He was fairly good friends with Roddy Piper, so he came by there often to visit with him, pick him up, or drop him off. Since Piper lived right above me, I saw both of them quite often.

As it turned out, Sgt. Slaughter, Roddy Piper, and I all had our birthdays in January. Our special day was near each other's. So, the three of us made it a tradition to celebrate getting older together. Our favorite place to go to have our birthday party was at the Red Lobster. We always ate so well, and we got so drunk. When the three of us got together sober, we didn't always act very mature, but when we were drunk, it was worse.

"Well, it's another birthday and another year," Sgt. Slaughter said, as he raised his arm while holding a glass of beer in his hand.

"Do you guys feel any older?" I asked.

"I feel older than you Harris, but that's easy to do since you act like a 10-year-old," Roddy joked.

"Keep it up Piper and I'll shove this lobster up your ass," I growled.

"That's what I've always wanted. How did you know?" He grinned.

"Which one is going to get us kicked out of this place this year?" The Sarge asked.

"It's always Piper," I replied.

"I wasn't the one who tried fishing the lobster out from their tank last year, Harris," Piper shouted.

"I don't remember doing that," I declared.

"How could you? You were so drunk that your beard passed out too," Roddy returned.

Our birthday celebrations were fun and memorable. At least for us. The employees at the restaurant always had their hands full. I must admit that we acted badly at times. One time, the three of us had a full-blown food fight in their dining room. We made a mess of the place, and we were asked to leave. We were incredibly lucky that the Police weren't called. Another time as we left the establishment after we ate dinner, Sarge and I decided to pull a practical joke on Piper. The Sarge and I were both on each side of him and we grabbed his arms and lifted Piper off the ground. Doing this was not an easy task, because Roddy was a fighter through and through. Our goal was to hang him by his clothing on the coat rack that was mounted on the wall in the lobby. We were successful, but we both received several elbows and forearms in doing so.

"Get me down from here you two," Roddy Shouted.

"How did you get up there Roddy?" The Sarge asked sarcastically.

"Harris, you better get me down from here!" He exclaimed.

The restaurant manager intervened and Roddy was let down. The ride back to the Days Inn was a little longer that night because Roddy was pissed. Roddy loved pulling his share of ribs, and he even laughed at a lot that were pulled on him. Being hung on the coat rack wasn't one that he appreciated.

The thing that I liked so much about Sgt. Slaughter was how giving he was of his advice. Back then, a lot of the boys were like that. The wrestlers that had been around a while seemed willing to share their knowledge with the newer boys. During that time in my career, aside from Piper, the Sarge was a great teacher to me. There were so many times when the two of us talked about wrestling in the dressing room, bars, car rides, or at our barbeques. One of the first pieces of advice the Sarge shared with me was this.

"Harris, you take too many bumps in one match," the Sarge insisted.

"I thought I was supposed to take bumps," I said with a confused look on my face.

"You're supposed to take bumps, but not as many as you take. I counted 40 bumps in your match with Charlie last night. Keep that up and you won't be able to wrestle another year," he explained.

"Okay, what do you suggest?" I asked.

"Take only 10 bumps in a match, but make those 10 bumps mean something," he advised. "You're flopping around like a fish for the sake of flopping around," the Sarge said.

"I'm just trying to put the babyface over," I told the Sarge.

"Put him over, but don't kill yourself in the meantime, Harris. Don't be a dummy," he shared.

From that point on, I listened to what the Sarge shared with me, but I have to admit that my body is paying for all my years of wrestling now. I hate to think what condition I could be in if I hadn't taken his advice when I did. Some of the other information he told me had to do with selling the punishment I received from my opponents during the matches.

"Harris, your face is a mask," the Sarge suggested.

"I'm not quite following you, Sarge," I replied.

"You can't be wearing a blank look on your face when you are in the ring. The people watching you won't know what you are feeling if you don't show them by your facial expressions," he confirmed.

"So, my face is a mask, and every different expression I put on it is a different mask?" I asked.

"How are the fans going to know what you are feeling if you don't show them with your face?" The Sarge questioned me.

"I guess they won't know if I don't show them," I said.

"Exactly, you have to think of that and never forget that you are on the stage," he stated.

"I need to get out there and show the people what I am feeling and going through!" I returned.

"Yes! You got it!" The Sarge exclaimed!

The Sarge helped me to be mindful that everything in wrestling had a purpose and it all meant something. When I wrestled for the Crocketts in 1981, Sgt. Slaughter was a heel. This is the time in his career when he and Don Kernodle were partners competing in an angle against Jay Youngblood and Ricky Steamboat for the National Wrestling Alliance Tag Team belts. The Sarge had a camouflaged limousine that he and Don traveled in. If you were a wrestling fan in the Carolinas back in the early 1980s, you knew of Sgt. Slaughter and his custom-made limo.

One night, I was traveling with the Sarge and Don, and we had a double shot that evening. The first event that we wrestled on was in Charlotte and then we had to drive to Fayetteville. On this night, Don was driving, and I was next to him in the passenger seat. The Sarge was so sick that night and he had a temperature of 103 degrees. So, the Sarge was in the backseat sleeping. Since Don knew the area well, he said that he could get us there much faster if he took the shortcuts. I didn't care how we got there as long as we arrived there safely and on time. Don drove on dirt roads that led to the old interstate highways, which took us through some of the most Podunk places I have ever been to. Trust me! I know Podunk! Since we were in a hurry, Don was driving faster than he should have been. At one point he flew by two pickup trucks that were full of Country Bumpkin-looking dudes. Trust me! I know what Country Bumpkin looks like! I looked into the side mirror on the outside of our car window and I saw the truck behind us flashed its lights. I knew then that we were in for some trouble!

"Did you see that?" I asked Don.

"Yes, he just flashed his lights?" He replied.

"Those guys are up to no good," I said.

"Yeah, but they are going to have to catch us first!" Don shouted.

At that moment, Don hit the gas. We went so fast that we made a huge cloud of dust that billowed behind us. I have no idea how the two vehicles were able to catch up with us, but it didn't take them long at all. At some point, one of the trucks pulled ahead of us and now our vehicle was between the two of them.

"We're in trouble now!" I yelled.

"We got this, Harris," Don laughed crazily.

"These guys have guns, knives, and tow chains. If we don't got this, we will be dead for sure!" I gasped.

"How do you know what they have? Do you know these people?" Don questioned me.

"No, but I know their kind!" I exclaimed.

Let me remind you that the Sarge is still sleeping in the back seat. I know he had to feel terrible, because how else could he have tolerated Don driving like a madman in such a desperate situation? I continuously looked into the mirrors and at Don. Don's crazed-looking face was as red as a tomato. He was growling and cussing, and beads of sweat were forming on his brow. Don was beyond intense. The truck that passed us, came to a stop a distance away from our limo. It looked as if they intended to block the road and make us stop. If we stopped, we could consider ourselves fishing bait!

"Stupid little boys! Stupid little boys!" Don yelled, but it sounded as if he was singing the phrase.

"Don, are you going to stop"? I asked with a serious tone.

"Why would I do that?" Don said which was then followed by an insane laugh.

I hadn't known him for very long at this point, but his behavior at that moment was a side of Don I had never expected to see. Up until this particular time, Don seemed somewhat quiet and reserved. Looking down the road, I saw that our adversaries were getting out of the pickup. When they realized that we weren't pulling over, they all scattered except one. The lone idiot jumped back into the truck and he tried to move it out of the way of our speeding limo. Since Don never decreased his speed, the driver never had a chance to completely get the truck off the roadway or close the door. WHAM!

"Are you crazy, Don?" I screamed!

"Bye, bye door. Bye, bye!" Don said in an evil tone.

"Now you've done it!" I shouted.

"Stupid little boys! Stupid little boys!" Don sang!

Don finally put his foot on the brake and we came to an abrupt stop. As I looked out my window a cloud of dust separated us from our adversaries. Don took off his seatbelt and he reached for the door handle of his car door. I grabbed his arm and gave him a stern look.

"Don! What the hell are you doing?" I asked.

"We're getting out," he said with a crazed grin on his face.

I must admit, I thought stopping and getting out of the limousine was the stupidest thing that we could do. However, I followed Don's lead. We both opened our doors and stepped out. Don stood on his side of the limo, and I stood on mine. Neither one of us said a word, we just watched what was happening in front of us. I counted at least 10 guys. They had to be in their late teens and or early 20s. They were all running around like chickens with their heads cut off. Whatever the hillbillies' intentions were about getting us to stop earlier, wasn't a thought in their heads at this moment. The young men picked pieces of the door that lay in the road, while others just stared at us. The guy that tried to move the truck had an obvious wet spot on the front of his pants. The look on his face was the dumbest one of all, I instantly realized he must have been the one who instigated everything.

"It looks like you boys are having a bad night," Don yelled to our aggressors.

"This guy has a pair," I thought to myself as my eyes locked on Don.

"Are you boys going to be alright?" Don yelled to the men once again.

"We're good," one of the guys answered back.

"I hope you boys have a safe night," Don returned with a smile.

Don and I got back into the limo, and we continued our drive to Fayetteville. I looked in the back seat to check on the Sarge and he was still sleeping. I was surprised that he didn't wake up, especially when Don took the truck door off its hinges. We got to our next event and Don and the Sarge wrestled Ricky and Jay one more time. After the match, we drove the Sarge straight to the emergency room. He was in bad shape and needed medical help. When the Sarge felt better, we told him about being chased by a bunch of stupid rednecks, he didn't believe us and he thought we were making the whole story up.

Don started wrestling with Rocky Kernodle more, who I believed to be his actual brother. To my knowledge, Don never went outside of the Mid-Atlantic area to wrestle. I could be wrong, but if he did, I never heard of it. A few years before Don's passing in 2021, I was at a wrestling convention in Winston-Salem, North Carolina, and both Rocky and Don came up to my table. At first, I didn't recognize either one of them. I always hate asking who somebody is at one of those events, but it's hard to remember someone after there has been a long period since you've seen them last. One of the men opened his mouth and started singing.

"Stupid little boys! Stupid little boys!"

Right away I knew that I was with Don, the crazy camouflaged limo driver. We talked and laughed about the times that we shared together and we even talked about Sarge. It felt good to relive and rehash some of the old stories. I had spent a lot of time in the Mid- Atlantic territory wrestling for the Crocketts over my career. Having to pleasure to get to know and work with Sarge and Don in the short time that I did, was something special for me.

Don truly did surprise me the night that Sarge was sick in the back seat of our vehicle. It was one of those outlandish stories that if I wasn't there, I might have to think twice about it myself. That incident with the hillbillies taught me not to judge a book by its cover! At first glance Don appeared to me as being a pretty mellow dude. However, I will gladly say that Don Kernodle HAD A PAIR OF NUTS! I guess it's the quiet ones that you have to watch out for!

CHAPTER 5 - MR. FUJI

Like I had said before, many people helped me along the way in my career. I don't think I could ever finish listing all of their names if I had to. I was grateful to meet Mr. Fuji in my first year in the Mid-Atlantic territory. By the time I arrived in North Carolina, Mr. Fuji had already been in wrestling for more than 10 years. Fuji was from Hawaii and he was of Japanese descent. I found Mr. Fuji to be a highly intelligent individual. He spoke great English, he was very polite, and he was a walking encyclopedia when it came to pro wrestling. Mr. Fuji could be the center of attention, but at other times he was so quiet, that it was almost as if he wasn't even in the room. It may have seemed as if he wasn't always paying attention to what was going on around him, but I assure you, Mr. Fuji was aware of everything! He seemed to be so in tune with pro wrestling, that it was almost like he had the answer before the question was even asked.

Everyone on the roster knew that I was a greenhorn. In wrestling, it wasn't just the new guys that got harassed, it was everybody, the newbies and the veterans. Though, the treatment of the two different classes wasn't always the same. When it came down to the practical jokes, they seemed to be fair game toward all wrestlers. The wrestlers that I knew were pulling all kinds of crazy pranks on each other. However, some of the guys took it well and some of them didn't. If there was a guy that didn't take it well, he got it worse. Again, this practice of absurd joking happened all the time. As for the new guys, it was a different kind of learning curve and it sucked! There were times when a veteran wrestler took a metal folding chair from the dressing room and placed it in the hallway. At that point, the rookie was told that area was his dressing room. A lot of times that went on until he earned the old-timer's respect. I have seen guys tortured by these types of immature antics, myself included.

One of the most annoying gags that I had to put up with was orchestrated by Mr. Fuji. From the time that I arrived in North Carolina until the time that Mr. Fuji left to wrestle elsewhere, I was haunted by tiny padlocks. In the beginning, the prank was tolerable. After it happened a couple of hundred times, not so much. As much as it irritated me, I put up with it as best I could. I thought if I didn't show that it bothered me, eventually Mr. Fuji might stop. However, he proved to be persistent and a man with a strong will. I found those locks on my luggage, my duffle bags, my boots, my clothing, and just about anywhere a lock could be placed. Trying to get through the airport was a bit of a hassle. It was when I went through the security gate was when I found most of the locks. Going to the airports with the heightened security measures in place today, would be almost impossible to get through. Even though I knew that Mr. Fuji was behind that prank, he always played it off as if he wasn't involved.

"Harris, it always takes you a long time to get through the airport," Mr. Fuji mentioned.

"I wonder why, Fuji?" I questioned with a strong tone.

"I don't understand why you have to put so many locks on the bags. Do you think someone is going to take your stuff?" He asked.

"No. I don't think anyone is going to take my stuff," I stated.

"Nobody wants your stuff, Harris. It's such a waste of time to use so many locks," Mr. Fuji said.

One of the worst practical jokes I have heard of had to be by Johnny Valentine. This was told to me by several wrestlers in the sport when I was coming up. Even I can't make a story like this up. Johnny took a crap and placed his waste into a plastic baggie. Back in the day, at certain motels, some of the beds had hollow metal posts on each of the corners. At the top of those posts that supported the headboard, had what might look to be a lid or a covering. Johnny took that baggie and poked it with holes, lifted the lid, and then dropped the bag of crap down that post. In the months when it got hot, I heard the smell was unbearable. This went on in different towns on the wrestling circuit. Sometimes it could have been weeks or months before someone from the roster stayed in one of those rooms. Eventually, they did and they always complained about the room smelling like crap. I don't know if Johnny ever admitted to doing that, or how the boys found out if it was him, but any person willing to do anything like that had to be very patient.

When it came to pulling off crazy stunts, I will give Mr. Fuji all the credit. I think the reason why I liked his jokes the best was the fact that he never let on that he was trying to fool anyone. He acted as if nothing out of the ordinary was going on. I can't tell you how many times I was on the receiving end of Mr. Fuji's pranks. One that I fell for a couple of different times took place in his Cadillac. Mr. Fuji often sprayed a lot of Armor-All on the backseats. It was not uncommon for Mr. Fuji to give me a ride to the wrestling shows. He always came to my place first. I was usually waiting outside as he arrived.

"Hello, Harris. How are you doing?" He asked through the open window on the driver's side.

"I'm doing well Mr. Fuji. How about yourself?" I asked as I walked toward the car.

"Harris, you have to sit in the back. I'm picking up one of the boys who has long legs. He needs to sit up front," Mr. Fuji explained.

"Not a problem. I don't mind sitting in the back," I replied.

I never suspected anything. I got in the back seat and we talked about our day and what was going to take place at the event. Mr. Fuji drove his Cadillac so fast and he took every turn so sharp, that my fat ass bounced from one side to the other. At first, I thought it was due to his reckless driving. Then I realized that I slid with such ease and I couldn't get my grip on anything. I figured out what he did. Of course, like classic Fuji, he never let on that he knew that there was a problem. He just acted like everything was just fine.

"It's a little slick back here Mr. Fuji," I spouted off.

"Oh, thank you very much," he replied.

"Mr. Fuji, can you please slow it down?" I requested.

"I cannot drive too slowly; I might cause an accident by doing that. I have to keep up with the traffic," Mr. Fuji responded.

Most of my rides with Fuji were just like that one. Even though I knew what I was in store for before I got into his vehicle, I seemed to fall for it every time.

After the matches, it was common for the boys to go to a bar or lounge to have some drinks before calling it a night. Fuji always made it a point to get there first so he could claim the big booth that wrapped around the table which sat in a corner of the room. Fuji always took his place in the middle, so there was always a wrestler sitting on each side of him. After several drinks, eventually, everyone sitting at the table got up to go to the bathroom to pee. Not Mr. Fuji, he always made it a point to pee on the person's leg sitting next to him, and if they were wearing cowboy boots, even better. Usually, most of us were too drunk to notice what had happened, but if anyone ever questioned why their pants felt wet; Fuji accused them of peeing their pants. It was a no-win situation. Walking to our car after drinking was always fun to see who was going to complain about their wet pants. Eventually, we all realized it was Fuji behind that one.

Fuji also invited me to his home several times. His wife was a very nice lady and she was so good to me. Her cooking was delicious, and she never let me go hungry. Every time I ate at their house, if I was about to finish what was on my plate, she always added more food onto it. I ate so well every single time I was their guest. I had to tell her to stop feeding me, but her food was so good. Mr. Fuji and I usually drank sake or rum after dinner. It truly was a good time. The most interesting thing about Mr. Fuji was that he didn't misbehave or play any practical jokes when he was at home or when his wife was around. He pretty much kept his act together then. The contrast of his character was quite different around the boys than it was while he was with his family. Most of the boys knew they couldn't get away with the crap that we did on the road, at home. Mr. Fuji was a lot of fun when we were at the wrestling matches, but at home he was a totally different person. I just assumed that his wife wasn't going to put up with any of his childlike behavior.

Fuji took me under his wing and his mentorship was vital to my growth in pro wrestling. I have to admit, when I first arrived in Charlotte, I felt as if I was in over my head. I appreciated the style of wrestling that Ivan had passed on to me. However, when I wrestled with the boys in the Mid-Atlantic territory, I seemed as if I was a step behind them. Mr. Fuji was instrumental in helping me with my choreography and he perfected the way that I called a match. The heels called the matches from start to finish back then.

In my first year in the Mid-Atlantic territory, I struggled with my thoughts when it came to my in-ring ability. Was I good enough? Was the booker happy with my work? Am I doing enough? As time went on, especially if I rode in the same car with Fuji from one town to the next, putting a match together was most of our conversation. Back then, the wrestlers didn't sit in the dressing room and talk about the match and plan it out step by step. We arrived at the venue, got into our wrestling gear, received the finish from the booker or referee, and my opponent and I went to the ring and we made the match look great! Mr. Fuji helped me make sense of things. It was like he was polishing a car, and I was the car. He was always showing me how to improve a hold or move and he shared all kinds of advice with me.

"Harris there are people in this business that will hurt you if you let them," Mr. Fuji mentioned.

"Do you think I'm going to let them hurt me, Mr. Fuji?" I asked.

"Knowing when it is time to defend yourself, is very important," He affirmed.

"Mr. Fuji, I know how to defend myself," I insisted.

"Harris, listen to me. When you are inside that ring, you need to know when it is a work and when it is a shoot. If you can't recognize the difference, you will get hurt. Do you understand? He questioned me with authority.

"Yes Sir, I understand now. Thank you very much," I grinned.

Fuji's advice might not have meant a whole lot to anyone else, but at that particular moment, it did to me. Some of the information he passed on, he only said once, and with other advice, he might have repeated it over and over again. However, he was patient with me and I didn't take his knowledge of pro wrestling for granted. I knew he was telling me the truth. I felt that I could accept and understand what he was trying to impress upon me. Spending time with Mr. Fuji was like going to school.

After being in the Carolinas for some time, Fuji warned me about certain guys. The one thing he impressed upon me about pro wrestling was that it was consumed with ego. Everybody thinks they can kick the other person's ass. There are legit tough guys in wrestling. From time to time, you'll take a payment and you'll give a receipt. Eventually, if you ever have a real beef with someone, over time, that stuff usually has a way of working itself out. Wrestling has always been like one big family, a brotherhood, and a sisterhood. There are times when actual family members do not always get along, and it's the same way in pro wrestling.

Sometime during this stint in the Carolinas, I started riding to the different towns with the Iron Sheik whose real name was Hossein Khosrow Ali Vaziri. The Iron Sheik was from Iran and he started wrestling in 1973 after he was trained by Verne Gagne. The Sheik had a long career and had an extensive run in the World Wrestling Federation. His notoriety as a heel wrestler was growing due to the events in the news that were happening around that time. With all the conflict that was happening in the early 1980s involving his country and the United States, Khosrow embraced the negative press that Iran was getting and he used it to his advantage. I liked the Sheik and we got along fine until I realized that he was taking advantage of me. Back then, if you shared a ride with another wrestler, you paid a trans fee. Usually, it was two to five cents per mile. The person who owned the car almost always drove it to the next town. The wrestlers traveling together also split the cost of the beer. That was the way it was supposed to happen, but that's not how the Iron Sheik did things. He made me drive his car, pay for gas, and buy the beer. If we were in my car, he didn't pay for anything. At first, I thought that was the way it was supposed to be since I was so new to the business. Someone eventually told me that I was being taken advantage of by the Sheik, when I found this out, I was hot!

So, I decided that I was going to confront him and whoop his ass. One night, at an event at a high school I was in the locker room and I was telling a few of the boys what my plan was for the Sheik. The Iron Sheik was on the other side of the dressing room and I'm pretty sure he had heard what I said. I didn't care if he had or not. So, I kept running my mouth. A minute or two passed and as I was putting my gear on for my match I glanced across the room and I spotted Mr. Fuji. Mr.

Fuji didn't say anything. He just stared at me and I realized that he was listening too. It was the weirdest damn thing. Just by Mr. Fuji staring at me, I knew that confronting the Sheik was a bad idea. Suddenly, Gene Anderson came into our dressing area with a blocking dummy normally used in football practice. Gene put me on the spot in front of everyone.

"Go ahead Harris, show us what you are going to do to Sheik, by demonstrating on the blocking dummy" Gene chuckled as he tossed the object onto thew floor.

"Yea Harris, we want to see how you're going to do it," Charlie Fulton shot at me with a smile

"Come on Harris!" Gene shouted.

I walked over to the dummy and I punched it and kicked it repetitively. I even did a couple elbow drops on it. After a minute of my demonstration, I spoke.

"That is what I'm going to do to the Iron Sheik, and anybody else if I have to," I boasted. "No one is going to take advantage of me!"

From where Gene was standing, he looked me straight in the eye and opened his mouth so everyone within earshot could hear.

"Harris, The Sheik will whoop your ass, plain and simple!" He chuckled.

Everyone in the locker room busted into laughter, even the Sheik. The Sheik and I both looked at each other, but nothing was said. However, at that moment it felt as if all the tension between the Sheik and I had melted away. My friendship from that point moving forward with the Sheik was a lot better. We developed a mutual respect for one another and from there on he helped me with the cost of travel. Had it not been for Mr. Fuji sharing his understanding of professional wrestling with me, my career could have been a lot different. I am very grateful for Mr. Fuji's friendship, and I will never forget him!

CHAPTER 6 - GEORGIA CHAMPIONSHIP WRESTLING

Wrestling in the Mid-Atlantic territory served me well, even if I was losing to everybody. I was working regularly and I had the opportunity to wrestle against a lot of the top names in the sport. I knew that I was improving every day because you can't wrestle against the best and not get any better. I have to admit, that I was getting pretty tired of putting everybody over. Back then, you have to remember, that pro wrestling was an everyday event. We just didn't wrestle on the weekends like a lot of wrestlers do today. Stepping into the ring night after night ensured that I was mastering my craft because I was doing it all the time.

Eventually, I began wrestling in Atlanta, Georgia on a more full-time basis, so I moved to downtown Atlanta at a motel called the Falcon's Rest. Most of the boys stayed there. It seemed as if a lot of the cities that had wrestling territories back then, had lodging where all the wrestlers seemed to congrergate. I have never wrestled in Portland, Oregon, but I have heard of stories about The Bomber Motel from a lot of the boys. Bonnie and I had been married only for a year at this time, and she went with me everywhere. Some of the wrestlers had their wives and families living in different cities or states, but I didn't want any part of that. I think that Bonnie enjoyed wrestling and being with the boys as much as I did.

Georgia Championship Wrestling also traveled into the states of Tennessee and Ohio quite often. Wrestling in various places and in front of different crowds was exciting. The talent that was on that roster was top-notch. Wrestlers such as Tommy Rich, Bob and Brad Armstrong, Mr. Wrestling II, and many others made my time in the Peach State educational. It was so good for me to compete against various people with an array of styles that I hadn't wrestled against before. I found out when I wrestled the same people over and over again, the routine got monotonous and the possibility of complacency had a better chance of setting in.

It was while I wrestled in Georgia Championship Wrestling, that I had the honor and pleasure of working inside the ring with both Ric Flair and Dusty Rhodes. Both men held the National Wrestling Alliance World Title throughout their careers. When I wrestled Dusty, he already had his first title run with the NWA strap. Meanwhile, Ric was being groomed to be champion. Wrestling both men on WTBS television was a highlight for me even though it wasn't for the NWA title at the time. Wrestlers in the profession knew of Ric and Dusty and what they were capable of doing for the business, so to have my name with theirs was special to me.

One of the first big cards that I wrestled on in the Georgia territory was on January 1st, 1982 at the Omni Coliseum in Atlanta. My opponent was Andre the Giant. Andre was the type of wrestler who came into any territory and he could wrestle anybody and the people went to the events just to see him. He was an attraction and that was the way he got booked. The promoters knew that he could draw people and bring in more money. There were a lot of big guys in the business when I wrestled, but nobody compared to Andre. He was something else. I remember the size of his hands. They were huge. I once received a chop from Andre that left a strong reminder of the strength that he possessed. It was enlightening, to say the least. I think I wore his handprint on my chest for a week. If he liked you, he called your boss, if he didn't like you, you were in trouble! Andre could make it easy for you inside the ring. If he was in a mood or if you were on his bad side, it could be a long night. Also on the card that evening was The Super Destroyer. My good buddy Scott Irwin. We spoke in the dressing room.

"I see you will be stepping in the ring with Andre," Scott smiled.

"I am. Is there anything I should know?" I asked.

"Don't die, and pray you come back in one piece," he laughed.

"Oh great," I mumbled.

"Andre's a real pro. He will take care of you in there. I don't think he has killed anyone yet," he added.

"Good to know," I replied with a smirk.

Scott partnered with the Masked Superstar, Bill Eadie in a tag team against Leroy Brown and Tommy Rich on that event. Tommy Rich was a fantastic talent in the ring. He was Jim Barnett's top wrestler and he got one hell of a push for many years in that territory. He was very popular with the fans, and the girls loved him. His youth, good looks, blonde hair, and a gift of gab were a part of his charm. In April of 1981, the National Wrestling Alliance put their World Heavyweight title on him after dethroning Harley Race. Only four days later, Harley got the belt back. I had heard the NWA made Tommy champion to help increase the business there and draw more fans into the Georgia territory. I believe the reason he didn't hold the belt any longer than he did was because, he was young, irresponsible, and partied too much. I think other wrestlers from my day would agree with me.

On February 7th, 1982 we were back at the Omni Coliseum once again and this time, I was in a match with Jerry Oates. It was one of the opening matches. By this time in Jerry's career, he had been wrestling for 10 years and our match ended in a draw. The night was special for me because I met Harley Race. Harley's opponent was Tommy Rich. Tommy was defending his NWA National Title against him. Being in the dressing room with Harley was an honor. I respected him for his unapologetic toughness and his passion for professional wrestling. If he ever thought one of the boys was disrespecting the sport, he said something about it. Harley had made quite the living with wrestling and he wasn't about to see anyone screw it up for him or anyone else. I liked Harley, he was a nice guy and he didn't come off as if he was the toughest dude in the sport. At least, I thought that he was! I approached him that night in the dressing room.

"Hello, I'm Rick Harris," I said as I stuck out my hand to shake his.

"Nice to meet you, I'm Harley, he replied.

"It's good to meet you," I returned.

"Where are you from, Rick?" Harley asked.

"I'm from Fort Worth, Texas," I told him.

"Oh, so, I imagine that you are familiar with Fritz and his boys," he commented.

"I am. It's hard not to know who they are," I grinned.

"That's a good family," he affirmed.

"I hope to work for Fritz someday," I said.

"Keep working hard Rick. You'll get there," he replied.

There were times that I had to pinch myself to assure I wasn't dreaming, that was one of them!

On February 28th, 1982, I had the honor of taking part in a tag team tournament for the vacant NWA Titles. I knew that I wasn't going to walk out of the building with one of the belts, but that didn't matter. Just to be involved in an event that included the Stan Hansen, The Funks, The Briscos, Kevin Sullivan, and many others made my heart feel good! My partner on that card was The Stomper, a wrestler of 20 years at that point in his career who was trained by Stu Hart. Our opponents that night was a pair of Japanese wrestlers, Jumbo Tsuruta and Tenryu. I didn't know much about Jumbo, except that I was told that he was good and he proved that to be true. Tenryu and I worked together in the Carolinas. The of two us drank a lot a beer together when we had our grilling parties at the Days Inn with the rest of the boys. I respected Tenryu and we considered each other good friends, and we had remained that way throughout our careers. I hadn't yet traveled to Japan in my career at that point, but the Stomper had. He made it a point to share some information with me before we stepped into the ring with our opponents.

"The Japanese wrestling style is a little stiff at times, but don't let that intimidate you, Harris," The Stomper assured.

"I'm no stranger to stiff wrestlers," I responded.

"Good to know. These two guys will keep us on our toes," he mentioned.

"Anything else I need to know," I asked.

"Whatever they give you in the ring, give it right back to them, they will respect you for it," he stated.

I thought our match went well and our opponents were professional in every way. Jumbo and Tenryu were what I consider technical wrestlers, so their style brought a certain kind of excitement to the contest. They went on to wrestle two more times that evening and they ended up losing to Ole Anderson and Stan Hansen. Anderson and Hansen walked away with the championship belts that night.

While I was in Georgia, I also had the pleasure of working with Bullet Bob Armstrong. He was a super nice guy. If you ever want to talk about people who have been pillars in professional wrestling, look no further. Bob Armstrong is that man. Bob was tough, but that wasn't always the first impression that you got from him. Bob came off as a kind and genuine person. At the same time, he could whoop your ass faster than a grasshopper could jump off a blade of grass. In the southeastern part of the country the Armstrong family name meant something in wrestling, just as the Von Erich name did in Texas. Bob was the patriarch and he had four sons named Scott, Brad, Steve, and Brian. Brian, later in his career he became better known as Road Dogg in World Wrestling Entertainment. They were all connected to pro wrestling one way or another over the years. I got along well with all of Bob's family. They were good to me and Bonnie. Brian was about

14 years old when I met him and he took a special liking to my wife. Bonnie often mentioned how sweet and thoughtful he was to her. It has been nice to follow Brian's career over the years. I guess pro wrestling has been a part of him his entire life.

On April 4th, 1982, I was scheduled for two matches. One was a contest with Brad Armstrong and the other was a Six Man Tag Team Match. Being in the ring with Brad, was just like going to a clinic. When I got done wrestling him or someone of his caliber, I always felt like my ring work improved in one way or another. I couldn't ask to work with a more gracious and selfless wrestler than Brad. Brad was one of the most underrated and under-utilized wrestlers that I have ever crossed paths with. Brad dedicated three decades of his life to pro wrestling and he had the skills and the knowledge to prove it. He had the looks, he had the personality, and the psychology for the business. I will never know why he never got the recognition he deserved. I know that many out there questioned that also. I remember chatting with him after our match.

"That was a lot of fun Harris," Brad grinned.

"It was. The crowd liked it too," I replied.

"How can you call this work?" He questioned.

"It doesn't feel like work at all," I said.

"It's the greatest job ever," He smiled.

I could relate to exactly what he was saying. Wrestling was what we did for a living, but it didn't feel like work at all. Later that night in the Six Man Tag Team Match, it was me, The Super Destroyer, and The Assassin wrestling against, Leroy Brown, Michael Hayes, and Mr. Wrestling II. Of course, my team lost, however, that night I won because I got paid for wrestling twice. Anytime I could wrestle twice in one day, I jumped at that opportunity to do that. I was already at the event anyway, and I was usually there the entire time, so it was nothing for me to step in the ring again if the booker needed me to.

Squaring off with Mr. Wrestling II was like having the night off. I learned a lot by wrestling against him. The way he moved and his attention to the details in the match, enhanced his storytelling. Mr. Wrestling II always wore his mask. Not one time did I ever see him without it. Underneath the hood, I knew the man's name was Johnny Walker. However, if I bumped into him on the street, I wouldn't have known it. He even wore his mask while he took a shower and he wore it inside the gas station when he bought his beer. Everybody knew who Mr. Wrestling II was and the fans loved him when he played the babyface. Johnny's wife made masks and jackets for the boys and made a pretty good business from it. Mr. Wrestling often advised me and several of the newer wrestlers. I listened with my ears wide open because I knew whatever he said was going to be useful.

"The expression on your face is everything. Let your face show emotion and the fans will know what you're saying when you are not even talking," Mr. Wrestling II shared.

"How do you do that since you are wearing a mask?" I asked.

"I let my body language do all the talking. I throw my arms in the air when I'm excited or I kick the ropes when I'm upset," he returned.

"I guess expressions and exaggerations can go a long way in this business," I stated.

"Indeed, they can Harris, indeed they can," he said.

I liked wrestling for Georgia Championship Wrestling. As my career continued, I crossed paths with a lot of the same wrestlers I knew. The wrestling family that I was a part of was getting bigger and bigger as time passed. I knew all my hard work that I was doing in the sport was going to pay off!

CHAPTER 7 - THE MID-SOUTH TERRITORY

I wrestled in the Georgia territory for a little over six months, and I enjoyed it. While I was there, I also had the good fortune to work with Terry Taylor, Tom Prichard, and Paul Orndorff. David Von Erich also spent some time wrestling in Georgia Championship Wrestling while I was there. Being from the same general area in North Texas and the fact that I knew his Daddy, gave us something to talk about. We discussed home, riding horses, and hunting and fishing. We were both country boys and we liked doing the same kind of pastimes when we weren't wrestling. I found it nice to talk to someone about the other things that I enjoyed doing in my life other than just wrestling.

I also had an opportunity to wrestle for a match in Tampa for a television taping for Championship Wrestling from Florida. My opponent was Wahoo McDaniel. Taking that shot with Eddie Graham's promotion was a chance for me to show him and Dusty how well I could work with a top talent. I thought my match with Wahoo went well. I took every chance I could to get as many eyeballs on my in-ring work as I could. I was fortunate to have good opportunities come my way that were very beneficial to me. However, at that time I had no idea that I was connecting some important pieces to my immediate future.

In May of 1982, I went back to Fort Worth to visit some of my friends and family. While I was there, I got in touch with Fritz and he put me on some shows. Wrestling in North Texas was easy for me because the shows were close to where my family was. Fritz always knew that I would jump at chance to work fulltime for him. Working a few matches in World Class allowed him to see the progress I was making. On that trip, I worked against The Spoiler, Frank Dusek, Al Madril, and The Great Kabuki. I had some interactions with

Kevin and Kerry Von Erich and I found out really quick that I had more in common with their brother David. When I met David for the first time, it felt like I had known him longer than I did. I think that was because we could easily talk about hunting and fishing. With Kevin and Kerry, it seemed that the only thing we had in common was the wrestling.

As Bonnie and I drove back to Georgia, we made it a point to stop in Shreveport, Louisiana to sit in on the television tapings for Mid-South Championship Wrestling. Mid-South Wrestling taped their matches at the Irish McNeil Boy's Club and the company was owned by Bill Watts. Bill wrestled well over 20 years and he was a legitimate tough guy. I don't think Bill was ever a part of pro wrestling, I think pro wrestling was a part of him!

In the summer, The Grappler, Skandor Akbar, and The One-Man Gang were all working in that territory. Any time that I had the time to see my friends and watch wrestling, it was always a plus for me. I met Akbar when I was training, and I crossed paths with The Grappler and Gang in the Carolinas. I also liked seeing how other wrestling companies did their business and how they prepped for television. Back then, we were expected to know how to wrestle for a T.V. taping, but it seemed like every promotion had their own way of doing things. Those differences were what helped set them apart from all the other wrestling programs.

As I made my way to where the boys were, I ran into the Grappler. Underneath the mask of The Grappler is Len Denton. The Grappler was one of the nicest guys that I have met in pro wrestling. When it came to wrestling and his in-ring style, he was one of the greatest technicians that ever laced up a pair of boots. The Grappler could have a great match with anyone.

"Hey Harris, how are you?" He asked.

"I'm doing very well. I wanted to stop in here before

heading back home," I said as I walked up to him and hugged him.

"It's good to see you. I can see that you are still staying out of the gym," The Grappler joked as he poked me in the stomach.

"So, how do you like this territory?" I inquired.

"It's good. The boys are good. The money is alright. The road trips will kill you, but the beer helps," he returned with a laugh.

"I hear that," I replied.

"Come over here Harris, I'd like to introduce you to someone," The Grappler said as he started to walk down the narrow hallway.

"Sure thing," I said as I followed him.

We walked into an open area, and they were a few people in there standing around and talking with each other. The person I had recognized without having to be told his name was, The Big Cat Ernie Ladd. Ernie stood six foot and 9 inches tall, and he was well over 300 pounds. Ernie played defensive tackle in the National Football League, and he was a good ball player. Now that he was working in pro wrestling, he had a great mind for the business and I honestly believed he thought about the in-ring sport constantly. He was a super nice guy; however, he could stomp a mudhole in somebody's ass if he needed to. If Ernie was in a bad mood, nobody wanted to deal with him until his attitude changed. Since he was a really big dude, he knew how to get his point across. At that time, he was the booker for Bill. Grizzly Smith, the father of Jake Roberts and Sam Houston, was the assistant booker. In all the years that I knew Grizzley, I never rode to the towns with him, but I can't even try to count how many rides I shared with his boys. Ernie and I had a good conversation the day I met him, and he asked me for my phone number. I gave it to him, but in pro wrestling, you tend to give your number out often with few returned calls. So, I had gotten used to not letting my expectations get too high. This time things were different. I must have been home for a couple of weeks when I received a phone call from Ernie.

"Hello, Harris. It's Ernie Ladd from Mid-South Championship Wrestling," he said in his soft but deep voice.

"Hi, Ernie. How are you?" I asked while anticipating why he called.

"Harris, Bill asked me to call you, he wants to bring you into Mid-South," Ernie explained.

"That sounds great, when do you need me to be there?" I questioned as waited for his response.

"The sooner the better," he returned.

I was glad to get the call. I was looking forward to be working with some of the wrestlers that I had made friends with over my first few years. I went to work in the Mid-South territory right away. Being around the caliber of talent that Bill had on the roster then, was exciting. Guys like Dick Murdoch, Mr. Olympia, Ted DeBiase, The Junkyard Dog, The Super Destroyer (Scott Irwin), and Dr. Death Steve Williams were there along with many others. I felt the energy that the entire crew brought to the table just by being with them. It was one more opportunity to take my game to the next level. I also got to see Mike Hudspeth again, one of the guys I trained with when I started with Ivan back in Dallas. Mike had been doing jobs and putting top names over just as long as I had been doing it. However, I was hoping all that was about to change working for Bill and Ernie.

Jim Ross was also working for Bill as a commentator, and he later became the booker for him. Jim wanted to be one of the boys and he tried to fit into that crowd, but he just couldn't do it. The boys looked at him as being a part of the office. All the wrestlers knew that he had ratted us out to Bill one time or another for something. Sometimes it seemed as if he set us up just so he could have some dirt on one of the boys. We grew not to trust Jim, and we kept him at a distance as much as possible. Jim was a brown-nosing stooge and boys didn't like him. However, I guess his way of doing things worked out for him, just look at how his career turned out.

Bill was a businessman and a promoter; he liked things to be a certain way…HIS WAY! Bill had the final say on everything and all the boys knew it. Inside the briefcase that he carried with him all the time was a handgun. Who knows if there were bullets in it or not? All the boys knew that he had it in there because he told us! I think that was one of his ways of holding some kind of control over the boys. I'm sure it was for security reasons considering a lot of money went in and out of that wrestling promotion. Bill had a strict rule when it came to fighting. Even though most of the boys from that era were big, there was always an idiot out in public ready and willing to challenge one of us! Bill fired wrestlers if they were ever beaten up in a bar because it watered down the believability factor. That is why a lot of us drank our beer on the car rides while going to the next town, or in our apartments and motel rooms. Knowing the consequences of Bill's rules detoured us from going to bars, but it didn't stop us!

Bill was horrible to work for, and he paid most of the boys like crap. The only person who was making money in the Mid-South territory was Bill. Looking back at it now, I understand that he was raising his family, and I'm sure he did what he thought was right. The only time that I ever saw Bill was at the television tapings or the big events. Other than that, he wasn't around. We all knew when we were in Shreveport at the Irish McNeil Boy's Club, that we had to be on our toes. If any wrestler slipped up, we got fined. I think the amount of the fine depended on the severity of the offense. Bill wanted us there an hour before the show started, if we were 30 minutes late, we got fined. Bill didn't have to be at the building to know who showed up on time or not, he had Grizzly keep track of that for him. I don't know if he deducted money from us to discipline us or so that he could save money, but I didn't agree with it. Bill never once docked my pay the entire time that I wrestled for him. Bonnie wasn't going to let that happen. Telling my wife that Bill kept a portion of my money wouldn't have worked out well for me if that ever happened. So, I behaved as much as possible.

The most challenging part of wrestling in the Mid-South territory was all the driving it entailed. It was quite the stretch. We started on a Monday, and we went to Baton Rouge, and then headed to Monroe. On Wednesday we were in Shreveport and in Oklahoma City on Thursday. We wrestled in Tulsa on Friday, and we were in East Texas on Saturday. It was on Sunday when we hit the small towns that bordered the Louisiana and Mississippi state lines. Of course, Monday we did it all over again. If a wrestler missed an event that he was scheduled for, he was fined $1,000. Riding in the car for as long as we did was a good time for camaraderie, discussing pro wrestling, and beer drinking. I learned so much by just listening to the talk about pro wrestling. Traveling for Bill reminded me of the same kind of long rides that I had to do when I worked for the Crocketts. I remember sharing a few trips with The Big Cat himself. Hearing about pro wrestling through Ernie's stories always left me feeling as if I had learned something new.

When wrestlers travel on the road as much as we did, especially for Bill, mechanical failures were bound to happen. Fortunately for us wrestlers, we had Sam Houston. If we ever had any troubles with our cars, we got ourselves to a pay phone and we called Grizzly. Then, Grizzly called his son so he could come out and get us back on the road. I can't tell you how many times we had to have Sam come out in the middle of nowhere to save us from being stranded. He truly was a wizard under the hood. I don't think there ever was a time that we called him, that he couldn't get us back on the road. Sam was the main reason why the Mid–South wrestlers rarely missed a show.

Bill made me a member of Devastation Inc. Working side by side with Akbar, Gang, and Scott (Super Destroyer) was always an adventure. Ray Traylor whose ring name was Big Bubba, acted as a bodyguard for Akbar. All of us called Ray, Boss Man. Akbar taught me more things than just about pro wrestling. If I kept an open mind every time he talked, I could easily learn something. He tried talking to me about my finances the entire time that I knew him. Akbar shared many ways of how I should save and invest my money, but I didn't listen.

As nice as Akbar was, he also had a temper. Usually, it showed up when our plans changed or when people made mistakes that affected him personally. To me, he seemed to have a little bit of trouble accepting change. Especially when it just happened. I remember a time when Devastation Inc. had to travel by plane for a few shots. Traveling that day was me, Akbar, Gang, Scott, and Big Bubba. We arrived at the airport early to avoid any unexpected problems. We had checked our bags in when we arrived, so, now we were just waiting to get on our plane. Gang, leaned back in his chair to get a little nap while the rest of us just chatted until it was time to board our flight. I think Akbar was the first one to notice that something wasn't right. He was watching people gather around the flight monitors appearing to be frustrated. Getting out of his seat, Akbar walked over to where the other passengers were standing, he looked up to see what all the other people were staring at. I got up out of my seat to join Akbar. I got a better look at the screen; I saw the word CANCELLED. Almost every single departure, including our flight was on that list. I turned my head to look at Akbar and when I did, he walked toward the service counter.

"Hello Sir, how can I help you?" A young man behind the counter asked.

"Can you tell me what's happening?" Akbar questioned.

"Sir, we are having a computer glitch, but we are hoping to get everything back into operation very soon," the man explained.

"So, I assume we will be flying out shortly?" Akbar inquired.

"Not exactly," returned the airport employee.

"Will we be flying out today?" Akbar asked as his face began to turn red.

"It doesn't look like any flights will be taking off, Sir," the man replied.

"We already checked in our bags, when can we get our bags?" Akbar fumed.

"Sir, we are working on returning everybody's luggage, but that could take a little while," he explained

I left Akbar's side to inform the other three wrestlers about what was taking place. Where the four of us waited, we weren't very close to where the counter was located. However, we could hear Akbar's voice was getting louder and we all could hear him very well. Gang who was relaxing lifted his head and looked in the direction where the yelling was coming from.

"Is that Akbar making all that noise?" Gang asked.

"Yes, it is," I said.

"What's happening?" Gang asked with a puzzled look on his face.

"The airport is canceling flights," I returned.

"Are we able to get our bag?" he questioned.

"That's what Akbar is working on," I replied.

"Well, then we should have them at any moment now," Gang grinned.

I walked back up to the counter to check on Akbar. As soon as my eyes got a glance at his face, I knew he was in a bad place. Akbar's face was as red as a tomato. Also, when he got mad, a vein in his forehead started to throb. When I saw Akbar in that state, I walked back over to Big Bubba, Gang, and Scott.

"Akbar is about to lose it," I told the boys.

"Is the vein doing pushups on his brow?" Scott questioned.

"Yes, and his top lip is sweating," I responded.

"The show should be starting anytime now," Gang commented.

"What show?" Big Bubba asked.

"You'll find out," Scott said with a laugh.

Up at the counter, I could see that Akbar was getting more animated, his arms were going up in the air and past his head as if he was reaching for something. His legs started moving and he wasn't standing still at all, it looked as if he had to pee badly.

"When can we get our bags?" Akbar yelled.

"Sir, you can have your bags when we get everything straightened out," the attendant said.

"I see them right there! I want those bags now! Akbar demanded.

"Which ones?" The young man asked.

"The blue suitcase! Those two black duffle bags, the red duffle bag, and the green backpack!" Akbar spouted off.

The man assisting Akbar set our bags on the opened section of the counter. As soon as the airport employee put one of the bags down, Akbar picked it up and threw it back over his head. He repeated this exercise until each of the bags were tossed in our direction. Luckily, since it's hard to hit a moving target, no one was struck by any of our flying luggage. I was a little surprised by that. The passengers in our area were in a state of disbelief and they were running in all directions to keep themselves safe!

"Oh, crap! I was afraid of this," I muttered.

"I told you it was showtime," Gang laughed.

"Does he always act like this?" Big Bubba inquired.

"You should see him when someone charges something to his credit card that he didn't ask for," Scott responded with a laugh.

Thank goodness nobody got hit by our luggage that day! Eventually, we got our traveling schedule back on track. It was always a little stressful traveling to different cities for shows. It was drilled into us back then that we honored our commitments no matter what. We were at the mercy of the airports, the weather, and unexpected situations. Even though Akbar got a little intense at times, it was friends like him that made my life that much more special!

CHAPTER 8 - MID-SOUTH WRESTLERS

I never thought that it was only one thing that made a wrestling promotion, a success. It is a multitude of elements such as: the fans, the booker, the storylines, and the talent working there. Bill Watts knew who he had on his roster and though he had the boys work under certain parameters, he trusted them to get their job done. During a certain period, the Mid-South promotion could do no wrong. I believe it was all due to the level of chemistry that existed among the boys.

When I wrestled in the Mid-South territory, I had the privilege of stepping in the ring with The Junkyard Dog nearly 50 different times. He was the one man who knew exactly how to bring the magic alive in that region. His real name was Sylvester Ritter, but I called him JYD. The charisma and personality he embodied were captivating. It didn't matter who his opponent was going to be, the crowd supported JYD no matter what. Standing in the middle of the ring while waiting for JYD to come to the ring was an experience in itself! Looking at the audience in a sold-out building, hearing them chant, "Who say they can beat the dog?" repeatedly, sent chills up and down my spine. He knew how to play to the audience. He sported a dog collar and chain as he danced through the aisles. I enjoyed working with him. Certain wrestlers back then in the 80s controlled certain wrestling territories. For the Von Erichs, it was Texas, for the Dusty Rhodes it was Florida, and for JYD, it was the Mid-South Territory. Everywhere that he went, the people adored him.

When I was there, one of JYD's biggest rivalries was Ted DeBiase and his fellow Rat Pack teammates, Matt Borne, and Jim Duggan. Duggan called himself the Big Cheese. Ted and JYD had some classic bouts in an array of gimmick matches which included Dog Collars, Dog Chains, No Disqualifications, and a Loser Leaves Town match. On

October 27th, 1982, Ted and Matt beat JYD and Mr. Olympia in a Loser Leaves-Town match and it set up an angle that put the Mid-South fans into a frenzy. In the days that followed that match, Bill had the idea of putting JYD under a mask and he now wrestled with the name Stagger Lee. Of course, everyone suspected that it was JYD wearing the hood. The anticipation of finding out if it was him or not just brought more people to the shows. There is no doubt that the contributions that JYD made to Bill's promotion had a lot to do with its success. JYD had charisma like no one I had ever seen! He truly was a special wrestler and person!

Every territory or promotion needed a good heel and Bill had Ted DiBiase. As a heel, their main job was to piss off the crowd. However, Ted rubbed the boys the wrong way too. A lot of that had to do with his personality and how he carried himself in and out of the ring. Most of the time, Ted just acted as if he was better than everyone else. We all thought he was arrogant. When Vince McMahon hired him to be The Million Dollar Man in the World Wrestling Federation, it fit him perfectly. The boys thought Ted acted like a spoiled brat. Vince got that right! Don't get me wrong, he was a hell of a wrestler in the ring, and he respected the business, but none of the boys wanted to hang out with him. When we both wrestled in Mid-South at the same time, the two of us made a couple of road trips together, but he never engaged in a conversation with me. When you are in a car driving with someone for 250 to 500 miles, a good conversation can help pass the time. I thought his disposition sucked! He was that way with everyone not just me. There has always been a strong brotherhood in wrestling, but I can tell you that not all the brothers get along, and sometimes nothing can change that. That seemed to be the case with me and Ted.

In 2016 or 2017, well after I retired from performing inside the ring, I got a call to make an appearance at

Wrestlecade in Winston-Salem, North Carolina. I know it was one of those two years because I had heart surgery in 2015 and it was after that. I was going to fly into Charlotte and then drive a rent-a-car to where the wrestling convention was to be held. The only catch to this whole thing: was I was asked to meet Ted at the same airport and take him with me. I have to admit, I didn't want to see Ted. I didn't like hanging out with him when we worked together at Mid-South, and I honestly didn't think things were going to be any different this time either. However, I agreed to meet Ted at the baggage claim which made a lot of sense since we both needed to go there and pick up our luggage. As I walked into the large area where the baggage carousels were located, I immediately spotted Ted. He was wearing a tracksuit and had his fanny pack around his waist like most of the boys from that era do. Of course, he had aged and had gained some weight like a lot of us have, but he had a smile on his face that I wasn't familiar with. This made me curious, so I looked down at my feet to make sure I wasn't dragging toilet paper on one of my shoes since I just visited the restroom. Thank goodness, I saw no toilet paper and I felt instant relief. As I got closer to him, Ted greeted me.

"Bart, how are you?" he wanted to know.

"I'm doing good, Ted," I replied. As he stretched out his arms to hug me. After we finished hugging, he stood right in front of me and still smiling from ear to ear.

"I can't tell you how good it is to see you, Bart," he commented.

"This can't be the same person from my days of working with Bill Watts," I thought to myself.

"It's good to see you, Ted," I returned. "Let me get my bag and we will be on our way."

The two of us walked over to the rent-a-car counter and got our transportation squared away. We both shared some small talk until got into the vehicle and started driving in the direction of where the wrestling convention was to be held. I enjoyed my time with Ted that day. He was a completely different person and he treated me as if we were both equals. That was something that I had never felt when I was with him before. I had heard that he dedicated his life to Christ. I don't know if that was why I noticed a huge difference in him, or if back in his wrestling days he was just living his gimmick. I saw a lot of the boys when I was wrestling take their character home with them and become that character. I played a mean heel, but I was able to turn that off when I was away from the business. Maybe back when Ted and I were working together, he wasn't able to turn it off. Who knows? On our road trip, he seemed extremely interested in everything I was talking about, and he asked questions about my family as well.

"How are your kids doing Bart?" He asked with a caring tone in his voice.

"They are good Ted, how about yours?" I returned.

"They are all doing well," he said.

"That is good to hear. I'm glad," I replied.

"So, what are you doing these days to stay busy and to keep yourself out of trouble," Ted grinned.

"Well, I make knives," I replied.

"What kind of knives? Are they hunting knives? He quizzed me.

"I make all different kinds and sizes. Some people use them for hunting, whittling, or just as a regular utility knife," I returned.

"How long have you been doing that, Bart?" He inquired.

"I have been making knives most of my life. My family has always done welding, so I have worked with metal since I was a kid. I can take a piece of metal and turn it into any shape or the size I want to," I explained.

"That sounds cool. What do you do for the handle?" Ted questioned.

"I usually use what I have. Sometimes I use a craved piece of wood, an ox bone, a deer antler, or even a ram's horn. You can use anything depending on how you want it to look," I commented.

When we arrived at the convention, we were greeted by the people who were putting on the event. They took us to where our tables were going to be. I can't tell you how many pictures I signed, but it was a lot and I remember having a great time seeing the boys and meeting with all the different wrestling fans. The ride with Ted back to the airport after the meet and greet, was just as pleasant as our first ride we had done earlier in the day. My impression of him changed. It was as if he wasn't even the same person that I had worked with so many years ago. I was so glad to have that time with Ted and to talk to him. It made my heart feel good. When we parted ways, we said goodbye with a hug.

"It was really good seeing you, Bart," he confided.

"I enjoyed it too, Ted. I hope we can do it again real soon," I said with a smile.

"I hope so too," he answered back.

"Until we meet again," I returned.

The two of us took one last look at each other before we turned away and made our way to our gates. I haven't seen Ted since, but I sure think of him often.

One of the class acts on Bill's roster was Steve "Dr. Death" Williams. If you have never had the pleasure to watch this man in the ring, you missed something special. When it came to tough guys, Steve Williams was one of the toughest in the wrestling business. Even the way that he looked at you was tough. It wasn't just his strength, physical attributes, and technical wrestling style that made him so great, but it was his big heart that I liked about him the most. He was a good guy, and he had a genuinely caring personality. If you were Steve's friend, you knew it, because you felt it!

I remember working with Steve at the beginning of his career. By this time, I had been wrestling for at least seven years, I worked with the newer guys a lot so I could be somewhat of a teacher to them. It was important for the greener talent to get comfortable wrestling in front of a crowd and that happened when they knew their opponent wasn't going to try to kill them. I had stepped into the ring with Steve numerous times, but one evening in Mississippi I believed I was going to become one of Dr. Death's victims! For Real! At some point in the match, I was going to make myself bleed, and I had the blade on my index finger covered with tape. As I removed the tape from the tip of my finger to cut my forehead, Steve came up behind me and he trapped my arms as he wrapped his around my torso placing me in a bearhug. Immediately, I turned my hand toward my thigh so, if anyone got cut, it was going to be me. I weighed 325 pounds and Steve picked me up as if I was a rag doll and he shook me up, down, and all around. My feet were completely off the ground and then I felt the pain in my leg shoot through my entire body.

"It's cutting me," I yelled.

"What?" Steve asked.

"My blade is cutting me. Let me go!" I exclaimed.

Immediately he dropped me in the middle of the ring like a hot rock. We finished the match soon after that. I looked at my leg and I saw blood. It was cut up pretty good and so was a new pair of tights, however, I lived to fight another day. However, the tights died! Going into the match we had the idea for the finish, and his bear hug wasn't a part of it. I remember confronting Steve in the locker room.

"Hey brother, what happened out there?" I asked.

"I don't know," Steve responded.

"If I had known you were going to wrap me up in a

bearhug like that, I wouldn't have uncovered my blade," I told him.

"Putting you into a bearhug just popped into my head," he replied.

"I'll pop you in the head," I murmured. "Stick with the plan. People can get hurt if we don't."

Stuff like that usually only happened with the new guys. Back then we were learning on the job. That was one of the main reasons why seasoned workers spent time with newer wrestlers coming into the business.

Years later, and just about a month before Steve passed away. I ran into him at an autograph signing in Shreveport, Louisiana. Several of the boys from the Mid-South promotion were there that day, but no one left an impression on me the way Steve did. I was sitting down at a table, and I was interacting with a few fans and signing some photos. Suddenly, I felt a couple of arms come around my neck to hug me from behind. I turned my head to see who it was, and it was Dr. Death. He was a little lighter in weight than the last time that I saw him, but his facial features, including his big warm smile, were just as I remembered them. The main difference in Steve that I recognized, was his throat and the sound of his voice. The two of us both shared the same bad habit, smokeless tobacco. I know for myself that I had never thought about the downside of using snuff. It truly hurt me to see him in that condition. It was hard not to look at the hole in his neck. As I looked at Steve as he held his hand to his throat as he spoke, I was blown away.

"Hi, Bart," Steve greeted.

"Dr. Death, Dadgum! I don't believe it!" I exclaimed.

"Bart, it is so good to see you," Steve said.

"It's good to see you too, Steve," I replied as stared at his throat.

"Bart, are you still dipping snuff?" He inquired.

"Yes, I am buddy," I admitted.

"Bart, quit dipping snuff!" He demanded.

I could easily see the effects that cancer had on him. Steve lost some weight; he just wasn't the size that I remember when we wrestled together. That was the last time that I ever saw Steve, his body might have been weak, but his spirit was as strong as ever. I will never forget his smile and the zeal that he had for life. Steve passed away from throat cancer on December 29, 2009. Shortly after that, with the support of my second wife Linda, I quit using tobacco just like he wanted me to. It wasn't easy, but it beats the alternative. I miss Dr. Death Steve Williams, there will never be anyone like him in or out of wrestling ever again! From class acts like Steve Williams to legendary icons like Andre the Giant, I had the pleasure of working with some of the very best wrestlers in history.

Andre and The Grappler got along very well. Anytime that Andre came to the Mid-South territory, he wanted to go to the bar with The Grappler before he left to wrestle in the next town. At this time, The Grappler was riding with Dick Murdoch and together the two of them could drink a lot of beer. It always seemed like there was a competition between The Grappler and Dick to see who guzzle down the most suds. After three days of being on the road with Dick, The Grappler was miserable! Sitting in the dressing room in Jackson, Mississippi on the heel side of the room was The Grappler. He was getting prepared to wrestle in his upcoming match with JYD. On the other side of the room where the good guys gathered to get ready, sat Andre.

"Hey, Boss!" Andre Shouted out to The Grappler. "You and me are going drinking tonight."

"Hi Andre," an unenthusiastic The Grappler returned from across the room.

"Wait for me, Boss. I go on last. We will leave together! The Giant exclaimed.

"Okay Andre," The Grappler replied.

Instead of waiting for Andre, when the Grappler was finished with his match against JYD, he left the building and sped back to Baton Rouge. The Grappler needed a day off from drinking. A couple of hours after the show, The Grappler came over to my trailer to ask for a favor.

"Harris, Andre wants to go drinking with me tonight. I can't do it. Can I stay in your spare room?" The Grappler wanted to know.

"Sure Buddy," I told him as I opened the door to let him in.

"I know the Giant won't find me here," he assured.

"Go get some rest brother. I will see you in the morning," I said.

The Grappler was on his side of the trailer sleeping and Bonnie and I were on our side. I have no idea what time it was, but as I slept, I was woken by a loud pounding on the front door. BOOM! BOOM! BOOM!

"Grappler, open the door, I know you are in here!" I heard Andre yell as I walked to the door just before I opened it.

My trailer had a little porch. I used it every day to get into my home, Andre on the other hand wasn't using the platform at all and his head went way past the top of the door frame.

"Andre, what's going on?" I asked.

"Is The Grappler here?" Andre questioned me.

"Yes, I believe he is sleeping," I answered.

"I want to talk to him," he demanded, and he pushed his large body into my trailer.

I didn't argue with Andre. Who is going to argue with a giant of a man like that? Not me! Andre made his way to where The Grappler's room was, and he opened the door only sticking his one arm inside. With one quick pull, Andre lifted The Grappler's bed and it flipped leaving the smaller man underneath it. The Grappler, who was in his underwear, stood to his feet just in time to receive a chop across the chest by Andre who couldn't get all of his body in the spare bedroom.

"You said you were going to drink with me," Andre shouted.

"I don't remember agreeing to that Andre. I need to take a break tonight and get some sleep," The Grappler pleaded.

"Get your pants on, we are going out!" Andre insisted. "You and Bonnie are going too Harris."

Andre got his way. The four of us went out and had some drinks. Andre could put them away too. Sometimes I don't know how he did it, but I had witnessed him pour a ton of alcohol into his body. I think his body size processed booze differently than the average man. Andre was a great big guy with a great big heart. Andre the Giant was one of a kind!

CHAPTER 9 - DICK MURDOCH

The men that seemed to be consistent in my wrestling career were The Grappler, Mike Davis, Sam Houston, and Dick Murdoch. I didn't always work with all of them at the same time, but in one way or another, those four men always seemed to be around, and they played a big part in my life. Guys like Dick, The Grappler, Sam, and Mike don't come around too often, but when they do, you better hope to keep friends like that.

Dick was one tough dude! To me, no matter where he might have traveled, I always associated Dick with Texas because that was where he was from and that was where I met him. I think the main reason why the two of us got along so well, was the fact that we were both from the Lone Star State, and we both were accustomed to being around the country lifestyle. That commonality gave us something to talk about when we weren't talking about wrestling. Dick had a ranch in Amarillo. He didn't have much of a Western look when I was around him, but he was a cowboy through and through.

I first met Dick in 1981, on a trip to visit my folks in Texas. I contacted Fritz so I could work a few spots for him. I think at that time Dick was working in Amarillo, but he had come in to do some matches for Fritz's promotion as well. It didn't take long for me to hit it off with Dick, after we both finished our obligations for Fritz, Dick asked me if I wanted to make some shows with him in West Texas. I gladly went. We worked in Sweetwater, Amarillo, and a couple of towns in between. The traveling that we did was just as fun as the wrestling was to me. The car rides gave us time to unwind and to learn from the stories we all shared about our profession.

I have always liked to drink beer, but in the early 80s, I tried to keep it quiet. I saw a lot of guys drink beer and they seemed to be open about it. I didn't feel comfortable about advertising my thirst for alcohol. I thought if the promoters knew that I liked to drink, they wouldn't use me due to concerns about me being a liability. I remember having a long talk about beer with Dick on that road trip.

"Do you drink beer or not Harris?" Dick asked.

"Yes, I drink beer, but I don't want everyone to know that I do," I told him.

"You don't want people to know? He inquired. What kind of dumb crap is that?"

"It's not dumb Dick, I want to keep on working and if a promoter finds out that I drink, they may judge me and not hire me," I explained.

"Do you know what it sounds like to me?" He asked.

"What"? I answered back.

"It sounds like you need to drink a beer, damn it!" Dick piped off. "I won't tell anyone I promise."

He reached into a brown grocery bag where he had a 12-pack. He pulled out a can and gave it to me. He handed me the can and I looked at it before I opened it.

"It's Coors," I mentioned.

"Yes. It's Coors. I'm glad you can read Harris." He shot back.

"I don't drink Coors. Coors tastes like cat piss," I insisted.

"Harris, if you know what cat piss tastes like, you'd be better off drinking Coors beer," Dick affirmed with a laugh.

"Is that all you have in there?" I inquired.

"Yes, that is all I have. I work for Coors, I'm a spokesman for them." He claimed. "I don't drink anything else."

"You work for Coors?" I asked.

"Yes. I'm a spokesman for the company. My job is to promote the beer and to help spread the distribution of their product," Dick said convincingly.

"You are so full of crap," I said.

"I'm telling you the truth. As I travel to wrestle at all

these venues, sports complexes, and arenas, if I see that they don't provide Coors beer at their facility, I talk to them." Dick explained.

"What do you mean that you go talk to them?" I asked with a puzzled look on my face.

"I set up a meeting with the owner to see how we can get Coors beer in there to sell at their facility," he confirmed. "I get paid to drink Coors beer."

I assumed that Dick made that story up, but he told it so well, it was hard not to believe it. In fact, of all the things that he and I talked about, that was the one story of his that was always consistent. Back then, I don't remember seeing Coors beer as available as it is today. I remember seeing Budweiser, Schlitz, Pabst Blue Ribbon, and Miller High Life almost everywhere that we went. In some parts of the country, you just couldn't find Coors. I didn't put too much stock into Dick's claim, since telling outrageous stories was just what we all did. We needed something to do to pass the time as we rode from one town to the other. Over the years as our wrestling careers continued, it seemed like all of the cities that never sold Coors beer did after Dick had spent so much time wrestling there. I noticed that in Mississippi, Georgia, North Carolina, and Puerto Rico. Again, I don't know if he was pulling my leg, but he sounded pretty believable when he talked about his affiliation with the beer company. These days, I can't see a can of Coors without thinking of Dick Murdoch.

The Mid-South office decided to put me, Hangman Rick Harris, in an angle with Dick Murdoch. This opportunity seemed to be what felt like my first big push in professional wrestling. I was excited to work with Dick because he was such a Ring General. He knew how to control a match and get it back on track if it needed that. He was damn good! At the time, I was a part of Devastation Inc. led by Skandor Akbar. If I'm going to be tagged with the name Hangman, I need to have a

Hangman's noose. I made one and I carried it with me to all my matches. It sure looked intimidating too. Over time, my name became synonymous with that rope. One night, I almost choked Dick to death with it on a television taping!

After the match with Dick and I had been going on for a little while, Akbar made his move. He jumped into the ring to interfere, and he joined me and helped beat the living tar out of Dick. Akbar aided me with my rope, and I proceeded to place it around the Dick's neck. Of course, I had the rope fixed in such a way that it wasn't going to choke him when I pulled on the lariat. Again, we didn't practice anything back then. It was all called in the ring. So, when we decided to do anything against each other, we committed to it. I wanted all of this to look good since it was being shot for T.V. I was standing in the ring and Murdoch was on the outside of the ring on the opposite side of the ropes that I was on. His feet were a couple of inches off the ground but most of his ass was resting on the ring apron. Gang at some point was to come out to assist me, but his main job was to elevate Dick to assure there was no real pressure being applied to his throat. However, the plan fell apart when Gang slipped on the slick wet floor around the ring. He lost his balance and his 400-pound body fell onto Dick pulling him toward the ground. Now we had a problem. Dick's face instantly turned colors. It went from red to purple quickly. Akbar and I immediately saw the severity of the situation. I think we both realized right away that we could kill Dick if our charade went on any longer, so I let go of the rope and Dick dropped to the floor. I had a lot of memorable matches in that territory, but that one with Dick I will never forget!

I don't know if I ever heard the story of how Dick got the name of Capitan Redneck. Currently, a nickname like that wouldn't fly because it isn't politically correct. Back then, we didn't think about that kind of stuff and people weren't so sensitive. We did our thing and if we were ever told to turn it down a notch, we did, but we pushed the envelope back then as far as we could to get a reaction. Sometime after I nearly hung Dick with my hangman's noose, we had another match on Mid-South television. As Captain Redneck, Dick carried a duffle bag full of all kinds of items. He had a six-pack of Coors beer in there, along with a shovel, a flashlight, a frying pan, and whatever else he needed in a survival kit. Our match was going along, and it was about time to finish it up. Everything went along as planned until I had turned my back to Dick, and I proceeded to leave the ring. Suddenly from out of nowhere, I felt something hit me in the back of my head and the entire place went dark. I thought that the building lost power, but the lights had gone out in me! I was out colder than a frozen pot roast! Waking up in the dressing room at the Irish McNeil Boys Club was a bit puzzling when I sat up and saw Dick smiling at me.

"What happened?" I asked as I raised my hand to the back of my head.

"That was your payback, Harris!" He exclaimed.

"My payback for what?" I inquired.

"The payback for nearly choking my ass to death with your Hangman's noose," Dick returned.

"I didn't know there was going to be a payback," I mouthed.

"Harris, in pro wrestling if you give a tater, you get a receipt. That was your payback," he grinned.

"What the hell did you hit me with Dick?" I wondered.

"That was my duffle bag. You owe me a can of beer by the way. It broke open when it connected with your hard skull," Dick laughed.

Dick taught me a valuable lesson that day. The main responsibility of every wrestler is to take care of one another when we were in the ring. If you didn't or if something went wrong, you could expect a surprise in return. This practice helped keep the boys honest.

I remember a time when Dick and I wrestled together on my only trip to Puerto Rico in 1992. We were both there on a two-week tour for Capitol Sports Promotions. I was hanging out in our room relaxing when Dick came in with a frozen pizza that he picked up from the grocery store. The pizza was a plain cheese pizza, but he planned to dress it up with extra ingredients that he also brought home. Usually, Dick grated extra cheese and sliced a whole stick of Pepperoni to add to it. From the kitchen area, he shouted out to me.

"Harris, do you like garlic?" He questioned.

"Yes, I do," I replied.

"Are you sure?" Dick asked again.

"Yes, I am sure. What part of, yes, I like garlic, do you not understand?" I shot back.

"Okay, I just thought I'd make sure," he responded.

When the pizza came out of the oven, I saw that Dick had put fresh cloves of garlic all over the pizza. He must have cut at least two or three bulbs of it and laid it on top of the pepperoni slices, which there was a lot of! I thought he was going to dash some garlic powder on it. I like garlic on my pizza, but not that much garlic! Our room smelled like we were in one of the Godfather movies! For the rest of matches that I had while I was there on the island, all my opponents knew what I ate that week. I smelled like an Italian restaurant.

Dick was a tremendous wrestler. Everything about pro wrestling fit him like a glove. He understood every aspect of the sport. Dick could do all the moves, he understood wrestling psychology, and he could talk on the microphone. Dick knew how to control the match and keep it going. He was that good. Dick could drink beer all night long with little sleep, and still go out and perform in front of a live crowd or on television and never skip a beat. He was a little unpredictable and a bit immature every now and then. There were times when Dick and I wrestled each other, and he tickled me in the stomach or my armpits, so he could make me laugh. Other times he pinched my nipples or my ass. I guess he did that stuff to me in the ring, to see how I'd react to it. At other times, as we were standing in our corners as the announcer to called our names, he'd make a goofy-looking face or cross his eyes to catch me off, guard. Despite his antics and the way that he did certain things, he was a lot of fun to be around. I truly believe he was the best Ring General in the business when I wrestled with him! I enjoyed every moment I spent with Dick.

CHAPTER 10 - SOUTHEASTERN CHAMPIONSHIP WRESTLING

In the winter of 1982, I left the Mid-South Territory. I returned to work for the Crocketts back in the Carolinas. I appreciated my time with Bill Watts because of the work that I had done in his company. However, Bill was a jerk, GOOD RIDDANCE! My second stint in the Mid-Atlantic area was just like my first tour of duty, I wasn't getting a push. One night, Gene Anderson came up to me in the dressing room and told me that I was going to win over Mike Davis. This blew my mind! For a moment, I thought that the office was finally giving me a push, but after I won that contest, I lost the rest of my matches for the next six months. I'd been wrestling for nearly eight years by this point, and I had done more losing than winning. Don't get me wrong, I loved what I was doing and there was nothing else that I wanted to be doing more, but I had paid my dues. The words that Ivan shared with me about a wrestler not getting a push were appearing to be true. I was starting to think the Crocketts didn't like me; however, the feeling was mutual. It was time for a change, and deep down within my soul, I felt like something was about to happen. I didn't know how and I didn't know when, I just knew it was about to happen!

Sometime near the summer of 1983, I heard from Bob Armstrong. Bob and I had been friends since meeting him two years prior when the Crocketts had me working in Georgia. Bob said that he wanted to talk to me and that he had an idea that I might be interested in. Bob was booking for the Fuller and Welch family in Southeastern Championship Wrestling territory which covered pretty much the entire state of Alabama and the top part of the state of Florida. Robert Fuller was the boss at that time or at least that was the impression I was under. The Grahams had control of the bottom half of Florida, so SECW didn't go into their territory. Back then, promoters respected boundaries and companies didn't go into someone else's territory to run a show. Of course, Vince McMahon Jr. ended up going against that code of ethics in the mid 80s, but that's another story. At one time, if a promoter overstepped their jurisdiction, they could expect strong repercussions such as flat tires on their ring trailer or whatever else it took to send a message. Promoters took that kind of stuff very seriously; it is all about the bottom line. Everybody wanted to feed their families. I was excited to talk with Bob because I enjoyed working alongside him and his boys when I wrestled for Georgia Championship Wrestling.

"Harris, do you have a minute to talk?" He asked.

"Sure, Bob. What can I do for you?" I returned.

"What do you think about coming to Pensacola, Florida, and wrestling for Southeastern Championship Wrestling.?" Bob inquired.

"It might be something I'd be interested in. Of course, I want to talk with Bonnie about it first," I said.

"Absolutely. I can understand that. We will be giving you a bit of a push too," he continued. "You won't have to be doing all of these squash jobs." He assured.

"I like the sound of that!" I replied.

"I think you will be a good fit over here, Harris," Bob added.

"When you say a bit of a push, what exactly do you mean by that?" I inquired.

"Main events, the belt, promos, you will be working on top," he promised.

"Wow! That sounds like something me and Bonnie will have to talk about!" I told Bob before hanging up the phone.

If I had learned anything in my first eight years of being in professional wrestling, the office will tell a wrestler whatever it is that they think he or she wants to hear. However, after I hung up the phone with Bob, I knew he was going to follow through with everything that he told me. It wasn't too hard for me to convince Bonnie that moving to Pensacola was a good idea. She knew that I was ready for the next step in my career. Bob saw that I had promise and I was grateful for that. When I showed up at Southeastern Championship Wrestling, they recorded a vignette of me so that they could introduce me to their audience. Upon my arrival at SECW, I was renamed Mountain Man Harris. Vignettes or promos were often used back then to acquaint the wrestler who was new to the territory with the local fans.

In this promo, my character was standing in a field digging up Mason Jars. Inside the jars was my treasure. They were full of my money. I have no idea how many jars the production team hid in the ground that day, but there were several. My progress was stopped when the Midnight Express spotted me as they drove on the nearby road. At that particular time, the Midnight Express consisted of Bobby Eaton, Randy Rose, and Norvell Austin. They acted surprised to see a man of my size and they invited me to go wrestle with them. Shooting the video for the introduction of Mountain Man Harris was a lot of fun and I was looking forward to the upcoming weeks of the television tapings!

The roster in the Southeastern Championship Wrestling was stacked nicely with talent. They had wrestlers such as Ken Lucas, Jerry Stubbs, Terry Gordy, Joe LeDuc, Jaques Rogeau, Ron Starr, Wayne Farris (The Honky Tonk Man), and so many others. I always found it interesting that even though the guys and gals were different in other territories, they were all very similar in one way or the other. There was a guy on the bottom, that was always going to be on the bottom, and there was a guy on the top who was probably always going to be on the top. There was mutual respect among the boys. However, if someone wanted your spot, and if they ended up taking it from you, they weren't going to lose sleep over it!

Holding a title was the one thing that I thought of doing since I started wrestling. Some guys may tell you that being a champion in wrestling isn't that big of a deal. It was for me! A champion is on top, he gets more exposure, and he can make more money. Being the champion meant that the office believed that wrestler could make money for the promotion. I always knew that I could do that. I took my first belt off of Ken Lucas and held it for 49 days. Staring at the National Wrestling Alliance Alabama Heavyweight Title after I won it, was quite the thrill for me and I believe it was for Bonnie too.

"Can you believe it, Bonnie?" I asked.

"Yes, I believe it. You've worked hard for that Dear," she congratulated me.

"It's nice to look at this belt up close like this," I said.

"It's the first of many, I'm proud of you," she replied.

She was right, the Alabama Heavyweight Title was the first of many, and staring at the belts after I won them never got old. Sometimes, I recognized certain details in the craftsmanship that I didn't notice the first 100 times I glared at them. To me, being the Champion meant something because the promoter was counting on me to be the draw. I knew that I was up for the job. It wasn't too long after I won the Alabama Championship, I went to Japan for my very first wrestling tour.

It was in August 1983, when I got the call to go overseas to wrestle with All Japan Pro Wrestling. Since I started wrestling, I had heard so many stories about the kind of money the boys were making there wrestling. All Japan Pro Wrestling was owned by Giant Baba. Giant Baba was nearly seven feet tall and he weighed 300 pounds. On two different occasions, Baba defeated Harley Race to win the National Wrestling Alliance Heavyweight title. One of those times was in 1979 and the other time was in 1980. Baba didn't hold on to the belt very long at all and Harley got it,. back from him each time. However, I'm sure that Baba's reign as the NWA Champion boosted the stock in his promotion. My tour to go to Japan was in the works well before I had ever left my second run with the Crocketts in the Summer of 1983. The idea to go over there was brought to me by Ricky Steamboat and Jay Youngblood. Those two guys were extremely popular in Japan. However, I do believe David Crockett ended up making the travel arraignments for me with Baba. The conversation I had with Jay and Ricky went something like this.

"Harris, are you ready to make a trip overseas? Ricky asked.

"I'll go wherever," I stated.

"I think you do well in Japan, Harris," Jay said.

"I guess there is one way to find out," I returned.

"You'll like it over there, plus the money is pretty good," Jay mentioned.

"What do I have to do?" I wanted to know.

"If you want to go, I will let the right people know," Ricky replied.

"I want to go," I told them.

The country of Japan and its spectators have a high regard for the sport. If the fans or the bookers don't like a specific wrestler, that wrestler won't get invited back. It's that simple. Not every American wrestler liked going to Japan, but the ones who did made a habit of working there often. The money I made there wasn't pretty good, it was damn good! I was very pleased with the payday that I came home with. I could always pay something off and sock some money away for a rainy day. Bonnie liked how I got paid in Japan also.

I don't know if all the boys from the States felt this way, but I was under the impression that the Japanese people resented the Americans who visited their country for the bombings they received from our government in 1945. Of course, it was a cultural shock for me because I couldn't speak the language. I did meet some people who spoke English, but a lot of times if I wanted something to eat, I felt like I was playing a game of Charades. The American wrestlers also stood out over there because I think the average height of a man in Japan is five feet and two inches, and to them, I'm sure we all looked like giants.

There were several American wrestlers on this particular trip with me. I remember that guys like Chavo Guerrero, Stan Hanson, Bruiser Brody, Buzz Tyler, Terry Gordy, Manny Fernandez, and Brad Rheingans were there most of the time that I was there. Tenryu was there too. It was great being able to catch up and visit with him. We could make each other laugh without even saying a word. I wrestled him that trip and it was an absolute treat for me. Unfortunately, while I was on the flight to go there, I came down with some kind of stomach bug. I recall being pretty sick the entire first week. There were some nights I didn't think I was going to get through my match without shitting myself, but luckily, I did. If you don't wrestle, you don't get paid. I wanted to get paid, so I wrestled. The wrestlers who were more experienced with the scene over there looked after me. It seemed as if Stan, Brody, and Tenryu had almost the same conversation with me every night.

"Don't let anyone back you into a corner," Brody said.

"If they do, you turn their ass around and do the same thing to them," Stan interjected.

"It's the same thing if someone does it in the States, but the difference here is that it happens often," Brody added.

"You're tough, don't be afraid to use your strength, you have to draw the line with some of these guys," Tenryu mentioned.

"I can fight if I have to," I boasted.

"We know you can fight, Harris," Tenryu continued. "Show your opponents that you can fight and you will be just fine."

My three friends couldn't have been more truthful. Everything played out in the ring just like they warned me. I don't think the Japanese wrestlers were trying to hurt their opponents, but I do think that they were trying to make some kind of a point. However, that was never really explained to me, but I knew if I wanted respect over there, it was going to be on a give-and-take basis. Believe me! I gave it and took it every chance I could!

I was introduced to Ribera Steak House. The place is iconic and it's a very popular eating spot for the boys. The steak is huge and so delicious. The meat is cooked to order and served with a square of butter on top and a side of corn. The owner is a huge wrestling fan and he covers the walls and ceiling with pictures of the wrestlers from all over the world who have been there. The restaurant isn't very big at all. Chavo Guerrero took me there and we had an amazing time. The steaks were huge and the entire staff treated us like kings. I still have my satin jacket from there. It's in my closet wrapped in plastic. Ribera was just one of those places that I always heard about from the other wrestlers, and somewhere I had to go before I left Japan.

Upon my return to the States, I immediately went back into my daily routine of wrestling and traveling for SECW. One of the things that I thought made living in Pensacola so special was the beautiful scenery and the accessibility to the Gulf of Mexico. The water was turquoise blue and the sand was as white as sugar. Spotting marine wildlife, such as sea turtles and dolphins was very common. It was a lot of fun to spend our downtime at the beach. My good friend in this territory was Terry Gordy, who later became one of the Fabulous Freebirds along with Michael Hayes and Buddy Roberts. Terry started wrestling when he was just 16 years old. I don't know how he got away with something like that back then. You had to have a license to wrestle and you had to be 18 to get it. The rules were pretty strict. I don't know if he had a phony document that proved he was of legal age, but he wrestled. He was darn good at it too. Terry lived the good life when I knew him. He lived in his van which he parked in Gulf Breeze. I think Terry paid a couple of bucks per day to stay at the Gulf Breeze Bridge, so I'm sure it was economically sound for him. The huge bridge is one that everyone referred to it as the Three Mile Bridge and it was what connected the cities of Pensacola and Gulf Breeze. We fished off and around that bridge often. Coming by the park daily was a food truck, a beer wagon, and a bait vendor, so, Terry had all the essentials that he needed!

On my days off, I drove down there with Bonnie to meet Terry. We only had fishing on our minds. It was a fun and relaxing way to unwind. We had several coolers. Some of them had been filled with ice to keep our drinks nice and cold and the others were just full of ice, to keep our catch nice and fresh. We spent a good bit of the day drinking beer and catching what became our feast for that evening. We caught a bunch of silver trout and I set out traps to catch crabs. It didn't take long until some of the other wrestlers that we worked with found out how we spent our time off. We were often met by Jody Hamilton (The Assassin), Peggy Lee, Leilani Kai, the Fabulous Moolah, the Armstrongs, and any of the other wrestlers that were around at that territory then. The kind of camaraderie that I had with the SECW roster was something very special and something I hold fondly in my memories today.

In the later part of my time in SECW, I wrestled under a mask and I was called El Lobo the Bull. I had never worn a mask inside the ring, but I was up for the task. I suppose one of the wrestlers left, quit, or got fired which opened a spot on the roster that the office had to fill. I remember being approached by Bob one day before a television taping in Mobile.

"Harris, how are you?" Bob asked.

"I'm doing well Bob, how are you?" I returned.

"Blessed, he said with a smile. "Would you be

interested in wrestling twice for us tonight?"

"Sure!" I responded.

"Once as Mountain Man Harris and once as El Lobo the Bull?" He hinted.

"El Lobo the who?" I questioned with a laugh.

"El Lobo the Bull. I need someone that I can count on to pull double duty when I need them to," Bob explained.

"No problem, Bob. Anything for you, my friend." I spoke.

"Great! And don't you worry, we will pay you for both matches," he made clear.

"I never doubted that for a minute, Bob," I replied.

I usually wrestled as El Lobo in the first or second match and later in the show, I'd be in the co-main event or the main event wrestling as Mountain Man Harris. Sometimes it was the other way around, but Mountain Man Harris usually had a better spot on the card than El Lobo did. The style of the mask covered the top of my skull, but there was an opening that exposed my beard and there was a hole in the back so my ponytail was exposed to the crowd. To me, it looked like Mountain Man Harris was wearing a mask on his head. Since I was getting paid extra, I didn't care what it looked like.

During this period, Bob was the top wrestler for SECW. I say this because he was the guy who was getting the push. He held the NWA Southeastern Heavyweight Title on several occasions and when Ric Flair came in to defend his world belt, he usually wrestled Bob. Bob was also in the main events, the big angles, and a lot of gimmick matches. Since he and Robert Fuller worked closely together in the office, I'm sure he understood Robert's vision for the company. Back then, the promoter or the promoter's family, or someone who was well trusted was put into the top spot. Plus, Bob was the booker. He could have any spot on the card that he wanted, everyone wanted to be on top!

The Armstrongs lived in Gulf Breeze, so if we ever had shots in Birmingham or Huntsville, I rode with Bob and Brad. Those rides were long so, it was nice to have their company. Most times, Bonnie dropped me off at a gas station or a convenience store where they agreed to pick me up. The store was about 10 miles from where Bonnie and I lived. One particular morning after she dropped me off while I was waiting for Bob and Brad, I decided to go to the restroom to take a piss. The restroom was on the outside of the building, but I had to go inside the store to get the key from the attendant. Walking back outside in the direction of the bathroom, I placed the key into the lock and opened the door. My expectation of finding a clean restroom at this gas station wasn't high. However, I have to admit that I was pleasantly surprised. I went into the stall so I could do my business and on the floor behind the toilet, I noticed what appeared to be money. I bent down and I picked it up and it was money alright. A wad of money! At that moment I didn't count it, but it appeared to be several hundred dollars all in 20-dollar bills. After I finished in the restroom, I returned the key and walked back outside. As I stood in front of the convenience store waiting for my ride, I noticed another twenty dollars blowing across the concrete. I followed it which led to a few more which led to more money scattered around the small building.

"What the hell happened?" I asked myself. "Maybe there was some kind of a robbery," I thought.

I continued to pick up all the money I saw without making it look like I was picking up money. I didn't know if I was being set up or what. It's not every day one stumbles across a payday like that one. I was walking around on the side of the gas station when Bob and Brad pulled up.

"Hey there Harris," Brad said.

"Hello gentlemen," I replied.

"Did you lose something out there? Bob asked.

"I thought I dropped a quarter, but I'm good. I'm ready to go," I replied as I jumped into the back seat of their car.

The money that I found at the store that morning was better than the payoff I made that night. To this day, I have no idea where that money came from, but Bonnie sure was happy that I found it.

A well-known masked wrestler in that area at the time was Mr. Olympia. He also worked in the Mid-South territory when I did. The man underneath the headgear was Jerry Stubbs. I got along with Jerry alright. Mr. Olympia was sometimes a good guy and sometimes a bad guy, the fans seemed to love him or hated him depending on his role. Mr. Olympia had a tag team partner in the Southeastern territory, and they had an angle in which they split from each other. The partner's name was Super Olympia, and under that mask was Arn Anderson. I liked Arn and I felt like we struck up a good friendship at SECW. We liked drinking beer together and I considered him to be one of the boys who was a "solid dude." When I met Arn, he might have been wrestling for two years at that time. He was good in the ring then, just as he was when his career progressed. Arn could wrestle a broomstick and have a good match with it. When people in the sport use that term to describe someone, it meant that wrestler could wrestle anyone. And Arn could wrestle anyone. He was that good. For the life of me, I don't know why Robert and Bob weren't giving him a better push in their company. I know that Arn wasn't happy with the way that the office was using him in the territory because the two of us spoke about it often.

"I feel like I could be doing more Harris," Arn confided.

"I think you're doing well. You're having good matches with good competition," I reminded him.

"I want great matches, Harris," he stated.

"They will come, Arn. It takes time. I was on the bottom for a long time," I explained.

"I'm Super Olympia, Harris," Arn growled.

"And I'm El Lobo. It's a job in pro wrestling. It's what we both wanted," I said.

"I feel like I could be doing more than Super Olympia," he responded.

"I'm sure everybody feels like that sometimes," I assured.

"You know the Crocketts and you know Dusty. Is there any way that you can help get into working with either of them?" Arn wondered.

"Send a tape to Dusty. Let him know who you are. Get on his radar," I insisted.

At that time in pro wrestling Dusty Rhodes was the man. He had a knack for going into areas and increasing their attendance. Not only at live shows but also with the television ratings as well. A lot of the boys wanted to work with him, because he had good ideas for wrestlers and wrestling gimmicks, and he could pull a storyline for two wrestlers out of thin air. At that time in his career, he was still with Florida Championship Wrestling. I kept encouraging Arn to send Dusty a tape with some promos and a few of his best matches on it. I'm not sure if Arn ever followed through with my advice at that time. The person that ended up getting a call from Dusty was me!

CHAPTER 11 - BECOMING BLACK BART

To have the opportunity to work with The American Dream, Dusty Rhodes in the early 1980s, was a wrestler's dream come true. Florida Championship Wrestling was owned and operated by Eddie Graham and the bookers at the time were Dusty and Kevin Sullivan. Separately, both bookers were geniuses, but together they were incredible! They kept the people anticipating what was going to happen next. I showed up there at the tail end of 1983. Before working full-time with Florida Championship Wrestling, if I was ever offered a match there, I took it. Florida was the place to be and the excitement that was being created in the storylines there was captivating. Not to mention the caliber of talent such as guys like Blackjack Mulligan, Barry Windham, The One-Man Gang, Billy Graham, Hector Guerrero, Denny Brown, Billy Jack Haynes, Kendo Nagasaki, Mike Davis, Mike Rotundo, and the referee Bill Alfonzo. Fans packed the Sportatorium in Tampa on Wednesday night, The Eddie Graham Sports Arena on Thursday night in Orlando, and we wrestled in Miami on Friday night. The rest of the nights of the week, we hit small towns with spot shows until we made our way back to Tampa for the next television taping.

Coming up the ranks of pro wrestling, I crossed paths with Dusty many times. Dusty was familiar with my work from my time in Georgia and Southeastern Championship Wrestling. It meant a lot to me that he even considered having me on his roster. In Eddie's territory, there was just a special kind of magic happening in pro wrestling around that time. So, when I got the call from Dusty, I must admit that I was excited about our conversation.

"Harris, this is Dusty Rhodes from down here in Orlando. How are you doing Baby?" Dusty asked.

"Hello, Dusty. I'm doing pretty good," I replied.

"That's a good Baby. That's good. Listen up Harris I have some good news Baby! We want to bring you into Florida Championship Wrestling." Dusty affirmed.

"Okay, that sounds good," I responded.

"I have an idea for you, Baby. I'm going to team you up with Ron Bass and I'm going to call you two the Long Riders. J.J. Dillon will be your manager. What do you think about all that?" Dusty questioned me.

"I think that all sounds great Dusty," I answered.

"That's good Baby. That's good. We want to call you Black Bart," Dusty said. "You good with that Baby?" He asked.

"I'm very good with that," I affirmed.

"I'm glad to hear that Bart," Dusty said in his soft southern tone.

I was right when I felt that good things were about to happen for me in my career! Here was an opportunity that doesn't come knocking too often. I immediately spoke with Bonnie about the conversation that I had with Dusty. I didn't think that there was a whole lot of convincing I was going to have to do with her. Bonnie and I had talked often about certain opportunities and what our decisions were going to be if they came our way. Bonnie knew who Dusty was. Anyone familiar with wrestling at that period did. Going to wrestle for Eddie Graham and Florida Championship Wrestling was a no-brainer. I was going and I couldn't wait to get there! Before heading to Tampa, I went back to Texas. I went back home to Fort Worth. I knew exactly what I needed for the Black Bart gimmick and I knew where to find it all. I was willing to put some cash down for some new gear. I needed a long-rider jacket, a new Stetson hat, and a pair of new boots. I went to the north side of Fort Worth which is called Cowtown because I knew that I was going to find everything that I was looking for there. It took me no time to find a cream-colored long-rider jacket and a nice cowboy hat. When it came to the boots that I wanted, which were the Triple Eagle Austin Halls, I didn't feel good about spending two to three grand on them at that moment. So, I went into a boot shop and purchased a nice pair of cowboy boots. I knew a guy who repaired shoes and boots and I asked him to remove the heels and replace them with a crape sole which would make the bottom of my boots flat. He did and they turned out to be an excellent pair of boots to wrestle in. Along with my attire, I had a few ropes and bullwhips made to assist me in making the Black Bart character more authentic.

Some of my first few matches with FCW were against Mike Davis. He was already familiar with the territory since he wrestled there two years prior. It had been a year or two since Mike and I worked in the same area together. However, it felt like we had picked up right where we had left off the last time, we saw each other.

"I glad you're here Harris," Mike grinned.

"I'm glad to be here too, but my name is Bart now. Get it right Mike," I insisted.

"Oh, excuse me, Black Bart, please don't hurt me with your bullwhip," he said sarcastically with a laugh.

"I will Black Bart you, Dummy!" I snapped.

"You're going to like it here. The territory is hot right now," he added.

"I know, just look at who is wrestling down here," I declared.

"Dusty knows exactly what to do when it comes to increasing the size of the crowd," Mike said. "He has the golden touch!"

Just as Dusty promised in our first conversation about me coming to Florida, I teamed up with Cowboy Ron Bass. The thing that stood out about Ron was his black colored handlebar mustache. He and I had worked together in the Carolinas. Ron was a ripper and a tearer. Meaning if he ever thought he had to defend himself, he could rip your face off without barely any effort. We had mutual respect for one another. However, when we felt like we had spent too much time with each other, we went our separate ways. The two of us were together so much and since we had to work so cohesively with each other, we didn't want to ruin a good thing. I had mentioned previously that Mike Davis and I were just like brothers, well, Ron Bass and I were like brothers too. Mike was the brother I usually got along with, and Ron was the brother I usually put up with, but I didn't love him any less. I just had a different kind of friendship with those two men. Ron was what I call a triple-tough dude. Not every wrestler wanted to work with him. It wasn't that Ron was hard to work with, but the boys knew if they pissed Ron off, he would let them know about it. Ron always sent his message hard and swiftly! Not too many people messed with Ron because they knew that he was going to beat their ass. I knew that he could have beat my ass, but he never did. I never wanted to go down that road with him. I knew what Ron was capable of doing and I respected him for that.

Ron and I, along with J.J. Dillon had a good thing going down in Florida. The three of us complimented each other very well. As a team, we were solid. We all could work in the ring, and we could all talk on the microphone. We also had respect for the profession, and we all had a solid understanding of the psychology of wrestling. J.J. was so good at stirring the pot and getting under the people's skin, that the fans couldn't help but hate him. I honestly believe he could piss off a Monk. Listening to J.J. cut a promo or hearing him set up a storyline was pure enjoyment. He was quite the talker.

Dusty constantly thought about how he could draw more people to the shows. He often moved guys around on the card, sometimes they were in the preliminary matches, sometimes they were in the mid-card, and sometimes they were in the main events. Dusty knew his roster well and he was familiar with their strength and weaknesses. There were an array of gimmick matches at the events in Florida. We had Bunkhouse, Taped Fists, Dog Collar, Bull Rope, Lumberjack, Kendo Stick, Indian Strap, Steel Cage, and Barbed Wire matches. The people who supported pro wrestling in Southern Florida came out in droves, and the reason why was because Dusty wasn't afraid to take risks. He could take a simple idea and twist it ever so slightly, and by doing that, he made that idea so much better. Dusty listened and he watched. If Dusty wasn't in the dressing room, he could be found hidden away in a dark corner of the venue, so, he could get a better feel for the crowd. Dusty wanted to hear what they cheered for and what they booed at. He truly had his finger on the pulse of professional wrestling. It wasn't just gimmick matches, it was the storylines that he and Kevin created there that helped stir up the emotions of fans. Dusty put himself under a hood and called himself the Midnight Rider. Everyone knew it was Dusty, but all those who came out wanted to know how the story was going to end. Dusty took the wrestling fans for a ride and they all enjoyed it!

Ron Bass was knee-deep in an angle with Barry Windham when I settled in southern Florida. They fought over a saddle which led to a Loser Leaves Town Match. Barry might have gotten Ron's saddle, but he was the one who lost the contest and ultimately, Barry had to leave town. To make things a little interesting with those two foes, Dusty put a mask on Barry and called him the Dirty Yellow Dog. The Yellow Dog gimmick might have only lasted a month before Barry returned as himself, but it was those kinds of storylines and ideas that made longtime customers of Eddie's promotion. While in CWF, I was in a series of gimmick matches with Barry. When I met Barry, he was tall and lanky. He hadn't filled out yet. As time went on, he put on some more weight, but in 1984, he was skinny! Despite his build, Barry was a tough kid, and he brought it every night. He was young and the girls liked him. Barry was the ultimate babyface. He could sell his punishment and he made everything he went through look believable. The fans empathized with him and the more that I tortured Barry, the more the people loved him. Sometimes returning to the dressing was a challenge for me after I beat Barry to a pulp. The fans bought what we were selling, hook line, and sinker and because of it, I got hit with cups of coke, snuff spit, and concession stand food that were all thrown at me.

When Ron and I started teaming together, our first set of opponents was Mike Davis and Mike Rotundo. We challenged them for their National Wrestling Alliance Florida United States Tag Team Championship. When they were champions, the championship was a trophy. It was almost as tall as they were and to take it to the next show, the trophy had to be dismantled and packed up. Every time the champions with the trophy arrived to a show for a title defense, they had to spend time putting the trophy together when they arrived at the venue. I almost didn't want to win the championship just because of that reason. However, on February 6th, 1984 in Palm Beach when Ron and I defeated Mike Rotundo and Mike Davis for the NWA Florida U.S. tag title, the promotion replaced the trophy with brand-new belts. I was relieved that Eddie did that. I didn't think that Ron and I had enough patience to mess with that trophy all the time. We had one heck of a laugh in the dressing room after the match.

"Isn't that some crap!" Mike Davis spouted off.

"Did you want to get a closer look at my belt, Davis?" I asked.

"I was hoping to watch you struggle while putting that trophy together," he continued. "That would have brought me great pleasure."

"I could put that trophy together with my eyes closed," I returned.

"Bart, you're so impatient. Eddie would have found that trophy in the dumpster if they gave it to you and Ron," Davis said.

"Well, that's where you can put it now because we have these new shiny belts," I laughed and grinned.

On May 17, 1984, as Black Bart, I had what seemed like a once-in-a-lifetime experience take place. I had the opportunity to wrestle Kerry Von Erich for the National Wrestling Alliance Heavyweight Championship Title in Melbourne, Florida. The match was special to me for a couple of reasons. It was my first time to wrestle for that particular belt. I was also stepping in the ring with Fritz Von Erich's son. I think what made that contest so significant was that we lost David Von Erich just three months prior. His unexpected death in Japan affected a lot of people all around the world. If David were alive today, there would still be a prominent wrestling company in the state of Texas. I guarantee it! I can't add to what has already been stated for the past four decades about David's death. I liked him a lot. David was tough as they come, and I thought he was the best wrestler of the whole bunch. Of all the brothers, David was the whole package. A good promoter and a good booker could build a company around a wrestler like him. I still think back to the times that I spent with him in Georgia Championship Wrestling. I know that it has been 40 years since his passing, but sometimes it feels just like it was just yesterday. David was something special. To see Kerry with that belt was cool, but I believed just like everyone else did at that time, that the NWA was planning to crown David with it. Those who never got to see David wrestle missed out! Seeing Kerry in the dressing room the day that we wrestled was nice. I hadn't seen a Von Erich since David died, so speaking with his brother was a bit emotional for the two of us.

"Hello Kerry," I greeted him.

"Hi Bart," How are you?" Kerry Asked.

"I'm doing good," I responded. "Kerry, I'm sorry about what happened to David."

"Thank you, Bart," he sighed.

"I still find it hard to accept the fact he's gone," I spoke.

"Honestly, I don't know if I will ever be able to accept it. I struggle with his absence all the time," Kerry shared.

At that moment, I felt a sadness come over me, not so much for David or myself, but for Kerry and his family members. It was a heartbreaking situation. Kerry successfully defended his title to me, and I was okay with that. Wrestling for the NWA Title put me on the biggest stage and I was thrilled to be able to do that. When I think back to that day, I have troubles remembering what we did in the match. However, I will never forget how I felt. Of course, I had butterflies in my stomach, but I have never been prouder to be a wrestler. Kerry lost the belt back to Ric Flair just seven days later in Japan.

Kevin, David, and Kerry Von Erich all brought something different to the ring with their wrestling styles. With David gone, there was a lot more pressure put on Kerry to fill the role that he left behind. Kerry was good, and he had the charisma and the personality of a true star. On top of that, his physique was amazing! Fritz expected his boys to be the best in pro wrestling. That expectation and the pressure they all felt from their father, had to be the toughest opponents the brothers ever faced!

CHAPTER 12 - FLORIDA CHAMPIONSHIP WRESTLERS

You could write a whole book on the talent that was in the Sunshine State during the eight months that I worked there. There was so much happening at that time, and that was the main reason why the territory was so popular. It's hard not to bring up the matches that Dusty Rhodes and Kevin Sullivan had against each other at that time. The chemistry that those two wrestlers had while working for Eddie was magical. Those two men not only came up with good ideas, but they also knew how to execute them and carry those storylines over a long stretch of time. They made a lot of money for Eddie, and the boys that were on the roster at that time did too.

In the summer of 1984 when Kevin was doing his devil gimmick, he had a motley crew to say the least. Kevin called his group the Army of Darkness. He had Bob Roop and Mark Lewin and a few others in that storyline. One person that sticks out to me, not only because she was pretty - and I cannot forget a pretty face - is Nancy Toffoloni. Nancy played the role of Kevin's valet, and she was called The Fallen Angel. I didn't have a lot of interaction with her, but we shared pleasantries, and she was always very kind and respectful to me. She was one of those people who genuinely cared about others. I know that her and Kevin got married, I just don't know if they were married when I worked with them. Kevin's group sometimes wore paint on their faces, carried snakes, and they acted like they were possessed. Every member was intriguing and they kept the Florida fans in disbelief!

A successful movie not only needs the top stars in the leading roles, but it also needs a great supporting cast, Florida Championship Wrestling could check all boxes. Mike Graham, what can I say? He was the promoter's son, but unlike other promoter's sons who I had worked with, he was the most reliable. Graham worked hard too, he wasn't the biggest guy in the dressing room, but he had a big pair of nuts! My good buddy, Gene Lewis was also there. To me, he was one of the best chameleons in the business of pro wrestling. Gene could take on a gimmick, and he became that character so well. Sometimes, when Gene morphed into a different persona, I forget that it was him. At World Class and in the Mid-South territories he was called the Mongol. In Florida, he wrestled as Molokai and Kharma, but in the mid-80s when he worked in the World Wrestling Federation, he wrestled as Cousin Junior along the sides of Uncle Elmer and Hillbilly Jim. Gene was a tremendous wrestler and a very good friend to me up until his death in 2013. Joe Lightfoot was a wrestler that I had some good matches with. When a promotion has a cowboy and an Indian gimmick running at the same time, a feud is there available at any time the box office needs a boost. Joe could work anywhere on the card and his two decades in the business proved that.

It was also in the Sunshine State that I met Buzz Sawyer. He spent 15 years in pro wrestling, and Buzz wrestled all over the place. The two of us crossed paths from time to time as we both worked our way around the territories. Buzz wasn't the biggest guy in wrestling, but I promise you that he was one of the toughest. Buzz had some notable feuds throughout his career. Some angles that come to my mind that he was involved in were Jim Duggan, Arn Anderson, and Dick Murdoch. However, wrestling fans in southern parts of the United States, especially, in the early 80s will never forget the bloodbaths that occurred between himself and Tommy Rich. For each gimmick match and every main event that those two men were a part of, they achieved the goal - they packed the venues with people. Their on-going battle lasted a year and a half if not longer!

I recall the time that Buzz came into the Florida territory. It was around Springtime of 1984. The way that I remember the story, Dusty brought him into Orlando, and the idea was to have Buzz interfere in the main event which paired Blackjack Mulligan against Kevin Sullivan. I suppose that Dusty had plans to use him in some big matches down the road. Unfortunately, not every plan in pro wrestling comes off without a hitch. The hitch that occurred on this particular day was that Buzz fell asleep! Buzz arrived in the afternoon before the event ever started. The idea that Dusty and Kevin came up with was to hide Buzz under the ring. When the final match ended, he was to come out from under the ring and surprise everyone with his presence. Helping Kevin attack Blackjack was the plan, but since Buzz dozed off waiting for his cue, it changed the finish of the match slightly. At the end of the night, Dusty was pissed off!

"Isn't that some shit?" Dusty fumed. "He had one damn job!"

"Where is he right now?" Eddie asked.

"The same place he has been since five o'clock," Dusty continued. "Sleeping under the ring!"

"Nobody has spoken to him yet?" Eddie questioned.

"Bill, go down there and wake Buzz's ass up!" Dusty yelled to Bill Alfonzo the referee. "I will fire his ass, damn it!" Dusty warned!

If Buzz did get fired that night, his termination didn't last long. If my memory serves me correctly, he worked in the territory for another month and a half.

If the memories that we were making were not taking place in the buildings that we worked in or inside the rings where we wrestled, they were happening on the car rides as well. Hanging out and sharing car rides with Mike Davis was always a fun time. The two of us found ourselves in a few crazy and unpredictable situations. A lot of these moments took place either going to or coming from a wrestling show. Mike and I both enjoyed fishing. We kept our fishing gear in the trunks of our vehicles for a spontaneous excursion. If we saw something that looked like we could fish in, we stopped and casted our lines. One evening, Mike and I were driving at night from Fort Myers to Hollywood on a highway known to the locals as Alligator Alley. That area is like one huge swamp. I made it a point to always carry a spotlight in my car. If we ever had to pull over at a rest stop, I wanted to be able to light up the area. I never wanted to walk upon a lurking alligator or Cottonmouth snake. This one night we pulled over and we stopped our vehicle near a body of water that we had fished in the past. From the side of the road, Mike and I could shine our spotlights off into the distance and see several pairs of red eyes staring back at us! After several minutes of observing, we lost count of how many sets of peepers disappeared and then returned. It might have only been one alligator blinking at us the entire time, though I doubt it. I walked back to the car and I sat down in the driver's seat, Mike yelled out to me.

"Are you going fishing?" He asked with a silly smirk on his face.

"I'm not going fishing. Get in the car," I insisted.

"Pop the trunk Bart, a few minutes of fishing isn't going to hurt anything," he pleaded.

"Are you going to try and catch an alligator, Dummy?" I asked as walked to the back of the car to open the trunk.

"I'm going to try," Mike replied.

"Okay, you're drunk. Maybe you should get back into the car," I suggested.

"Maybe you're the only drunk person here, Dad!" He said sarcastically as he grabbed the fishing gear from the trunk, as he walked away from my vehicle.

At this point, I knew there was no way of convincing Mike that fishing at this moment was a bad idea, so I joined him. We found a spot near the side of the highway. Since it was dark, I was taking turns between shining the light on what Mike was doing with the fishing poles, and keeping an eye on our surroundings for any unwanted visitors. In doing all this, I noticed Mike had taken one of my favorite fishing lures from my tackle box to use on his line.

"Mike! Is that my $8 fishing lure that I see on your pole?" I wondered.

"Maybe," he answered back.

"Take it off right now!" I exclaimed. "That lure is for bass fishing!"

"I'm bass fishing," he returned.

"With all those eyes that we see, the only thing that you're going to catch is an alligator," I told him sharply.

"Well then, I guess I'm catching an alligator tonight," Mike replied.

Mike had his mind set on fishing, so, it was a lot easier just to let him do it. Mike had his fishing pole ready to go. I had my light shined on him and I could my shiny lure. I knew that was the last time I was going to see it.

"Mike, if you lose my lure, you will owe me $8," I demanded.

"I'm not going to lose your stupid lure. You are sounding like my dad right now, Dad" Mike went on.

Mike walked over to the edge of the shore to cast his line. He stood there at first looking like a professional angler until he felt a tug on his line. He could hardly contain himself as he began to jump up and down as if he had to pee.

"Look here! I got something," he declared. "We'll be eating bass tonight!"

"If you're lucky you caught a bass. Your line is either caught on something or you caught an alligator," I commented.

At that moment, Mike started fighting with the pole. I thought he was just trying to be funny. As time passed, I took him more seriously. Mike turned to me in my direction.

"Bart! Get over here and help me!" He shouted.

I ran over to where Mike was and I stood right behind him. I reached my arms around his body, and I put my hands next to his on the pole. We both started pulling with all our might.

"You got an alligator, Dummy," I yelled.

"We will be eating alligator tonight!" Mike blurted.

Suddenly the rod flew out of our grasps, and we heard a splash into the water. I quickly grabbed the spotlight and shined it into the water where I thought that I heard the rod land.

"Holy cow! My fishing pole is taking off! He exclaimed.

"An alligator took it," I replied.

"I liked that rod and reel," he pouted.

"I liked that lure too! You owe me $ 8, Mike!" I fumed!

"Go get it from the alligator. I'm going back to the car," Mike spoke as he walked away from where I stood.

The two of us laughed about that night of fishing for quite some time. Whenever we went fishing after that incident, we always asked each other if we had planned to fish for bass or alligator. Mike never paid me for the lure that he lost, and the alligator never reimbursed Mike for his fishing pole.

When I wasn't fishing, I was back in the ring. Ron and I were defending our Florida U.S. Tag Belts. For Mike Davis, he went on a tour to Japan and when he returned, he transformed himself into a new persona. It is one of the more entertaining storylines that I can remember. The story was put out that while Mike was in Japan, he suffered a traumatic head injury which altered his personality. Mike began to portray a spitting image of Dusty Rhodes. However, his Dusty Rhodes wasn't a babyface, he was a heel, and he ran around with Kevin and his twisted little group. Mike was hilarious in this role, and it went on for several months. In my opinion, Mike did a better Dusty than Dusty. It was too funny!

Now that Mike Davis was being used differently in the territory, Mike Rotundo needed a partner and they put him with Barry Windham. Barry and Rotundo went on to have a long and intense series of matches with Ron and me. Whether they were tag matches or single events they always brought out the best in all of us. Those belts switched hands several times and there was a lot of blood spilled between our teams. Mike Rotundo was a real wrestler; he could stretch me and Ron at the same time. If one wasn't paying attention, people might mistake Mike for a pretzel maker because that was how he made Ron and I look most nights.

Rotundo and Barry were amazing wrestling talents. At some point, Mike married Barry's sister so, they were in-laws. They both were athletic, good-looking, and tough. It was easy for Ron and I to get heat when we wrestled them. The Florida fans really got into the matches that we had against the two young babyfaces. The people hated us! J.J. Dillion as our manager, well, nobody squirted fuel on the fire better than he did! All the storylines that Dusty and Kevin created were entertaining to our fanbase.

People could not stop watching CWF and new fans were being pulled in just by word of mouth. We started doing shots in smaller towns because our product was in high demand. We did double shots on Friday, Saturday, and Sunday. The schedule was a bit of a challenge, yet at the same time, it was exhilarating. I loved the adrenaline rush that I got from the audience! I remember talking to Ron while leaving a gymnasium after a match that we had with Barry and Rotundo.

"Ron, how many people do you think were in that gym tonight?" I questioned.

"I don't know. 500 or 600 hundred maybe. It wasn't that big of a space, but it was packed," Ron said.

"It was standing room only," I gasped.

"I think the crowds are getting bigger. That's a good sign, Bart," Ron continued. "Be concerned when the crowd is not big."

A lot of the conversations I had with Ron were like that. He knew the pro wrestling business well enough to share what he knew and he was able to share his experiences. Ron and I weren't ones to share our feeling with each other, but we talked about the stuff that we thought was important when we had to.

Barry and I had some wars! In the dressing room we got the finish, but I called the match in the ring. He followed my direction very well. I had a great match every time I wrestled Barry. He always made things that easy. Barry didn't have an ego when I worked with him, he was as humble as humble could be. I had some dog collar matches with Barry that I thought were some of the best gimmick matches I had been a part of. In a dog collar match, you need to trust your opponent and have common sense. Barry and I could check both boxes. There are certain things that a wrestler cannot do with a collar around his neck. The same thing goes for a strap or rope tied around your wrist. Nobody wants to severely hurt or even kill his opponent. I learned all that the hard way when I nearly choked Dick Murdoch to death. So, I felt good about knowing how to keep Barry safe. Depending on what venue we were in, we could be in the same dressing area as our opponents. Of course, when that was the case, the heels and babyfaces usually went in and came out of different doors. Sometimes if I saw Barry in there before or after our match, we often chatted it up.

"That was a damn good match, Barry," I exclaimed!

"Thank you, Bart. I appreciate you saying that" Barry returned with a smile.

"I know your Daddy didn't teach you how to throw a

punch because I feel his when they land," I huffed.

"Yeah, I hear my dad is a little stiff in the ring when it comes to punching," he said.

"A little stiff?" I'm still looking for a couple of my teeth, Barry," I laughed.

When it came to getting in the ring with Blackjack, I always expected a street fight. He wrestled very stiff and tight. I knew that he wasn't going to kill me, but sometimes I wished he had. I never had a problem selling anything that he threw at me. My reactions and my expressions all looked natural with Blackjack because he was really kicking my ass! Blackjack hit me so hard that it hurt. However, he expected me to give it back to him the same way. Barry on the other hand, wasn't stiff inside the ring at all when I worked with him. A fly landing on my nose hit harder than Barry did, but somehow, he always made it look like he was taking me to my limit.

Blackjack had come up in the business a few years before I did. He too was a Texas boy, and he was billed from Sweetwater. If that was the case, he didn't drink enough of it because at times he was as mean as a snake. A lot of the boys accepted him for who he was. Mean, moody, and set in his ways, was a good description that fit Blackjack well. For a time, the two of us fought over the NWA Brass Knuckles Championship. Each bout was a war! In one contest, when I held the belt, we started fighting in the locker room. That match was a bloodbath. Blackjack had another son that wrestled in the area too. His name was Kendall, and he was as skinny as a stick when he started. I never understood why Blackjack wrestled with the last name Mulligan, and Barry and Kendall wrestled with the last name Windham. I never asked. It's just one of those things I don't have the answer for. Back then, a lot of us didn't use our real last names. I didn't use mine. Barry and his Daddy, Blackjack Mulligan shared a lot of similarities. The father and son were both professional through and through.

Blackjack and Barry loved the business, and they knew it quite well. At that time, along with Dusty and Mike Rotundo, I'd have to say that they were the babyfaces that ruled the place. The difference between Blackjack and his son, Barry was nice and a pleasure to be around, Blackjack not so much! If you ever wanted a mudhole stomped into your ass, Mulligan was the guy to do it!

Another wrestler that stands out to me when I think of Florida is Sam Houston. My friend that I met in the Mid-South territory. I'm not sure if Florida was his first territory or if he had already done some matches for Bill Watts, but Sam hadn't been wrestling long at this time. One night, we were in Tampa for a show that we were shooting for television. Ron and I along with J.J. Dillon were in our area of the dressing room, and Sam was nearby getting ready for his match with The One-Man Gang. A little time passed when Dusty came to talk to us about our finishes. Don't ask me why, but when Dusty came to talk to us in the dressing room, he wore only a t-shirt and a pair of tennis shoes. He didn't wear any underwear, shorts, or anything! Dusty had his personal business hanging out for the whole world to see! His t-shirt was always two sizes too small. So, just imagine, Dusty's chubby body being half naked while trying to talk serious business with the boys. It was hard to keep a straight face with him sometimes when he did things like that. He was known for his bleach blonde hair and the soft southern tones of his voice, but those characteristics took a backseat to his private parts most nights in the dressing room.

"Damn! Dusty, put some pants on!" I exclaimed!

"I'm all natural. My doctor says I shouldn't let myself get too sweaty down there. Nobody wants a rash on their twig and berries, now do they Baby?" Dusty smiled.

"What do you have for us?" Ron asked.

"Where is Sammy Baby?" Dusty questioned as he looked over at Sam taping up his wrist.

"I'm right here, Dusty," Sam said.

"I want you to get some color tonight, Sammy Baby," Dusty directed.

"You want me to bleed?" Sam returned.

"No, Baby, I want you to get some color," Dusty soothed. "The One-Man Gang going to the moon, Baby. We want to make him look good, Sammy," Dusty said and then he walked away from our small group.

"I never cut myself Bart," Sam fretted.

"I'll do it for you Sam, I'll cut you," J.J. spoke up.

"No, no! Nobody is cutting anybody," I insisted. "Sam, you need to do it yourself."

"I don't want to do it, Bart," Sam refused.

"I got it Sam, you're in good hands," J.J. smiled.

"What a joke?" Ron spoke under his breath.

When it was time the match with Sam and Gang, J.J. went to be in Gang's corner that evening. The contest had been going for a couple of minutes and it wasn't expected to go long at all. It came to the point in the match when Gang was about to end the contest. After Gang had tossed Sam like a rag doll a couple more times, Sam laid on the mat near the side of the ring with his head underneath the ropes hanging over the edge of the apron. His head was facing down so he could see the floor. At that moment, J.J. went in for the attack and he made it look like he hit Sam with a foreign object. In an instant, J.J. cut Sam at the top of his forehead from ear to ear. Sam got off the mat quicker than a jackrabbit running for its life! The fans were in a state of shock when they saw how bad he was bleeding. Sam was standing in the middle of the ring and every time his heart took a beat, blood squirted out of his forehead, over the top rope and into the crowd of onlooking fans. It was obvious that J.J. hit a vein! Gang put Sam to the mat, performed his 747 splash and ended the match right away. The referee Bill Alfonzo was in disbelief!

Bill signaled for the timekeeper to ring the bell. That action might have ended the match; however, it didn't stop Sam from bleeding! I was afraid that he was going to die right there inside the ring! In all my years of pro wrestling, I had never seen anybody bleed quite that bad before. Bill immediately went to check on Sam. Eventually, my friend was escorted to the back of the building where we could get a better assessment of his condition. Once inside the dressing room, Kevin and some of the other boys took turns applying pressure on Sam's wound to help stop it from bleeding. Sam never got any stiches. Instead, he continued to wrestle Gang for the rest of the week. In the matches that came after that initial incident, Sam bled easily without the help from anyone's blade. J.J. did a number on Sam, and he was nowhere to be found for the rest of that night. I believe he left the building as soon as the match ended. I do not believe that J.J. intentionally cut a vein on Sam's head, but I think he meant to make it a point that your supposed to do that task yourself. After that, Sam was able to cut himself, he never trusted anybody else to do it for him, especially J.J. Dillon!

CHAPTER 13 – WHITE HOT HEAT

There is nothing like pro wrestling to get the blood pumping! The adrenalin runs through your veins, and you feel invincible! One may begin to believe that they can beat up the toughest guy on the roster. I'm just talking about the fan right now; I'm not talking about any of the wrestlers. Wrestling is a game of emotions! It has always been that way. People who watch professional wrestling become invested in their favorite competitors. When passionate fans come out to live events where beer is almost always sold, it can become a powder keg! That emotional firestorm that stems from stupidity combined with a dash of fan interaction, is what the boys call "white hot heat." It is a certain point during a show when the crowd becomes so involved with what is taking place, the entire scene nearly erupts into a riot. It just takes one person to act stupid for the fireworks to go off! Rarely do large riots transpire. However, I was once part of a show in Orlando that was going in that direction. I was fighting Blackjack Mulligan and he hit me so hard that he knocked me out! I always knew that he and I were never going to play patty-cake inside the ring. On the other hand, I never thought Mulligan would hit me as hard as he did. The referee and the boys in the back knew how the match was supposed to go, and it wasn't supposed to go like that! So, when I didn't get up to my feet, the other wrestlers knew that they needed to get me out of there. I think I started to come to my senses when the boys came inside the ring and began moving me around. When I have been knocked out like that previously, which has only been a couple of times, it always felt as if I was drunk.

"Bart, wake up. It's me, Mike," Mike Davis said.

"Bart, we are going to get you out of here," Kevin assured.

"What happened?" I asked. "Did somebody turn off

the lights?"

"Yes, Blackjack did. He turned off your lights," Mike said with a grin.

At that moment, I couldn't name all of the guys who assisted me, but I later found out that it was Mike Davis, Kevin Sullivan, Buzz Sawyer, Ron Bass, and The Guerrero Brothers (Hector & Chavo). As we made our way back to the dressing room, my colleagues helped carry and support me to make sure that I didn't fall to the floor. Suddenly, I felt my head go backward as a fan we passed from the crowd yanked on my hair. We never put our hands on the fans, until they put their hands on us first. If someone in the audience touched me or one of the boys, it was open season. Fans were up on their feet, and I was getting hit with cups and everything else. One of the wrestlers assisting me retaliated with a swing and it all started from there. That incident unfolded quickly. I was told 36 fights broke out that night, I'm sure that there were a lot of arrests too. The Police got the wrestlers out of the building in a speedy fashion to ensure our safety. Incidences like that didn't happen often, but there was always a chance. Most times, if I thought I was being challenged by a spectator, I could stand my ground a yell at them, that tactic rarely failed.

Playing the role of the heel, was fun, however, you had to be always aware of your surroundings. If the fans knew what type of cars we drove, our vehicles were vandalized or tampered with. So, we got wise and drove rent-a-cars. At the larger events, there are usually more police officers on duty, and the parking lot was more secure, but at the smaller events it was different. If we wrestled at a recreation center or a high school gym, we parked in the same parking lot as the fans did. So, their accessibility to us and our vehicles was so much easier. We always had to be on our toes.

One day, Ron and I were double booked against Barry Windham and Mike Rotundo in a tag team event. Our second show was scheduled at the Eddie Graham Sports Arena later that evening. We had just finished up our afternoon event and we had about 100 miles to drive until we arrived in Orlando. As soon as Ron and I exited the back door of the building, a fan who was at the show approached us. The man had to be in his early to mid-20 and he wasn't alone. The instigator had three friends that were with him. They were not right next to him but standing maybe 10 or 15 feet away. In an instant, the guy stepped right in front of Ron and blocked him from going forward. The obnoxious fan got mouthy and he disrespected Ron.

"You're a piece of crap!" The man yelled.

"The show is over. It's time to go home. Thank you for coming out," Ron said as he proceeded to walk to our car.

"Don't walk away from me when I'm talking to you," the fan provoked.

"I don't know you, it's time for you to go home, Ron replied as he kept walking.

"Keep walking you piece of crap! Your whole family is a piece of crap," the man taunted.

At that moment, Ron was done talking. Without saying a word, Ron dropped his traveling bag and grabbed the guy who disrespected him with one hand. With his other hand, Ron punched him in the face repeatedly. Ron outweighed the fan by 30 or 40 pounds. However, it appeared that the fan might have been intoxicated. I'm sure that helped him with his bravery. I never liked tangling with someone drunk because they didn't quit fighting unless you physically stopped them. Ron was landing some hard hits on his adversary, but it didn't look like the guy was letting up. He tried to return Ron blow for blow. While all that was happening, I looked in the direction of where the attacker's friends were. They cheered on their buddy, but none of them mustered up enough stupidness to join in. From where the fight started near the back door of the building, it quickly moved near the Lincoln town car that we rented. Ron and the fan were standing by the vehicle when both men lost their footing and they fell to the ground. Rolling around in the parking lot the men made their way right next to our car. The fan positioned himself on top of Ron. With one hand, I watched Ron place his index finger in the man's eye socket and his thumb was applying pressure to the soft part of his nose. Ron's other hand was pulling the dude's ear away from his head. That was what I meant about ripping and tearing. Ron Bass was one of the best to do those types of tactics. In no time Ron gained control of the fight and he stood back on his feet. My friend yanked his foe by his hair and picked him up to body slam him. Standing right in front of our rent-a-car, I could envision what was to happen next!

"Not on the car!" I shouted.

Right after those words came out of my mouth, Ron dropped his attacker on the hood of the Lincoln. That was it! The fight was over! The man that Ron beat up lay defeated on the front end of our vehicle. The attacker's friends and I were in shock by what we had just witnessed. Ron walked over to the spot in the parking lot where his hat was lying on the ground, and he bent over and picked it up. As Ron placed his Stetson back on his head, he looked at the three other guys who were there.

"Hey girls, come get this piece of trash off my car!" Ron demanded.

"Yes Sir," one of the guys said as they all followed through with Ron's order.

The friends helped the man off the car, and they walked away from our vehicle. I have no idea how long the fight lasted, but I know who won! Ron and I made our way to the car and we both got inside, and we drove to our next show in Orlando. When we had arrived at the second venue of the day, we finally stopped talking about the incident that happened just two hours before. However, Ron and I were reminded of the fight the moment we made our way to the ring. The two of us noticed the four men we encountered earlier that day sitting in the front row. I must admit, my partner and I were a bit surprised by what we saw. Standing in the corner of the ring while the announcer addressed the crowd, Ron and I spoke to each other.

"Isn't that something?" I said to Ron gesturing to the guys with the familiar faces.

"It's unbelievable! He returned.

"They must be true fans," I perplexed.

"If they want to go again, it's your turn," Ron insisted.

"I wouldn't want to deprive you of all that fun," I joked.

"I will show them what fun is, Bart," he growled.

The four guys we encountered earlier that day didn't say anything to either of us at that event. Ron and I concentrated on the task at hand and we had another great match with Barry and Mike. We never took an eye off the guys we had trouble with, but Ron and I had a pretty good feeling they weren't going to try us again, and they didn't. That was one story that Ron and talked about quite often as we traveled.

Another fight I recall that took place happened in the dressing room in Tampa. This confrontation involved Billy Jack Haynes and Barry, but mostly Billy Jack. Billy was a popular wrestler who had just been in the business for a couple of years when I met him. He had a muscled-up body, a full black beard, and hair of the same color. Billy wore a black cowboy hat with a flat brim. The hat was the same style worn by actor Tom Laughlin who starred as Billy Jack in the movie drama series. There was a big contrast between Billy's body and Barry's. Billy had a body builder's look to him, as for Barry he was more like a beanpole. There was also a contrast in the two wrestler's personalities. Barry was nice, polite, and easy to get along with, Billy wasn't. Since we were taping for television that day, Ron and I, along with several of the other boys, had shown up early to do interviews and cut promos. I was in my spot in the dressing area with Ron getting ready for our upcoming contest. I was sitting there putting tape on my wrists and fingers while I shared a casual conversation with Ron. I was distracted by a noise several feet away from the other corner of the room. The sound that I heard was like an object contacting the wall combined with yelling. The yelling came from Billy who pushed Barry. I looked in that direction and I noticed Billy Jack trying to corner Barry as he took off his jacket. By this time, the altercation had captured Ron's attention as well. Ron and I looked at it each other and I'm sure we both had puzzled expressions on our faces. Most times when a couple of wrestlers had an issue with each other, the other boys let them solve it among themselves. However, Ron and I knew that Blackjack was going to show up at any minute and we assumed that he would step in and defend his son.

"Barry's daddy is not going to like the looks of that," I said.

"I agree," Ron returned.

"I'm glad my name isn't Billy Jack," I mentioned.

Billy turned up the heat with Barry and the physicality escalated. Billy pushed Barry again and as he did, Barry lost his balance and went to the floor. Billy pretty much dominated Barry in the dressing room, but that was mostly because Barry retreated from his attacker. I was surprised that Barry was being so passive. I had been in the ring with Barry several times by this point, and that kid could take it and give it, however, this day he did all the taking. It was about that time when Blackjack came in, he set his duffle bag on the bench next to me and he proceeded to take off his shirt. Blackjack noticed the disagreement between Billy and Barry, and then he looked at me and Ron.

"What did Barry do?" Blackjack asked.

"I don't know," Ron replied.

"Well, he did something. No one gets pushed around like that for no reason," he said.

"Are you going to do something Blackjack?" I questioned.

"No. Barry is a grown man. He doesn't need me to fight his battles," Blackjack maintained.

"That's your boy over there," I insisted.

"Bart, if the police need to be called, I'm sure someone will do that. Until then, they need to work things out. It looks like Billy is trying to do that," Blackjack said.

Billy eventually stopped beating up Barry and things resumed to their normal state. The funny thing was that Billy and Barry wrestled against Ron and me that night in a tag team match. No one in the crowd who watched the contest could tell that they had a match of their own before the show even started. Barry and Billy acted as if nothing happened, and they appeared to the fans as if they were friends. Billy was a bit of a hothead. Most of the wrestlers, bookers, and promoters found him difficult to work with.

Back in the 80s, professional wrestling was a lot different than it is today. Kayfabe was held in high regard. Thanks to Vince McMahon and his idea of Sports Entertainment, he let that secret out of the bag a long time ago. In my heyday, if I was seen in the same restaurant with a wrestler, I was in an angle with meant that I could have been fired. We were expected to always keep up our gimmick in the ring and outside of it. If I saw the babyface wrestler in a place that I was at or going into, I left. It didn't matter if I was washing my truck or shopping at a store. Since we pushed everything that we did to be real, I'm sure the fans wanted to see us fight outside of the T.V. program too.

Mike Davis and I talked about the inner workings of

professional wrestling quite often. Some fans wanted to watch wrestling and they wanted to believe it, then some fans wanted to figure everything out. The wrestlers had to stay one step ahead of the people. I can't tell you how many times fans have shared their ideas with me on how we bled. Just look at our foreheads! The blood wasn't fake, and neither was the wound it came from.

"There was a guy in the front row watching me closely when my head made contact with the corner post," I explained to Mike.

"I think I know who you are referring to," he replied. "Was he wearing a red baseball cap?"

"Yes, that's the guy that I'm talking about," I said. "I knew he wanted to catch me doing something when I laid face down on the concrete floor," I mentioned.

"That was the same guy who asked if I was hurt when I got thrown out of the ring," Mike recounted.

"Some of these people are too funny," I laughed.

"I agree, Bart," Mike said.

If we weren't fighting someone or protecting the integrity of professional wrestling, we were doing a bunch of silly stuff that could have led to our deaths or gotten us into a lot of trouble. I'm reminded of a story that happened in Yeehaw Junction, Florida. The town itself isn't very big. Back in the 80s, I remember there being only one caution light, a restaurant, a little store, and a gas station. In 1968, the government used Yeehaw Junction as a testing ground for biological warfare. However, when I think of Yeehaw Junction, I think of something totally different, and it has nothing to do with the government and chemical testing.

One evening in 1984, a bunch of us were coming back from Tampa after a television taping, and we were headed to Orlando. Since there were so many of us traveling, we were all in four separate vehicles. Dusty and his oldest son Dustin

Rhodes were on one of the rides. Ron, I, and J.J. Dillion were together. Barry, Mike Rotundo, and Mike Davis were grouped up, and Blackjack and Kendall were driving in the fourth vehicle. Back then, we had Citizens Band Radios or CBs which they are commonly called. Yeehaw Junction is 75 miles south of Orlando, and since we had been drinking and driving for an hour and a half, I think some of the boys were getting restless. Behind the gas station in Yeehaw Junction, was a fenced-in pasture where bulls were kept. It was well past midnight when chatter began trading back and forth over the airwaves.

"Hello, hello, it's the American Dream," Dusty said in his familiar Southern soulful voice.

"Go ahead Dusty, it's Blackjack," Blackjack returned.

"We're coming up on Yeehaw Junction in just a few miles. Is anybody in the mood for some bull riding?" Dusty asked with a mischievous laugh.

"Are you serious, Dusty?" Ron questioned.

"Oh Baby, I'm so serious that I'm willing to put some money down" Dusty assured.

"I think he had too many beers already," I turned to Ron and told him as he was driving. Ron spoke into the mic one more time.

"Bart said he is going to take all your money, Dusty," Ron grinned.

"Don't be saying crap like that," I said to Ron.

"Oh, he did? Well, look here, Black Bart. I better not get yelled at by your wife after you come home without any money," Dusty promised.

"Look what you started, Ron," I fumed.

"Bart said it's your wife who is going to yell at your broke ass," Ron laughed.

"Unbelievable!" I mouthed.

"We'll see about that Cowboy!" Dusty returned.

After minutes of talking on the radio, we arrived at Yeehaw Junction. We all parked in the gas station parking lot. It was dark and quiet, except for an occasional moo from the pasture. We made our way next fence to get a glimpse of the bulls. Being from Texas, I knew a few things about bulls and various other farm animals. The main thing to keep in mind with a bull is that they can become aggressive around other cows and strangers. WE WERE STRANGERS! I felt that this was a bad idea from the very beginning. Barbed wire lined the fence from post to post. I made it clear to everyone that I wasn't going into the pasture because I drank a lot of beer. Everybody threw twenty dollars down into someone's hat. The money was to go to the wrestler who was able to stay on the bull the longest. Dusty, Ron, Dustin, Blackjack, and Barry all made their way through the fence and entered the pasture. As soon as the five men got to the other side of the fence, the bulls nearby were startled, and they all went wild by running around frantically. Within seconds, Ron, Blackjack, Barry, and Dustin returned to the safe side of the fence. J.J., I, Mike Rotundo, and Mike Davis laughed hysterically watching our four friends make their escape to safety. After the laughter subsided, we all realized that Dusty was still in the pasture.

"Where the hell is Dusty?" Ron asked.

At that moment, off into the distance we all could hear yells made by Dusty. He had grabbed onto one of the bulls, but Dusty was only halfway on him. We watched the huge animal take off with our friend. I'm guessing Dusty weighed around 260 pounds at the time, but that bull made him look like he was a rag doll. I really don't know if being dragged constitutes as riding, but if anyone came close to mounting one on the bulls that night, it was Dusty. I can't tell you for how long Dusty held on and rode the bull, but it was longer than anyone else was able to do. Eventually, Dusty fell off the bull, and he ran in our direction with a purpose. The look on his face was a combination of fear and amazement. I can't tell you if I ever saw Dusty move that quickly. Laughter mixed with cheers came from my side of the barrier as Dusty neared where we waited. As Dusty made his way up and over the barbed wire fence, excitement and joy could be heard in his voice.

"I did it! I did it! I won the money! I rode the bull!" Dusty exclaimed.

Some of us were in shock that Dusty followed through with his plan. I was surprised that anyone crossed the fence in the first place, but I guess that we all fell victim under the spell of alcohol that evening. I have to give to Dusty; he definitely had a pair of balls on him! I can promise you that everyone who was there that night laughed until we got to our destination, and long after that! The story that came from the night that we stopped in Yeehaw Junction, has been told and retold for the last 40 years.

CHAPTER 14 - LORDS OF THE RING

I always thought that pro wrestling was about taking risks, building for the next event, and rolling the dice. Promoters wanted to attract the person who normally wouldn't come to a live event. On June 30th, 1984, that is exactly what Eddie Graham had set out to do. The stage was set at The Orange Bowl in Miami, Florida for the Lord of the Rings. The main event was to pair the National Wrestling Alliance World Champion, Ric Flair against the challenger, Dusty Rhodes. The winner was to be presented with a gold and diamond-covered ring and walk away with the NWA Title. Dusty had a knack for coming up with some catchy names for the shows. Dusty had the mind for the Pay-Per-View shows and the big events. He came up with The Great American Bash, Starrcade, and several other well-known named events when he later worked for Vince McMahon Jr. in World Wrestling Entertainment. I remember chatting with Dusty about his creative ideas.

"Dusty, how in the world do you come up with all this stuff," I wondered.

"Well, Baby, one good idea leads to another idea, and it keeps going from there," Dusty replied.

"You have a lot of good ideas when it comes to wrestling," I stated.

"I've had a lot of bad ideas too, I just don't talk about them too much Baby," he replied with a laugh.

"How do you come up with themes for the events, Dusty?" I asked.

"They're like little movies. I think about creating a movie and promoting it like a movie," he affirmed.

Up until that point in my career, I have never wrestled in a football stadium before. I had no clue what to expect. Knowing that the Orange Bowl sat 75,000 people, a sellout wasn't expected, but I was anxious to see how many people were going to attend. I was later told the attendance was close to 20,000 people. One side of the facility was filled from one end zone to the other. Seeing what the setup on the field looked like piqued my curiosity, so I went to take a look at it a few hours before the event ever started. Seeing all the chairs on the field for the first time, even though fans hadn't arrived at the show yet, I still got goosebumps!

"Wow!" I thought to myself.

I was in awe. I couldn't believe that I was going to wrestle in a building that size. Thoughts of my days of working with Ivan flooded into my mind. I was blown away! What a contrast! It is hard to put my feelings into words. I was so glad to have the opportunity to be a part of this. An event like Lord of the Rings has feuds, gimmick matches, and several high-profile wrestlers come to perform.

When it came to the Lord of the Rings, the entire card was stacked with talent from top to bottom. More than a dozen matches were scheduled. The card included the likes of Blackjack Mulligan, Kevin Sullivan, The One-Man Gang, Billy Jack Haynes, Superstar Billy Graham, The Road Warriors, Hector & Chavo Guerrero, Mike Rotundo, Barry Windham, Dick Slater, and many others. The match I was in was a Six-Man Tag Match. With J.J. Dillion in our corner, I teamed with Ron Bass and Angelo Mosco. Our opponents were Wahoo McDaniel, Jimmy Valiant, and The Junkyard Dog. The match wasn't anything special. There wasn't a title on the line or a score to settle in that particular contest, but the fans seemed to be excited about it. I spoke with Ron in the dressing room.

"Here we go again, Bass. It's showtime," I said with a confident smile.

"It's going to be fun," Ron returned.

"I'm looking forward to it. This is most people I've

ever worked in front of," I commented.

"Enjoy it, Bart. Big stages come and go," he answered back.

"I'm not taking it for granted, that's for damn sure," I confirmed.

"I'm glad to hear it because houses like this beat the Outlaw circuit," he grinned.

"Yes, they do," I replied.

When it came time for us to enter the field for our match, I felt a rush of adrenaline going through my entire body. That specific feeling wasn't new to me; however, the intensity was! Walking out of the tunnel and stepping onto the field to make my way to the ring was electric. The ring was near the 50-yard line and though it didn't seem like it was that far of a walk, it almost seemed as if time was moving in slow motion. The crowd was so loud that I couldn't make much sense of what they were saying. I know they are booing J.J., Ron, Angelo, and myself. I expected the fans to taunt us, but I never experienced it at that level until that day. When I was inside the ring and I saw the crowd of people from there, it was an exciting moment for me. The noise level was so loud in the building that it felt as if the ring was vibrating. I guess I could compare it to a mini earthquake, but just not as violent. The buzzing never stopped and the communication with the boys during the match wasn't easy. I had some spots with Jimmy in that contest. At one point, I was lying on my back in the ring with thoughts running through my head.

"I can't believe all of these people are here," I thought.

My team lost. I can't remember the exact finish because a lot of that match is a blur to me. I was taken aback by the entire atmosphere. It was as if I was wrestling on auto pilot, and I was just going through the motions of the match. A feeling of satisfaction came to me when we all walked back to the dressing room through the sea of people. The fans booed us as we left the ring and they were all giving us the thumbs-down gesture. I loved nothing more than seeing the disdain that the fans had for me. I loved it!

After the Lords of the Ring event, there was a fall-out! For years, I thought it was because of an argument over payouts or the lack thereof that the boys received from the show that day. I know that I had a discussion with Ron about our pay from that specific show. At the time, some of the other boys I had conversations with had some questions about their pay as well. Recently, Kevin Sullivan claimed that there was a disagreement between Dusty and Hiro Matsuda. Hiro worked in Eddie's office, and he was the one who paid the wrestlers in the promotion. Supposedly, their conflict had nothing to do with the Lord of the Rings payroll. However, shortly after the Lords of the Ring, Dusty left Florida and started booking for the Crocketts in the Carolinas for their Mid-Atlantic promotion. Fellow wrestler Denny Brown backs up the claim that everyone left Florida due to their disappointment with their payoff from that same event. Denny shared this conversation with me that he had with Dusty and Kevin in Tampa right before a slew of the boys headed out of the Florida territory.

"Denny, do you have a moment?" Kevin asked.

"Why sure, Kevin? What's up?" Denny inquired.

"Can you make a town next week" he wanted to know.

"What do you mean can I make a town?" Denny questioned with a puzzled look on his face. "I work for you guys."

"He won't be there," Dusty chimed in. "He will be in Charlotte with me."

Denny was one of the first wrestlers to go with Dusty, but I don't think anyone had a clue as to what was going to happen next. Within six months between July and December of 1984, Dusty and 15 other wrestlers quit working for Eddie and almost all of them followed Dusty. I can't speak for everyone regarding the specific reasons why they left. I know the boys that I spoke with thought they deserved more money from the Orange Bowl card. Perhaps some left for personal reasons that they made concerning their families or otherwise. I know this, while I was in Florida in the summer of 1984, the promotion was on fire! The shows were selling out, the storylines were incredible, new fans were coming out to the events, and the money was rolling in. However, when it was all said and done, within a year nothing was left except smoldering embers.

The list of names that left the Sunshine State when Dusty did was Dick Slater, Billy Graham, Joe Lightfoot, Gang, Billy Jack Haynes, J.J. Dillion, Mike Davis, Brian Adias, Ron Bass, Denny Brown, Mike Fever, Angelo Mosco Jr., Mike Rotundo, Barry Windham, and myself. A promotion cannot lose that many talented wrestlers and expect to survive. I knew Dusty had the golden touch when it came to professional wrestling, and I wanted to be wherever he was at.

On January 21st, 1985, Eddie Graham was found dead with what appeared to be a self-inflicted gun wound to the head. Eddie was only 55 years old. I thought about his son Mike because he wrestled with us, I felt like I knew him a little bit. I was sad for Mike and his family. Of course, all kinds of stories and rumors circled around Eddie's death, and some of the chatter was absurd. Shortly after hearing the news, I talked with Ron about Eddie's passing while making a road trip.

"So, Ron, what do think about Eddie? I questioned.

"Do you mean, what do I think about him being dead?" Ron asked.

"Yeah," I replied.

"Well, he was dealing with a lot of people, and he was dealing with a lot of money. I'm sure that can bring a lot of stress on a man," he mentioned.

"Yeah, you're right about all that," I said.

"What do you think about all of it, Bart?" Ron inquired.

"I have no idea what to think. It's kind of weird, it's pretty sad," I returned.

"You are right about that, Bart. It's pretty sad," he sighed.

Though I didn't have a lot of interaction with Eddie during the time that I worked with him, he was good to me when the two of us were together. I believed that he loved pro wrestling, I don't think anyone can invest that much of their life into the sport and not love it. Eddie had a big heart, he cared about people and he gave to his community. I know that he was recognized for his philanthropic activities and because of them, lives of people were impacted. I find the entire situation upsetting, he was only 55 and obviously he was hurting... And because of his death, a lot of his friends and family were left hurting too.

CHAPTER 15 – GOODBYE TO FLORIDA

Florida Championship Wrestling had a great run, and it had a great fall. The Graham's wrestling promotion had been running strong for so long, I'm sure many never thought that it would ever fizzle out like that. For the faithful fans who came out to the live events and who followed the product on television, they got to see it all unfold. For the fans who read about the wrestling territories through the magazines, they might have been scratching their heads and wondering what might have happened with all of that. I am sure that the fans who loved and supported that show were heartbroken. It was sad to see Florida Championship Wrestling in that kind of shape. There was a mass exodus that took place in Florida, but it didn't all happen at once. Let me say it like this, the bomb went off and it took a few months for the dust to settle! In the end, Graham's promotion crumbled, and the Crockett's company flourished.

In West Palms Beach, Florida on August 6th, 1984, Ron, and I lost a bout against Blackjack Mulligan and the One-Man Gang. The stipulation was that the losers had to leave town. So, the Long Riders along with J.J. Dillon packed up their belongings and we moved on. Back then, it was big matches like that how a booker ended a feud between wrestlers. Loser leaving town matches was also another great way for a wrestler to go off to another wrestling territory. The devoted fan didn't want to miss out on that kind of storytelling. That sort of marketing tactic was taken from the carnival, and it was something that the veteran workers in the business understood very well. Leaving Florida to go to the Carolinas was monumental. Not just for Dusty, but for everyone who went with him, and for the world of pro wrestling itself! It was the ending of one chapter and the beginning of another. However, I don't think anyone knew exactly what was in store for us! Wrestlers believed in Dusty, and a lot of them wanted to work with him. If he liked you, he made a spot on the card for you. There was no way that I was going to stay behind in Florida. I knew that I had to go with Dusty. The transformation I had from Hangman Rick Harris to the Black Bart character was life-changing for me! It might have been a small tweak to what I already had going on, but it was Dusty who helped me with that small tweak.

If it hadn't been for Dusty going to the Mid-Atlantic territory, I wouldn't have gone back there. I had worked with the Crocketts for a couple of years already and they never pushed me once. If Dusty wanted to push a wrestler to the top of the card, he did it. He didn't care if nobody else agreed with him or not. It was hard to argue the business of pro wrestling with Dusty because he just knew it so well. Some of the wrestlers when I arrived, were: Mark and Jay Youngblood, Ricky Steamboat, Ivan and Nikita Koloff, Wahoo McDaniel, and my buddies Charlie Fulton and Don Kernodle were still up there. For the wrestlers who felt that their jobs were in jeopardy now that Dusty was running the show, they left to go somewhere else. Not everybody got along with Dusty, and I think that was because he called the shots. On the other hand, I can name countless wrestlers who were loyal to him because of what he did for their careers.

Arn Anderson arrived in the Carolinas right around the same time that I did. I assume he finally took the advice that I gave him when we both worked for Ron Fuller. I'm sure when Dusty and the Crocketts got to see Arn in action, they probably wished that they brought him in sooner. Little did anyone know that his career was about to be taken to new heights. Those who didn't yet know of Arn Anderson were about to never forget him! He solidified his name and legacy in this great sport through his hard work, dedication, and his love for the business!

The Crocketts might have owned Mid-Atlantic and World Championship Wrestling, but Dusty ran those companies. He was the boss and there was no mistake about that! It was apparent when he called for a team meeting. The meeting was for the boys, the Crocketts were not invited. If David or Jim ever walked into the dressing room while Dusty was having such a gathering with us, the Crocketts knew to say hello and then they moved on. They were not privy to what Dusty shared with the wrestlers during those meetings. To the boys, it was a definite sign of who the real boss was. Dusty and his boys made a ton of money for that family.

Dusty was an innovative thinker, and his wrestling mind kept elevating pro wrestling to new levels. Dusty's vision for professional wrestling was always evolving. I can't say that I always understood his methods for growing our in-ring sport, but I fully believed in everything that he did. The Crocketts' wrestling territory was huge. They had a hold on the Carolinas, Georgia, and everywhere within the surrounding areas. Simulcasting was introduced to wrestling and it was a game-changer. Fans in Atlanta at the Omni could pay for and watch an event on a screen that was being put on in real-time from the Coliseum in Charlotte. At first, I had trouble wrapping my mind around that concept, because I always believed that the fans wanted to see the live shows in person. Dusty believed that people just wanted to watch wrestling regardless, and now there was a way to make that happen.

"Can you see it, Baby?" Dusty asked.

"Can I see what? Are you talking about the huge movie screen we are looking at?" Yes, "I see it," I responded to him.

"No, Black Bart, can you see the future?" He questioned.

"No. I see a big screen," I replied.

"Focus Baby, focus! Our business is going to be

strongly distributed by technology. One day pro wrestling is going to be doing nothing except television. Mark my words, Baby," Dusty cooed.

I must admit, his words that day didn't sit well with me. If I wrestled in a match for a television taping, I got paid $50. I could wrestle in four matches for television and make $200. If I was at a live show, I could make $200 or more for just one match. It didn't take me very long to do the math on that problem. I wanted to work on the live events. However, Dusty was right again and if you look at the landscape of our sport today, television and pay-per-view shows are a big part of it all. A MAJOR PART OF IT! Wrestling can be watched on T.V. and online at any time of the day in any given week. It was not like that in my day. People wanted to come out to the live shows, and today they almost don't have to.

In pro wrestling when a booker had an idea for two wrestlers, or even multiple wrestlers to have a long-term program with each other, they always baited the fans. Making sure that the audience was invested in the upcoming story was crucial for ticket sales. An idea that was handed to Ron and me at this time was to start wrestling against Ricky Steamboat and his brother Victor. Ricky was one of the top stars in the area at that time. To me, I thought that Ricky was the whole package when it came to a professional wrestler. He could talk, he could wrestle, and he had a good look for television. In my opinion, very few wrestlers compare to him. As this angle was just getting underway, Ricky was wrestling in Japan. Someone in the office had an idea for Ron, J.J., and me to go down to Steamboat's gym and record us doing a workout in there. I was told that we had permission from both Victor and Ricky to shoot the vignette. So, one day the three of us and a production guy went to get some video footage of us training in there. We were being silly with our antics and we were taunting Victor. It was pro wrestling in its truest form! We even made it look like we left Victor trapped on a bench with a heavy bar of weights on his chest. Returning home, Ricky wasn't happy about what took place in his facility while he was wrestling overseas. He expressed his opinion against the entire situation. Shortly after that, I heard that there was a change in plans about moving forward with the Steamboat's and the Long Rider's feud. I really don't know why Ricky became so upset and why we never started the program that was planned. The four of us never fought and that was a series of matches that I was very excited about being a part of.

In 1984 at a television taping in North Carolina, a match between Ricky Steamboat and Ron Bass is one many fans will never forget. It wasn't so much what happened with Ron and Ricky, but what happened to J.J. Dillon that day. Comedy can be a big part of pro wrestling and when it is presented well, it always looks like it was unplanned. However, a lot of thought goes into a great storyline and getting a pop from the crowd. In this contest, J.J. and I entered the ring, and we attacked Ricky. While the three of us whooped up on Ricky, his friend Dick Slater came out from the back to assist him. In a matter of seconds, Dick and Ricky cleared the ring and Ron and I took off to the dressing room. At that moment, J.J. suddenly realized that he was alone at ringside. As he and Dick traded words with each other, Dusty snuck up behind J.J. and threw him into the ring while Ricky waited with anticipation. All eyes are on the center of the ring as Ricky tussled with J.J. Unexpectantly, as Ricky pulled at J.J.'s pants, they came off his body to reveal women's underwear and stockings. The look on referee, Tommy Young's face was priceless, and the crowd went nuts! Even the announcers, David Crockett and Bob Caudle who called the action at ringside seemed to be caught off guard. It was one of those moments in wrestling that lasted less than a couple of minutes. However, the story of J.J. wearing ladies' lingerie has stayed around to this very day.

J.J. didn't want to do that spot and I know that he tried talking Dusty out of making him do it. Since J.J. had always been a dedicated worker to the sport of pro wrestling, he did it anyway. When Dusty had an idea in his head that he believed was going to work, he stuck to his guns. I know that Dusty tried something similar with J.J. when we were all in Florida, however, it didn't quite get the reaction as it did in the Mid-Atlantic territory.

Ron and I went on to have a series of matches with Ricky and Dick, but in a short time that run stalled in its tracks. I mark that period of time as the end of the Long Riders. I say that only because so many changes took place then. Ricky went to wrestle for the World Wrestling Federation, Ron and I started to wrestle in more singles matches, and J.J. went to manage the Four Horsemen!

Greg Bowle Collection

Nature Boy Ric Flair

Photo by Duane Long

Barry Windham vs.Black Bart

Greg Bowle Collection

Black Bart , J.J. Dillon & Ron Bass

Photo Courtesy of Rick Harris

Rick at age 14

Photo Courtesy of Rick Harris

Rick's father Leon

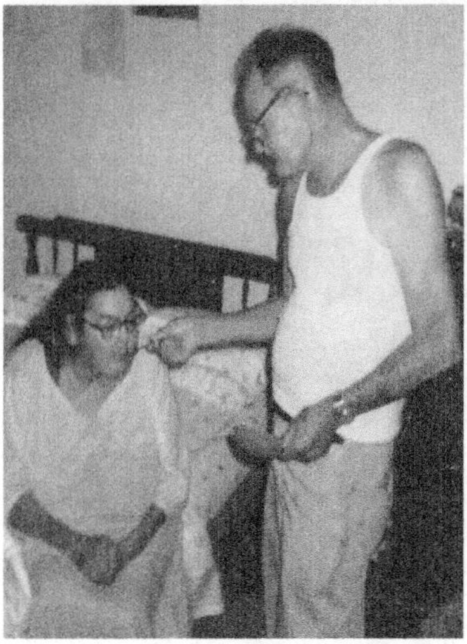

Photo Courtesy of Rick Harris

Rick's parents Ruby & Leon

Photo Courtesy of Rick Harris

Rick & mother Ruby

Photo Courtesy of Rick Harris

Rick with his brothers Leon (left) John (right)

Photo Courtesy of Rick Harris

Mary (Sister) Ruby (Mother) Linda (Sister)
Judy Carol (Sister)

Photo Courtesy of Rick Harris

Rick's first wife Bonnie, Buddy, & Rick

Photo Courtesy of Rick Harris

Rick with his kids

Photo Courtesy of Rick Harris

Rick's second Wife Linda

Photo Courtesy of Rick Harris

The Arkansas Strangler

Photo Courtesy of Rick Harris

The Arkansas Strangler & Johnny McBrown

Photo Courtesy of Rick Harris

Hangman Rick Harris

Photo Courtesy of Rick Harris

Mountain Man Harris

Photo Courtesy of Rick Harris

Jimmy Snuka

Photo Courtesy of Rick Harris

Tommy Young

Photo Courtesy of Rick Harris

Rick with Mr. Fuji

Photo Courtesy of Rick Harris

Charlie Fulton

Photo Courtesy of Rick Harris

Gene Lewis

Greg Bowle Collection

Sgt. Slaughter & Don Kernodle

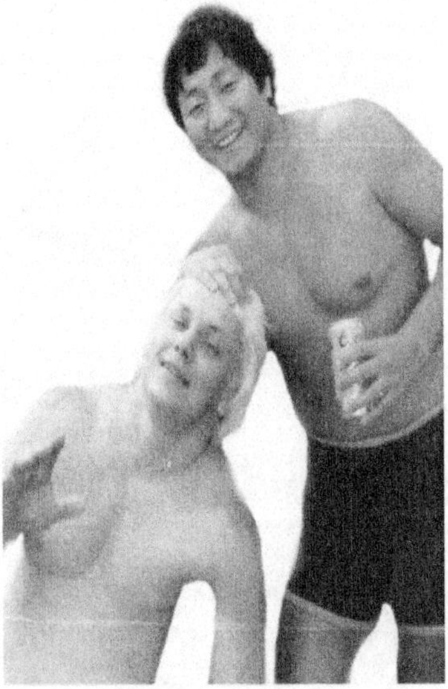

Photo Courtesy of Rick Harris

Ken Timbs & Genichiro Tenyru

Greg Bowle Collection

The Junkyard Dog (JYD)

Courtesy of Len Denton

The Grappler – Len Denton

Greg Bowle Collection

Big Cat Ernie Ladd

Courtesy of Sam Houston

Sam Houston

Photo Courtesy of Rick Harris

Mountain Man Harris vs. Bob Armstrong

Photo Courtesy of Rick Harris

Terry Gordy vs. Brad Armstrong

Photo by Duane Long

J.J. Dillion & Black Bart

Photo by Duane Long

Ron Bass & Black Bart

Greg Bowle Collection

Buzz Sawyer

Photos by Peter Lederberg

Black Bart vs. Dusty Rhodes

Photo by Duane Long

Billy Jack Haynes & Bart

Photo by Duane Long

Barry Windham, Bill Alfonso & Black Bart

Photo by Duane Long

Bart vs. Blackjack Mulligan

Photo Courtesy by Denny Brown

Denny Brown

Photo Courtesy of Sheree Sawyer

Buzz Tyler

Photo By Ric Davies

Terry Taylor & Bart

Photo Courtesy of Rick Harris

David Allen Coe & Rick Harris

Photos by Peter Lederberg

Dustin Rhodes & Bart

Mike Lano wreslano@aol.com

Bruiser Brody

Photo Courtesy of Bill Irwin

Wild Bill Irwin

Mike Lano wreslano@aol.com

Kerry & Kevin Von Erich

Mike Lano wreslano@aol.com

Kevin, Mike, & Lance Von Erich

Photo Courtesy of James Beard

Black Bart, James Beard, & Kerry Von Erich

Photo Courtesy of Rick Harris

Bart vs. Kerry Von Erich

Photo Courtesy of Rick Harris

Bart vs. Kerry Von Erich

Greg Bowle Collection

The Barbarian

Photo Courtesy of James Beard

Chazz Taylor, Johnny Hawk, & James Beard

Photo Courtesy of Rick Harris

Skandor Akbar, Johnny Mantell, & Black Bart

Jon-Paul LeBlance

Charlie Haas & Black Bart

M. Roof Photography

Tim Storm & Black Bart

Photo Courtesy of Rick Harris

Ron Bass & Bonnie Harris

Jon-Paul LeBlance & 4 Corners Photography

The Iron Sheik

Photo Courtesy of Andrew Anderson

Bart, Andrew Anderson, & Sam Houston

Photo Courtesy of Mike Andrews

Preacher aka: Gen. Von Hessler

Jon-Paul LeBlance & 4 Corners Photography

Bart signing pictures at a show

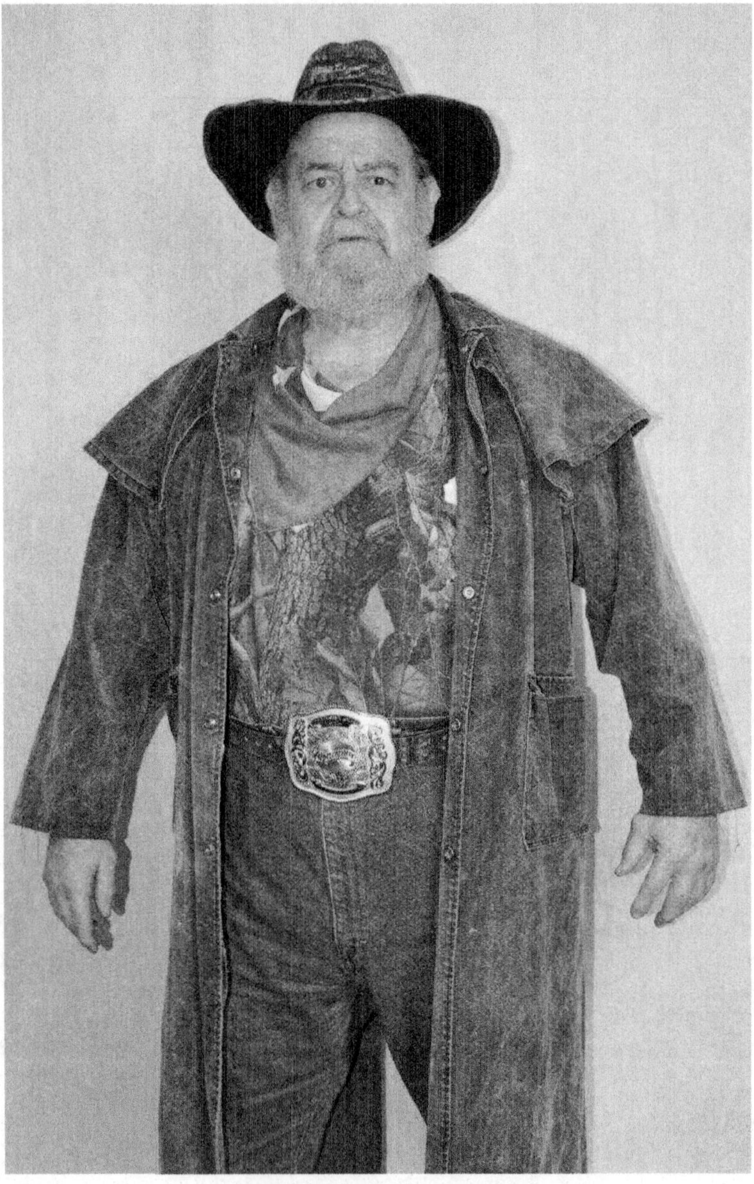

Jon-Paul LeBlance & 4 Corners Photography

Black Bart in 2016

CHAPTER 16 – THE FOUR HORSEMEN

The professional wrestling product in the Summer of 1985 was on fire! Vince McMahon had just debuted WrestleMania and recruited new fans by combining mainstream talent with the likes of Muhamad Ali, Cyndi Lauper, Mr. T., Liberace, Billy Martin, and the Rockettes. This event gave pro wrestling the shot in the arm that it needed. I think it was the show that separated the men from the boys. A lot of the companies tried to duplicate what Vince had just done, but they missed the target. It was around this time that Vince started scooping up all the major talent and because of that action, the smaller wrestling companies were struggling to survive. The Crockett's promotion was still thriving. The Crocketts had key factors that played in their favor. Not only did they have experience in the wrestling business, they also had an incredible pool of talent to draw from. Most importantly though, they had Dusty Rhodes as their booker. Even though the world was still buzzing from Wrestlemania, Dusty had an ace up his sleeve with the Great American Bash. Vince had just shown the world that wrestling could go to a whole new level and Dusty wasn't going to sit back and just watch it happen. He too, was going to show the fans that wrestling and entertainment were a good mix. On July 6, 1985, at the American Legion Memorial Stadium in Charlotte, North Carolina the stage was set. This show was one of many that solidified Dusty's wrestling credibility. David Allen Coe even performed a one-hour concert at the event. Watching David Allen perform that day and getting to meet him backstage was a real treat for me. A lot of his music was the soundtrack for my life. David was friendly and he was easy going. I appreciated that he visited with me and took a picture with me.

The card that day was stacked and the Crocketts had

been promoting the heck out of it, the anticipation for a huge crowd was expected. It was said that 27,000 people came out to see their favorite superstars go into action that day. Jimmy Valiant faced off with Paul Jones in a dog collar match. The Road Warriors went against the Russians, Ivan Koloff, and Krusher Khrushchev. Ric Flair defended his NWA World Heavyweight Title against Nikita Koloff, and Dusty fought Tully Blanchard in a steel cage match. If the NWA and the WWF hadn't officially said that they were at war with each other, everybody just assumed that they were. Oh, did I mention that Crocketts also had the Four Horsemen? In 1985 the Four Horsemen consisted of Ric Flair, Tully Blanchard, Ole & Arn Anderson, along with their manager J.J. Dillon. Over the years, other wrestlers stepped into that role, but it was hard to replace the original members.

Ron and I started to see the writing on the wall about Dusty going in a different direction with our team. The two of us still wrestled with each other, but we began doing a lot more one-on-one matches against other opponents. Even though J.J. wasn't with us as much, Ron and I were still getting a good push. However, it was just being done differently. J.J. on the other hand was in a good spot. He was overseeing four top-billed wrestlers and they were in angles with the likes of Dusty Rhodes and Magnum T.A. The amount of money the Crocketts were bringing in at that time was substantial due to the fact their entire roster was top-notch.

When you talk about a wrestler like Ric Flair, what can you say? At that time, he was the best wrestler in the business, and he can easily be classified as the greatest of all time. Fans wanted to see Ric Flair on the card, just so they could say that they saw him wrestle in person. I can understand that since I had the honor of standing across the ring with him. Fans were in awe of his greatness and his confidence reenforced it. His attire inside and outside of the ring was exquisite. The robes that he wore, I heard were in the range of $10,000. The feathers, rhinestones, and sequins sewed to the fabric gave him a touch of excellence, whether he needed it or not. His day-to-day wardrobe, he sported from head to toe was of high quality and it had class. His braggadocio attitude was always present and wrestling fans expected it! His ability to step into the ring and wrestle the top talent of his day was the reason why he became the top man in the sport! His charisma and personality were second to none. Those were the main reasons why the NWA had put their title on him. He worked hard, he was reliable, and he knew how to make the wrestlers he challenged look good. Ric could go into every town, win the match, keep his belt, and still make the fans love their hometown hero more than they had before the contest started. That was the magic that Ric possessed. He just looked like a champion. His entire demeanor screamed World Champion!

I have always thought highly of Arn Anderson. Even in his early days in the business, I considered him to be a superb wrestler. He was always so smooth in the ring and he did everything right on time. Arn's and my friendship picked up in the Carolinas where it left off in Southeastern Championship Wrestling. I traveled the roads with Arn and I was with him the day that his grandmother was buried. He called her Nana. Arn was an absolute mess that day and we had to drive nearly 200 miles in one direction to Bluefield West Virginia for a match at an armory. I suspected that Arn had been drinking when I picked him up. However, he removed all doubt when he insisted that we stop and get some more beer for the ride to the show. I knew that he was depressed, and I could see his grief. I felt bad for him. As I drove to Bluefield, he sat next to me in the passenger seat with a case of beer between his legs. Whenever we passed a car on the highway, Arn shot the middle finger at the other drivers.

"What are you looking at, Jerk?" Arn yelled.

"Arn, take it easy. Those people didn't do anything to you," I stated.

"They are looking at me," he slurred.

"Arn, I think you had enough beer. Stop drinking and take a nap," I suggested.

"My Nana died," He howled.

"I know she did," I comforted.

"I don't want to wrestle, but I'm in the main event. I want to go to the funeral," he babbled. "But I have to wrestle."

"Try taking a nap Arn," I pleaded.

"I don't want to take a nap. I want to drink. My Nana died," he sobbed.

If I were to guess, he had 40 beers before he wrestled Ricky Steamboat in the main event that evening. Knowing of Arn's condition, I thought that it was going to be a hard match to watch, but his performance that night was amazing. I was in awe of how he composed himself inside the ring. I thought the match he had with Ricky deserved five stars. Referee Tommy Young suspected that Arn was under the influence, only because he smelled like a brewery.

After the show, Tommy approached me in the dressing room.

"Bart, what's going on with Arn?" Tommy asked.

"His Nana was buried today. He wanted to go to the funeral. He's in a bad place," I replied.

"Bart, he is drunk off his ass," he claimed.

"My Nana died Tommy. You can kiss it, Tommy," Arn growled.

"Bart, I'm going to have to tell the office about this," Tommy insisted.

"I don't care who you tell, Tommy. No wrestler in this company can go out there and have a match like he just did, not sober or drunk!" I affirmed.

"My Nana died Tommy," Arn mumbled.

I don't know if Tommy ever said anything to the

Crocketts or not about Arn being drunk. Back then we all drank. I never saw anyone drink as much as Arn did that day and ever wrestle that well. It was mind-blowing to me!

Ole Anderson was the booker in the Carolinas for a long time. However, prior to that he was brought into to be a part of the Minnesota Wrecking Crew alongside of Gene Anderson. Ole was a replacement for Lars Anderson. Anderson is just a wrestling name. These three men, including Arn were not blood related. Ole also was a talented wrestler; however, his style was a bit of a throwback. His in-ring delivery reminded me sort of the style that Ivan passed on to me. His wrestling was good, but it was just from a different era. His people skills were from a different era too. I think Ole believed in the motto "I don't give a shit!" That was just the way he came off to me. I believe that Ole liked being the puppet master and he used that power to his advantage. Ole screwed some wrestlers by not booking them the way they deserved or he didn't book them at all. I don't think he could have done one of the boys a favor even if he tried. I watched wrestlers walk away from the sport because they couldn't support their families due to how Ole was booking them and using them on the shows. It was disheartening to see. The last time that I saw Ole was in a hotel in downtown Charlotte at an autograph signing. He was sitting in the lobby degrading pro wrestling. Ole was talking negatively about our business in a loud, disrespectful, arrogant tone. Ole is a prick and an embarrassment to our sport! He got back everything that he deserved for how he treated the boys who proudly worked in pro wrestling.

The fourth man that helped make up this wrestling group was Tully Blanchard. Tully was a damn good technician in the ring. He was from Texas and his Father, Joe Blanchard, was the owner and promoter of Southwest Championship Wrestling based out of San Antonio. To me, Tully suffered from what most second-generation wrestlers seem afflicted with, "Do you know who my father is?" It was just something I learned to accept. It was almost like this type of wrestler seemed as if they deserved some sort of entitlement. Tully had a hell of a run with Dusty during that period. I remember when I first met Tully. Ron and I wrestled on the same card with him in Richmond, Virginia. After our matches that evening, several of the boys went into the bar of the motel that we were staying in. Tully showed up to meet us all dressed up like he was going somewhere fancier than the dive we were already drinking at. He was sitting with Ron and me as he began to speak about himself.

"You see this watch, Bart?" Tully asked.

"I do," I replied.

"That watch cost me $5,000," he bragged.

"Wow!" I exclaimed sarcastically.

"Do you want to know how much this gold necklace and the diamond rings are worth?" he questioned me.

"Not really," I mouthed.

Tully started to talk once again when he was interrupted by Ron. I quickly realized that Ron and Tully must have already been familiar with each other and Ron wasn't too keen on him sitting with us.

"Tully, Bart isn't one damn bit impressed with any of that crap," Ron snapped. "I don't give a crap about it either."

"Excuse me, Ron," Tully shot back.

"Since you seem to have so much money burning a hole in your pocket, why don't you buy me and Bart another round of drinks?" Ron wanted to know.

Tully didn't say another word. He took one last look at Ron and I and he got up from our table and walked away. To me, Tully always came off like he thought he was better than everyone else. I didn't spend too much time with him outside of wrestling because he wasn't the easiest person to get along with. I just gave Tully his space as much as I could. Oh, and by the way, he didn't buy Ron and me any drinks that evening.

In the early part of my career, especially when I worked alongside Mr. Fuji, I witnessed a lot of ribs being done to me and others around me. I get it, everybody likes to have a good laugh, but some of the stuff we had done to each other crossed the line. As the years passed in my career the jokes kept coming and they were almost always accompanied by hard feelings. One prank I remember very well was done to me by J.J. Dillon. We were in Charlotte for the Great American Bash when J.J. destroyed my $300 Stetson Cowboy hat. When I found it, it was pressed between J.J.'s briefcase and a bench inside the dressing room. To me, it looked as if someone had tried to flatten it out by applying pressure to it. The once nice Stetson was as flat as a pancake. There was no denying that it was done deliberately. Several of the boys pointed the finger at J.J. However, when I confronted him about it, J.J. made all kinds of excuses about how it couldn't have been him.

"J.J., do you want to explain what happened with my hat?" I asked.

"What's up, Bart?" J.J questioned.

"Don't, what's up me J.J.," I hissed.

"What are you talking about?" He demanded.

"Look at my hat J.J., It was under your briefcase!" I shouted.

"Bart, it could have been anyone in the dressing room! Don't try to pin this crap on me!" J.J. fired back.

I was so pissed off that I took the matter to Dusty. He was in the babyface dressing room when I found him. I walked right up to him.

"Bart, what are you doing in here, Baby," Dusty spoke.

"Look at my hat Dusty," I hissed.

"Bart, that thing looks like a pancake. Are you sure that's a cowboy hat?" Dusty asked with a laugh.

"Dusty, that's a $300 hat," I declared.

"I know they can be expensive, Baby. I have a couple myself," he said.

"I know it was J.J.," I accused.

"Did you see him do it, Bart?" Dusty continued. "It could have been any of the wrestlers, Baby. You know how the boys can get sometimes. They're just having some fun," he grinned.

"So, I guess I'm going to have to go out and buy a new hat!" I exclaimed.

"Black Bart needs a black hat, Baby. The two go together just like Bonnie and Clyde," Dusty explained.

J.J. never admitted to destroying my hat, but over the years I have found out that some of the other ribs that were done to me during my career, were mostly done by J.J. Had I known that he was doing all that crap to me when it was happening, I would have kicked a hole in his ass back then. J.J. had a mean streak in him and it strongly went against the character that he wanted everyone to see.

The Crocketts made a lot of money with the Four Horsemen gimmick. Though many came into the group after the original four. In my opinion, If I were to pick two of the best replacements that later came into that faction, I'd name Barry Windham and Chris Benoit. The Four Horsemen was a huge part of professional wrestling and its history. I honestly thought the gimmick was poor booking. I believed by having that many wrestlers in one faction cut into the undercard's pay. When you have guys like Tully, Ric, Ole, and Arn, a promoter is going to have to pay them top dollar, and let's not forget J.J., that's five, and all of those people have to get paid. Paying that many people took money and spots away from lower-card or mid-card wrestlers. Having only two Horsemen would have made better sense financially to me if the Crocketts and Dusty had gone that route. Having five guys in one spot didn't seem very wise to me!

CHAPTER 17 - BUZZ TYLER

I believe the magic that was made in pro wrestling, started with the booking of the matches. It is wise for the person in that position to know the talent that is on the roster very well. That will help decide on the wrestlers who would be a good fit with each other. Any Bozo can throw two guys in a ring and have them fight each other, but is it going to make sense? Is it going to draw money? Let's face it, that certain working chemistry to pull off a long-standing feud with a pair of guys and gals, is either there or it's not. It is that simple! While working in the Mid-Atlantic territory in January of 1985, I had a chance to work against Buzz Tyler. Buzz was nearly six feet tall, and he had to weigh around 280 pounds. He was big and he had a barrel-sized chest. Buzz reminded me of a powerlifter because of his body structure and the natural strength that he possessed. He sported a beard and mustache, which matched the color of his black hair. He often wore a singlet when he wrestled. To me, Buzz was a special wrestler, of course, this is something I discovered after we were booked in an angle with each other.

At the time, I had never wrestled against Buzz. In 1983 when I went to Japan for the first time, he was on that tour too. I didn't have a lot of interaction with him on that trip. He showed up to the Crocketts promotion around the Fall of 1984. Before then, Buzz had wrestled for the NWA Central States Wrestling territory for some time. CSW ran a lot of shows in Kansas and Missouri, along some of the states that surrounded them. In that period, collectively he had wrestled Dusty Rhodes, Harley Race, Ric Flair, and Bob Backlund for their respected World Titles at least a dozen times. Just knowing that information and the fact he worked in Japan on multiple tours, told me that his contribution to this sport is appreciated and admired by his peers. Pro wrestling is and always has been an extremely competitive business and not everyone makes it to World Champion status. However, Buzz Tyler was a damn good wrestler! It is by no mistake that he worked against the top named wrestlers of his day!

It was at a television taping in Spartanburg, South Carolina when we worked together for the first time. When I arrived at the arena, I was approached by Dusty Rhodes. Dusty's mind was always thinking about wrestling. It was fascinating to hear his ideas and to watch the facial expressions he made when he talked about the sport that he loved so much. I don't know how he did it. He knew exactly what it took to make a spark that could ignite a fire.

"Hey Bart, I need to talk to you Baby," Dusty said to me as I was getting ready for my match before the show.

"What's up, Dusty?" I asked.

"I'm thinking about doing an angle with you and Buzz Tyler," he suggested.

"Okay," I replied.

"Do you know Buzz? He questioned.

"I Know him a little bit," I told Dusty.

"I have a feeling the two of you will work well together. I have something in mind that which I think will play out beautifully," Dusty smiled.

I have no idea how long Dusty might have been thinking about this idea, but it seemed as if it came together rather quickly. I do know that on January 12, 1985, a segment was recorded with David Crockett as he presented a gift-wrapped box to Buzz during a televised interview. The gift was said to be from the fans in Spartanburg and Buzz went ahead and opened it with David on television. When Buzz reached inside the box, he pulled out a white t-shirt that sported the college team, the South Carolina Gamecocks. Buzz over played the gesture with such excitement that it resembled a child getting a Christmas present! His gratitude was sincere and his smile was ear to ear! Little did the fans know that this was all part of our plan. Since we were wrestling in Spartanburg which, was Buzz's hometown, he automatically earned sympathy points from the audience. A lot of people think pro wrestling is about fighting and flying around in the ring. To me though, the art of professional wrestling is being able to tug at the heart strings of the fans and draw out their emotions. If you don't have a crowd that is emotionally attached, you only have two people rolling around in a ring. It was the little things that we did in pro wrestling that made the big things bigger. All these segments were taped in Spartanburg in one day, but they played out on television over the next couple of weeks. Everything was falling into place when Buzz came out wearing a different shirt. This one was a black short-sleeved South Carolina Gamecocks t-shirt. Once again, he was told that it also came from his loyal hometown supporters.

While on the studio set, Buzz spoke with Bob Caudle. Bob listened as the 280-pound wrestler showed his love to fans who treated him. In wrestling, these types of segments are obvious to some of the spectators. While others get blindsided by what is about to happen next. This is where the fun began. As Buzz was in the ring wrestling against Bill Alexander, I went over to where Bob Caudle was standing on the set. I grabbed the microphone from him. Buzz had tossed out the bait by thanking all the kind people from Spartanburg for giving him the shirts. I was about to catch the entire crowd, hook, line, and sinker!" Off camera, I was heard disrespecting Buzz and the fans of Spartanburg. I called the people scum bags and I told them how much I hated them. I definitely made my presence known and, in an instant, I got under the skin of Buzz's supporters.

At that instant, I was shown on camera standing with Bob on the set. I received my cue, and I started tearing the shirt. The funny thing about it was, that I thought someone on the production crew might have gimmicked the shirt with pre-cuts to make it easier for me to destroy. Nobody prepped the shirt at all, so I had to put some effort into it to tear it. Within seconds, I tore into pieces. It took a little extra effort, but I got the job done. Bob acted if he was wanting to stop me, but I was determined to piss everyone off in that building and that was exactly what I did. Instantly, I walked off set.

Everything for our upcoming feud was put into place. Dusty formulated his idea. He gave Buzz and I the instructions, and we did our parts. Fans were so mad at me that I was hit in the face with somebody's hot dog! Sometimes the fans took it too far and they threw their keys, rocks, and even batteries at us. Thank God that it was only a hot dog that day! The heat that was created by that one simple action had almost everyone in South Carolina, who liked wrestling, hate me! Now everything was pending on what Buzz was going to do next. After Buzz's match with Bill Alexander was finished, he made his way to the interview set. Buzz was fired up!

Buzz was yelling and he was very animated. His emotions ran high and he defended his fans. Buzz took my actions toward him and the people of South Carolina very personal. His promo probably lasted around two minutes long. Buzz was passionate and his words were clear and what he was saying made sense. He convinced people that he was going to tear my head off for tearing up his t-shirt! When he finished his rant, he threatened me on television by stating that he was going to put me on a slab!

I have always believed that the interview Buzz did that day about me, was by far one of the best I have ever heard. The ability that Buzz had to draw the fans in emotionally proved to me why he was making a living in professional wrestling. Back then, we didn't practice what we were going to say over and over, we had an idea of what the booker had in his mind, and we ran with it. I don't think it's that way anymore. Cutting promos is a thing of the past. I do have to admit that I was a little taken aback when Buzz said he was going to put me on a slab! For tearing up a damn a t-shirt? You got to love pro wrestling! That was the spark that started the explosion. Buzz and I had great in-ring chemistry together. Neither one of us held back either. We gave it to each other as hard as we could stand it without knocking each other's teeth out. That was one of the main reasons why I liked working with him so much. I'm not sure if Dusty knew what was going to come out of putting Buzz and me into an angle with each other, but I'm guessing that our matches exceeded everyone's expectations.

As Buzz and I feuded, the booking office received a ton of requests from the local promoters for Buzz and me to be on their cards. There were about seven small wrestling promotions in the Carolinas that were covered by the C-team. I believe it was known as the Raleigh circuit; the boys called it Mama Crockett's territory. I guess instead of monopolizing the region, Mrs. Crockett, worked with the smaller companies so they could stay in business as well. Buzz and I became a big hit with those promoters, and as long we were in the main event, they didn't care who else was on the card. I was blown away at some of the crowds that came out to watch Buzz and I go after each other. Our matches caught on in those small towns where the shows were held in high school gymnasiums. As our battles continued, we wrestled out on the football field to accommodate the large crowds that we attracted.

During that time in wrestling, if you had two good wrestlers working together in an angle, the bookers took it to the bitter end. If the storyline ever became stale, they mixed things up or ended it. Many of the wrestling feuds that took place during the territory era could last beyond a year or more. However, that was not the case with me and Buzz. As quick as our rivalry started, it ended just as fast. Buzz and I might have wrestled for at least two months, if it even went that long. The funny thing about it, no one ever said anything to me or Buzz why we stopped wrestling against each other. Dusty never said why it was over. It just ended!

After my feud with Buzz, I immediately went into a run for the NWA National Heavyweight Title. Some of my opponents during that title run were Brett Sawyer, Terry Taylor, Ronnie Garvin, and Jimmy Valiant. The strangest thing about my feud with Buzz was when it ended, it was just two weeks later that Ron Bass was in an angle with him. The two of them went on to have several gimmick matches, such as a Texas Death match, a Taped Fists match, and several Texas Bull Rope matches. Buzz and I didn't have those kinds of matches, because we didn't need to have matches like that. It makes no sense to me why the office would stop a feud like the one that Buzz and I had. Especially, when we packed the venues and put butts into the seats! I always wonder if someone on the roster thought that we were getting too much attention, or even if Ron had said something to Dusty. I know that Ron and Dusty were friends for a lot longer than Dusty and I were. It wasn't uncommon for wrestlers' egos to get bruised along with their bodies while they wrestled. Maybe Ron wanted some of that action. Well, he got it. The two things that always seemed to be present in pro wrestling were egos and politics. If the both of them didn't rear their ugly head, at least one of them would eventually!

CHAPTER 18 - RONNIE & RON

Bookers are always trying to keep wrestling programs fresh and exciting. The booker's penicil had a lot of power. A name could be added to a program with the tip of the pencil or it could be removed with the eraser. The person in that position, if he is good, is willing to think outside the box. Dusty was like that and so were other men like Kevin Sullivan, Gary Hart, George Scott, and Skandor Akbar. Every booker was a little different in the way that they did certain storylines, but the goal was always the same: sell tickets! One day, I was approached by J.J. To the fans, he was mine and Ron's manager, but he had a role in the office. J.J. worked under Dusty at that time and helped him manage the boys.

"We need you to tell Bass to pick it up," J.J. suggested.

"Run that by me again?" I asked.

"Ron needs to step it up, Bart. You're pulling all the weight for the Long Riders," he implied.

"Bass is a hell of a hand, he's a good worker and a loyal employee," I declared.

"We think he can be doing more," J.J. claimed.

"So, you want me to tell Ron that he is going to be fired if he doesn't straighten up? "I questioned.

"We want you to tell him to exert himself some more," he advised.

"That isn't my job. That's a job for you or Dusty. I won't do it," I insisted.

I didn't like being asked to do that. If Bass needed to do more, which I didn't believe that he did, that was the job for the office to say something. NOT ME! Ron and I had wrestled in a lot of matches together at that point and though we didn't always agree on everything, we had a mutual respect for each other. We made good money together. It wasn't long after that, Ron and I stopped teaming together and we both began wrestling only in singles matches against other guys on the roster. That wasn't anything that Ron and I asked for, I assume that was coming from Dusty and his pencil. I wasn't too thrilled about it at first, but Dusty ended up putting the NWA National Heavyweight Title on me and I liked that aspect of the change. I was a little surprised by that decision only because during that time, there were so many talented wrestlers that surrounded me in that territory. I could give a list of names that were deserving of holding the National belt, but I sure was appreciative that Dusty chose me. In those days, there were three titles that were considered as being prestigious among the boys. They were the NWA World Heavyweight, the National Heavyweight, and the North American Heavyweight belts. I was always honored when a promoter put a belt on me. A belt said more than any number of words ever could say. Having a belt around your waist, said that you were the man! I always felt like there was a lot of responsibility that went along with being a champion, so, I always took my title runs seriously.

Before I held the National belt, Ronnie Garvin had it. Ronnie's nickname was "The Hands of Stone," and that was no joke. Mulligan hit hard, but when it came to Ronnie Garvin throwing a punch, HELLO! I can't count the number of stars that I saw with each punch to my face. It was painful. Leading up to the title change, I taunted my opponent and caused a bunch of trouble. I started challenging Ronnie and while in a match with Ron Bass, I went to ringside and I shared some choice words with the Champion. To make matters worse, I grabbed Ronnie's National title, put it around my waist, and walked off with it. That was all I needed to do! A week later, I was in a loser leaves town match with Ronnie, and I took the belt from him. I didn't know all the particulars surrounding Ronnie's personal life at the time, but it was my understanding that he needed to return home for some family business. So, that was the reason the loser leaves town stipulation was placed in that contest.

Eventually, when Ronnie returned from his absence, the two of us engaged in several matches. Whenever I stepped into the ring with Ronnie, if we didn't wrestle a full hour, we went to 40 or 50 minutes every time. Wrestling him got me into the best wrestling shape of my career. One night in Wheeling, West Virginia, we wrestled in a taped fist match. Normally the boys taped their fists with white tape, like first aid tape. However, this night was different. My friend and the referee for our match, Tommy Young was the person who gave me a heads-up about what Ronnie was up to.

"Hello, Bart. How are you this evening?" Tommy asked.

"I'm good buddy. I'm just getting ready for my match with Ronnie," I returned.

"Hey Bart, I need to tell you something," Tommy whispered.

"What's up, Tommy?" I inquired.

"Ronnie isn't using that kind of tape that you are taping your fists with," he informed.

"What's he using?" I wanted to know.

"He wrapped his hands with duct tape," Tommy filled me in.

"That dirty dog! I don't have any duct tape," I fettered.

"Good luck," Tommy said to me as he walked away.

As I sat on the dressing room bench feeling like a dumbass, I stared at my hands. I knew if I didn't get a roll of duct tape, I had no business getting into the ring with Ronnie, and that wasn't going to happen. I wanted to kick Ronnie's ass even more at this point. My mind was racing!

"What am I going to do?" I thought to myself.

I just sat there and looked around the room. I dared to leave the building, but where was I going to find a store quick enough that had duct tape? Leaving the building was never a good idea because I never wanted to miss a match. So, I continued to sit. Suddenly, I noticed the air that was coming through the vent from the ceiling. The building we were wrestling in that night was a decent-sized coliseum, so I knew I had to find the storage closet. I had done some air conditioning work back home, so if I could get my hands on tape used in that industry, I'd be in good shape. The tape used for air condition units is made from aluminum, so I looked feverishly for a roll. I walked through the halls of the building and with the help of a maintenance worker, I obtained the tape that I was looking for. Back in the dressing room, I went to work on taping my fists. When I finished the layer of aluminum tape, I covered it with a layer of white tape. I was ready! I couldn't wait until I got into the ring that night. The bell rang and the two of us went at each other with a purpose. The second after I hit Ronnie in the head, he looked straight into my eyes as if he were puzzled. The fight was on and oddly enough, a part of me felt as if I had won before our match was even over! WE BEAT THE PISS OUT OF EACH OTHER THAT NIGHT! We were both covered with so much blood, that we couldn't tell if it was his or mine! I can't remember if I ever told Ronnie about how I taped my hands that night. I would have been in big trouble had I not evened the playing field. I'm guessing Ronnie could have changed his name from the "The Hands of Stone," to "The Hands of Duct Tape!"

After that match, it was brought to my attention that I had the support of fans there in that city. Some people there had formed the Black Bart Fan Club. I never knew anything like that ever existed. Usually, heel wrestlers don't get that kind of attention from the ticket buyers, so, I had to go out and see my supporters for myself. They had pictures of me and posters made for me. A couple of the guys were even dressed like me, they were decked out wearing dusters and cowboy hats. Several of the members who gathered with me that evening asked me to sign some photos for them. They wanted to talk to me and tell me who they were and where they were from. I must admit it was flattering!

Ronnie and I had another memorable taped fist match, this time it was held in Marietta, Georgia. It wasn't eventful for the tape that we put on our fists; it was what happened during the match that was so unforgettable. After 10 minutes of intense fighting inside the ring, we found ourselves on the floor outside of it. The action continued as we made our way further and further away from the ring. Fighting in the foyer of the building where the people came in and went out was not off-limits. Neither was the concessions stand area. The fans who had watched us fight inside the venue came to where we were brawling in the hallways. We were surrounded by a sea of people in a matter of moments, which is not a very safe place to be in. Ronnie picked up one of the old metal cylinder ashtrays. They stood about three feet tall and were weighted down with sand. He connected that heavy object to the top of my head and cut me open worse than I already was. NO BLADE! We call that doing it the hard way! I felt the warm blood run down my face, and it went straight into my eyes. I did the best I could to use my wrist and forearm to push the blood away, so, I could see better. It was helping only a little bit. As Ronnie and I continued to fight, I noticed a guy in his mid-20s walking toward me with intention. To me, he looked like a country bumpkin. The fan was wearing blue jeans, a western shirt, a baseball cap, and cowboy boots. I think I know a country bumpkin when I see one. Out of nowhere, this guy took a swing at me. When he threw his punch, I timed it exactly right and I leaned back. With my movement, I avoided his punch and I retaliated by busting him in the nose. He dropped to the floor and I went over to where he was. I began to use the blade on his face that I had concealed on my index finger. The idiot screamed and two of his friends came in my direction. Ronnie assisted me with those two bozos, and he kept them at a distance. Eventually, the antagonists retreated. Ronnie and I quickly made our way back to the ring and we finished the match.

Once I made my way back to the dressing room, the medical staff treated the wound I received from the ashtray. The bleeding had stopped, and the cut was closed with butterfly stitches. After I cleaned myself up from being covered with blood, I got dressed and proceeded to leave. When I walked out of the dressing room, I was met by law enforcement. Two of the men were city cops and the other was a highway patrol officer. I instantly thought that I was in trouble. So, I lifted my arms and put them in front of me placing my hands together.

"Hello gentleman, I'm ready to do my part," I said.

"What are you doing, Bart?" One of the police officers questioned.

"Aren't you here to take me to jail?" I asked.

"Bart, we saw the entire incident. We came to ask if you want to press charges on that man," the cop returned.'

"No. I don't want to do that," I informed the policemen.

"Are you sure?" The highway patrolman asked.

"I'm sure. How is that guy doing?" I inquired.

"I don't think he will be doing that again," one of the policemen said.

I was glad the cops didn't take me to jail. I know how pissed off I was when that fan attempted his attack on me, so I was concerned that I might have hurt him badly in the heat of the battle.

When I wrapped up my series with Ronnie, I started another one with Terry Taylor. That storyline didn't last too long either, but I liked wrestling Terry when I got the chance. A lot of the babyface wrestlers could be what I described as "candy-ass." Many complained about their hair being pulled too hard, or a punch being delivered with too much force. Ric Flair and Hulk Hogan were like that, but not Terry Taylor. I first met Terry when I wrestled in Georgia. Terry looked like a model, and he had a great look for television. At first glance, some might underestimate him, however, he was as tough as they came, he could take care of himself if had to, and I had a ton of respect for him. Shortly after we started our series, I dropped the NWA National Title to him, and from that point, I transitioned into a feud with Outlaw Ron Bass. Yes! My longtime tag team partner Ron Bass!

Ron and I had been doing our own thing for several months at this point. Our tag team partnership was long dissolved with no hopes of its return. The two of us had our feud with Buzz Tyler and then we had battles with other guys as well. When I fought Ronnie and Terry, Ron had his hands full with Buddy Landel. I remember being in the dressing room having a conversation with Ron. Dusty approached us, and as

usual he was naked from the waist down. He seemed to be in a pleasant mood. His jovial demeanor and big smile on his face were a dead giveaway.

"There they are my two favorite outlaws," Dusty cooed.

"Hey there, Dusty," I replied.

"So, we have a change," he added.

"What kind of a change?" Ron asked.

"Black Bart and the Outlaw Ron Bass are going to have a little feud," Dusty informed.

"What? Is there no chance of us ever working together again?" I wanted to know.

"You're not going to be the Long Riders no more, Baby," he advised.

"When is this going to happen?" Ron wondered.

"Right away. Right now. It already happened, Baby," Dusty went on.

A part of me was confused and the other part of me understood that it was pro wrestling. Change is just about the one thing you can count on when it comes to this sport. I think Ron felt the same way that I did about Dusty's idea. Now, the stage was set for Ron and me. The Outlaw versus Black Bart. I was the heel, and he was now the babyface. Of Course, J.J. was my manager. Breaking up a team and having two former friends fight in a feud is common in pro wrestling. I think it's too common and an overused angle in the business, but it seems to be something the fans like to watch. I can tell you right now, that neither one of us wanted to wrestle each other. I thought that Ron and I had good chemistry as a team, but when it came to us being opponents, it just wasn't there. I think the two of us had been heels for so long and we were so used to calling the match inside the ring, we constantly battled for control. It was natural for both of us to want to be the Ring General when we competed. I remember speaking to Ron about our matches after they happened on several different occasions.

"What's your opinion of that match, Ron?" I asked curiously.

"I thought it was crap," Ron replied.

"I agree. I can't seem to find my rhythm," I explained.

"If it's not broken, don't fix it." Ron continued. "The Long Riders weren't broken."

"What is the office thinking?" I inquired.

"They aren't thinking, Bart, and that's the problem!" Ron snapped.

For nearly six months the two of us wrestled all over the southeastern part of the United States. Night after night it was the same, it felt as if we were forcing a square peg into a round hole. We attempted some gimmick matches and they fell flat too. It wasn't until November 28, 1985, in Greensboro, North Carolina the Crocketts and Dusty put on Starrcade.

This was the time that I felt some kind of magic with The Outlaw. Ron and I faced off in a Bull rope match. By this time in my career, I had been in several matches of this type, and Ron had too. So, I think I should know what a good rope match is compared to a bad one. This night was special for me, Ron was going to walk away the winner, and the stipulation was for him to get J.J. in the ring for five minutes when the contest was over. I remember the exchange of words that Ron and I had in the dressing room before the show started.

"Good evening, Bart," Ron said.

"Hi Ron," I returned.

"Are you ready for this?" He asked.

"I'm ready for the aftermath," I replied with a smile.

"Me too," he grinned.

"Be sure that you give him one for me," I pleaded.

"Bart, since I like you so much, I will give him two," Ron smiled.

Just like it was planned, Ron won our match and he was going to have his way with J.J. Pulling stunts like that always helped draw more of a crowd to the shows. With this being a big event, it helped assure that fans would want to come out and pay good money to see Ron kick J.J.'s ass. After Ron won, I exited the ring and sold my punishment. As I lay on the floor on the outside of the ring, Ron started going at J.J. like flies on honey. I couldn't see what Ron was doing to J.J., but I could hear the commotion and it sounded painful. I knew that Ron was going to take pleasure in torturing his former manager. I was taking great pleasure in it as well because J.J. needed a good-ass whooping! After all, he had it coming! I was supposed to run in and stop Ron's assault before the five minutes ran out, but I waited as long as I could. No one gave me a cue to enter the ring, so I just estimated, and I estimated long! After the match, and once inside the dressing room, I didn't say anything to Ron about his time with J.J. However, we both shared a smile and that said everything!

That Bull rope match at Starrcade with Ron was one of my favorites. It was by far the best match that the two of us had when we battled. We wrestled each other for the next couple of months, but nothing came close to that contest in Greensboro. I feel that we actually found a rhythm that we hadn't experienced before until that point. I'm not sure if it was the style of the match that we fought in or the fact that J.J. had to face Bass when it was over. I still think about that match to this very day. It truly was a classic bout for Ron and me. While all that was going on with Ronnie Garvin, Terry Taylor, and Ron Bass, I was also doing spots with Sam Houston. I couldn't have been happier! The matches that I had with Sam were absolute classics! SAM HOUSTON AND I COULD TEAR A PLACE DOWN!

CHAPTER 19 - SAM HOUSTON

If I had to pick just one wrestler from my entire career who I thought I had some of my best matches with, I'd have to say it is Sam Houston! I think it had a lot to do with the trust we had for one another. Sam knew that he could trust his body with me, and I trusted mine with him. We also wanted to go out there and prove a point. We knew that we were just as good as the other wrestlers on the roster, and when people saw our matches, no one could deny it! Sam and I might have had the mid-card spot when we were first put together. However, we were put in semi-main and the main event matches as time progressed. When the fans saw that Sam and I were wrestling each other on an upcoming card, they knew that they were going to get their money's worth. It truly was mind-blowing to see how the fans were so invested in our matches. When the office had us fighting over the Mid-Atlantic title, it added more fuel to the fire, and it gave a stronger purpose to our battles. Every match we had was different than the last one. We knew what to do to get the crowd back into our contest if their attention drifted. It was exhilarating to be able to feel the response that the fans gave us every time we stepped in the ring with each other!

On April 26, 1986, Crockett Promotions took a show to the Civic Center in Baltimore, Maryland for a crowd of nearly 7,000 people. The card was packed solid with top talents such as The Midnight Express, Manny Fernandez, The Road Warriors, Ivan and Nikita Koloff, Arn Anderson, Ronnie Garvin, Don Kernodle, Denny Brown, and several others. That night Sam and I squared off in a Texas Death match. In this type of contest, we had no rules and neither of us could be disqualified. To say that Sam and I tore the house down was an understatement! We gave it our all! The two of us were covered in blood, and at one point during our battle I believe we both operated on just our will and instincts.

Before the match finished, Sam and I were ambushed by a few men who worked for the Athletic Commission. They did what they could do to stop us from fighting, but they failed miserably. After several minutes of the official's interference, our match ended. We were properly introduced to our new friends when we returned to the dressing room. The commission was not happy that Sam and I took a bloodbath. If Sam and I were supposed to bleed in our matches, WE GOT BLOODY! The officials had some words with Dusty, but I never heard too much about what they discussed with him about that particular match. I do know the Commission was not happy with the direction that Sam I took our contest.

In May of that same year, we returned to Baltimore to wrestle at the Civic Center once again. Sam and I were scheduled to face off at that event as well. The fans who got to watch us wrestle the month prior were anticipating another amazing fight between us! I was feeling overwhelmed with excitement until I entered the dressing room. I quickly found out that Sam and I were wrestling in the second match of the night. My opponent and I were surprised. We couldn't understand why our match was placed so low on the card. Especially, because of what happened that last time the two of us fought each other in Baltimore. Sam and I found Dusty to talk with him about it.

"Hey, Dusty do you have a minute to talk to us?" I asked.

"I always have a minute to talk to Black Bart and Sammy Baby, but not tonight, I'm busy fellas. Sorry, I have to take care of something," Dusty responded.

"Dusty, is this correct?" I questioned him as I showed him the booking sheet.

"Is what correct, Baby?" he wondered.

"Are we in the second match?" Sam inquired.

"That is correct, Baby. You two have a good match. I know you will," Dusty replied as he turned to walk away.

"Dusty we almost destroyed this place last month in a Texas Death match," I shouted.

"You sure did! It was a damn good match too," he said.

"You know the fans want to see us do the same thing tonight. How are we supposed to follow our last match?" Sam asked.

"The best way you know how, Baby. The best way that you know how," Dusty said as he walked away.

"Dusty, is that it?" I asked.

"No, that's not it. The Athletic Commission said no blood, Baby, no blood!" Dusty spoke.

At first, Sam and I were a bit puzzled. It took us no time to realize what we needed to do. We knew what the fans were expecting from us. They wanted to see us go out there and top what did on our last visit. Despite being the second match of the night, Sam and I took Dusty's advice. We followed our last match the best way that we knew how! We were determined to have the match of the night! Our match started out like a regular opening match. We did regular moves that weren't too extravagant. It only took us a couple of minutes until we got things heated up in our battle! Once again, the two of us made our way to the outside of the ring and we nearly killed each other. The Athletic Commission had tables set all around each side of the ring. So, for us to get out of the ring and onto the floor, we had to get on or go over the tables. When we were both standing on the floor, I slammed Sam's head into a table, and he hit the floor. When Sam stood back up, he was bleeding badly. He came back with a chair to my head, and I dropped to my knees. When I got back to my feet, streams of blood ran down my face. This match had rules, so, to keep the referee from stopping the match, one of us had to get back into the ring to stop the official's count. For us to do that we either had to step on or move the official's tables out of our way. Since Sam and I had so many tables at our disposal, we used them on each other too. These tables were not rigged in any way, they were hard and sturdy and the two of us felt every bit of them. The fans were on their feet and in awe of what they were watching.

Once again, three guys from the Maryland State Athletic Commission came over to us to stop Sam and me from fighting. Shortly thereafter, we went back into the ring and finished our match. I might have won, but the officials from the state of Maryland were determined to throw their weight around.

In the dressing room, the saga continued when one of the officials from the commission came to lay down the law. It was apparent that the man that came to see us was upset. His red face, and body language was a dead giveaway.

"Where is he?" Where is Dusty?" the man shouted out with authority.

"I'm right here, Baby. What seems to be the problem?" Dusty wanted to know.

"The problem is right there! Those two guys right there!" The official shouted as he pointed in Sam's and my direction.

"What on earth did those two guys right there do?" Dusty asked.

"Don't play dumb with me! We said no blood! Look at them they're covered with it!" The man fumed.

"What would you like me to do now?" Dusty inquired.

"That's it! It's over. The show is over!" He demanded.

"Do you realize how many people are out there?" Dusty asked with a puzzled look on his face.

"You need to take your fat ass out there right now and tell the audience that the show is over!" he ordered directly to Dusty.

"If you want to cancel the show you need to take your ass out there and do it yourself!" Dusty shot back. "But I won't be responsible when they riot"!

"Those two are never to wrestle each other in the state of Maryland ever again!" he commanded. Is that understood? The official shouted.

"It's understood, Baby. I understood everything you said," Dusty answered in a half-sarcastic and half-annoyed tone.

For a moment there was silence. Dusty and the commissioner stared intensely at each other. Suddenly Dusty spoke.

"Are you done talking? If so, get out of my dressing room!" Dusty demanded!

Dusty knew that if the show didn't continue, the people in that place would have been pissed off! The man left the back of the building and the show resumed. However, the rest of the night was quite different after Sam, and I wrestled. The audience was so invested in our match that they were emotionally spent when it was over. The fans had no more energy left. Sam and I followed our last match the best way that we knew how. I'm sure the other athletes on the show that night went out there and gave it their best, however, Sam and I had the best match of the night. The fans were ready to go home before the main event. The state of Maryland held to its promise. Sam and I were never allowed to wrestle against each other there ever again. That was a rule the commission took very seriously and one that they never wavered on it.

Another similar situation happened in Philadelphia, Pennsylvania. The Athletic Commission in Pennsylvania was a pain in the ass to work with also. All the wrestlers had to have physicals and their blood pressure had to be taken before they wrestled. We needed to have a license to wrestle there too, and the officials always seemed to be watching us. The atmosphere every time we went to Philadelphia or any other city in that state seemed different than the other places that we wrestled in. I remember Dusty talking to Sam and me before we went out to the ring to wrestle.

"Alright, where are my cowboys? I want to talk to you about your match, Baby," Dusty cooed.

"What's up, Dusty?" I asked.

"Where is Sammy, Baby?" he wanted to know.

"He's over there," I said as I pointed in the opposite direction of the dressing room.

"Come over here Sammy, Baby. I want to talk to you and Black Bart," Dusty spoke before Sam headed to where we were.

"Hey there Dusty," Sam said.

"Alright, boys. I want you two to go out there and give them a show. I want you to use tables, I want you to use chairs, I want some color. I want the works," Dusty affirmed. "Can you do that for me, cowboys?"

"We got it," I answered.

"Do you get it, Sammy, Baby?" Dusty said with a big smile on his face.

"Yes Sir," Sam replied.

"That's good, it's going to be good, Baby. It's going to be just like the OK Corral, but when it's done, we are all going back to the ranch!" Dusty spoke out loud as he walked away to another part of the dressing room.

I had a feeling that the Athletic Commission in the Keystone State was getting on Dusty's last nerve, and he wanted to make it a point to stick it to them. He permitted us to push the envelope, so Sam and I went all out! The moment the bell rang for our bout, the fireworks went off! We beat the crap out of each other, in the ring and out of the ring. We both attacked each other with chairs and tables, and at one point, I threatened to hit Sam with the timekeeper's hammer that was used to strike the bell with. Once again, our match was off the charts, and the fans went nuts! It wasn't hard to notice that the state officials at ringside were not happy with our wrestling style that night. I had a feeling that once we returned to the dressing room, Sam and I would hear something from them. As I predicted, we did. The door to the dressing room opened and, in the doorway, stood one of the guys who worked with the commission.

"Who's in charge?" the man asked in a loud and stern tone.

"That would be me," Dusty replied as he walked to where the man was standing.

"The show is over!" he demanded.

"The show is over?" Dusty questioned the man with a perplexed look on his face.

"Yes! It's over!" the official responded.

"I say this with all due respect. The people here in Philly are a little crazy. Not in a bad way crazy, but in a good way crazy. They like Rocky, steak sandwiches, and their wrestling. You can't take away their wrestling," Dusty replied in a calm and soothing voice.

"The show is over!" the man shouted.

"If the show is over there will be a riot. Not in a good way, but in a bad way," Dusty was convinced.

The man stared at Dusty for a moment as if he was thinking about what Dusty just told him.

"Okay, the show will continue. There will be no more blood and no more violence!" the commission worker insisted.

"Not a problem. I will take care of everything from here. Thank you so much for the visit," Dusty responded sarcastically as he led the man through the door and out of our area

"Those are the rules. You will obey them!" he said as

Dusty closed the door on him. Dusty turned away from the door and looked at all of us who just listened in on the conversation he just had.

"You heard the man. Go out there and wrestle!" Dusty stated.

Just as it was in the state of Maryland, Sam and I were told that weren't allowed to wrestle each other in the state of Pennsylvania ever again either. When Sam and I first started working together, I usually was the wrestler who won, however, as things started to heat up between us, that changed. Often there were times, that Magnum T.A. or Dusty ran to the ring to distract the referee, and changed the finish of the match on the fly. We all knew if Sam didn't win some of the matches that he and I were in, the fans would tear the place down. Sometimes, Sam and I decided to switch the finish despite what Dusty told us to do, based on the vibe we were feeling from the crowd. To this day, Sam and I often talk about the matches that we had in Maryland and Pennsylvania.

"Sam, do you remember the matches that the athletic commissions got involved in?" I asked.

"Are you kidding? How can I forget those battles?" he responded with a laugh.

"That was a good time," I answered back.

"That was a great time. It was so great that they didn't want us to come back," he chuckled.

"Great times for sure," I reminisced.

I can't guess how many times Sam and I had wrestled each other over our careers. I can honestly say that we never had a bad one. The two of us wanted to steal the show every night and we did that! Even though the matches that we had together were very physical, they were fun, and it felt like a night off. Knowing Sam has not only made me a better wrestler, but a better person as well. I am blessed to have the friend that I do in Sam.

CHAPTER 20 – WORLD CLASS CHAMPIONSHIP WRESTLING

World Class Championship Wrestling had changed drastically since I met David Von Erich when I wrestled in Georgia in 1982. In 1986, some of the wrestlers that were in the Dallas territory were guys like Scott Casey, Buzz Sawyer, Matt Borne, Steve Simpson, Mark and Chris Youngblood, Brian Adias, Tim Brooks, The Grappler, and The Dingo Warrior, who went the World Wrestling Federation under the name of The Ultimate Warrior. Of course, you had the Von Erichs. When it came to working with Kevin, Kerry, and Mike Von Erich at World Class I wasn't a fan. I didn't spend a lot of time talking to them unless it was about our matches. I didn't want to be around them. Not just because I was a heel, the boys who wrestled them had to candy-coat their careers and make them look better in the ring than they actually were. Kevin, Kerry, and Mike had no respect for time and schedules, and they acted as if they could do whatever they wanted to. To me, they came off as immature and childish. Since their dad, Fritz Von Erich was the boss, we all had to put up with it.

I respected David. I enjoyed the short time that I worked with him in Georgia. Unfortunately, due to David's unexpected death in February 1984, while he was wrestling in Japan, I wasn't able to spend any more time with him. In September of 1985, Mike Von Erich went to the hospital, for a shoulder surgery. While he was in the hospital, he contracted Toxic Shock Syndrome. He nearly died because of the whole ordeal, but by God's grace, he pulled through. He eventually came back to wrestling, but he was never the same after that. Truth be told, Mike didn't want to be a wrestler. I heard that he wanted to be in a band or be a part of the production crew for the wrestling program. However, Fritz had other plans for Mike, and that was for him to be a professional wrestler just like the rest of the family.

In June of 1986, Kerry was involved in a severe motorcycle accident when he hit a police car. Referee Rick Hazzard was one of the first people who met him at the hospital. Rick was shocked to see the condition of Kerry's right foot. The highlight of Kerry's career was when he took the NWA belt off of Ric Flair at Texas Stadium in May of 1984. The National Wrestling Alliance didn't keep the belt on him for too long. Some of the boys were surprised that his title reign wasn't longer while others questioned why they gave the belt to him in the first place. To be a World Champion, a wrestler really needed to be a Ring General. Controlling every aspect of the match wasn't Kerry's strength. However, that accomplishment for Kerry seemed a million light years away from where he was now! The severity of Kerry's injury had many questions if he would every return to the ring. Determination, more setbacks, and a long road of recovery seemed to describe Kerry's reality and immediate future.

It was important for Fritz to have the Von Erich name on every wrestling card when his company ran shows. Back then, World Class ran two shows a night, and due to the Von Erich's popularity, they drew a lot of money for their company. Unfortunately, because of these unforeseen illnesses and accidents, booking the Von Erich boys wasn't always possible. The office put a lot of thought into keeping the attendance up at the events. Welcome in Lance Von Erich! Lance was not related to the Von Erichs at all. His real name was Kevin Vaughan, but Fritz named him Lance and he was the kayfabe cousin. Lance wasn't a wrestler, he was a bodybuilder, but when it came to wrestling, he put in the effort to get better. The good thing about wrestling against Lance was that he was easy to work with in the ring. I couldn't say the same about Kevin or Kerry.

Lance was discovered in the Summer of 1984 by

David Manning, but he didn't start wrestling for World Class until October of 1985. Before Fritz had him wrestling in Dallas full-time, Lance was sent to wrestle in Portland, Oregon to work with promoter Don Owen. Back then, a wrestler could go somewhere like the Pacific Northwest and wrestle under a different name and still remain under the radar. In Portland Don called Lance, Ricky Vaughn. Lance didn't have the wrestling skills that Kevin and Kerry had, but he was more reliable than the Von Erich brothers ever were!

In the mid to late 80s, the wrestling territories that once thrived were experiencing smaller house draws than ever before. Many of them could no longer keep up with what Vince McMahon was doing and remain in business. World Class had its share of problems. Fritz pulled away from the National Wrestling Alliance, which in my opinion weakened his product. I had heard that Fritz felt that his boys weren't getting their fair share of matches for the NWA Title belt, that he believed they deserved. So, he created his own World Title for the territory. The crowds got smaller as time went on, but the boys working there were doing all they could to keep the wrestling product alive!

Mike Von Erich was the youngest brother wrestling at this time. Chris who was a couple of years behind Mike was around the business quite a bit. Chris didn't start wrestling until 1990, but he and Mike were pretty tight, so he was always around or it seemed that way to me. Mike didn't have the body of a wrestler. Mike's body type was similar to his older brother David's. However, David was tall and very athletic. To me, Mike always looked too frail and too skinny, and he looked very unhealthy in the Summer of 1986.

That Summer, before I started working for Fritz permanently, I wrestled against Mike somewhere in Louisiana at a show. Bonnie and I were still living in Georgia and we drove to Fort Worth to visit my family. I called Fritz to see if he had a match I could pick up and he made a spot for me without hesitation. The event seemed to be in the middle of nowhere, but somehow Bonnie and I found it. I arrived at the venue, and it was in an old tin building. It looked like a huge warehouse or an old airplane hangar. If the facility had air conditioning in it, it wasn't working properly that evening. Inside the ring, it felt like 140 degrees. However, there were several hundred people in attendance, and they didn't seem to mind sitting in a sauna. I was told that I was wrestling Mike Von Erich. I had never met him before this encounter, and it didn't dawn on me that this was the same Von Erich brother who suffered from the bout with Toxic Shock Syndrome. I hadn't been around the territory for any length of time at this point, so, I was clueless about a lot of details concerning the wrestlers that worked for Fritz. Anytime that I knew I was wrestling against one of Fritz's boys, it meant only one thing to me, the wrestler not named Von Erich was going to lose! Since the heel's main job is to make his opponent look good, I was prepared to do that in this bout with Mike.

The heat inside the ring was affecting me. Our bodies were sweaty, and it was difficult to lock up or put a hold on one another because we slipped out of every move. Plus, the sweat was running into my eyes and that was causing me issues that I didn't expect with my vision. I never lost my concentration in a match like this before, but this night all I could think of was drinking a cold beer. I'm sure Mike was experiencing the same troubles that I was. On top of all that, he was as white as a sheet of paper. Despite the challenges that we faced in that match, we were scheduled to go 20 minutes, so we had to make it work. Somewhere around the 10-minute mark of the match, I noticed the scar on Mike's shoulder. I can't tell you why I didn't notice it earlier, but it was then that I realized that this was the same Von Erich that nearly died from the bacteri-
al

infection the previous year. I started to question why Fritz was having Mike work at all, considering what he had gone through. I became concerned for my opponent's' well-being and I walked over to referee Rick Hazzard to talk to him.

"Isn't this the same Von Erich that was sick?" I questioned.

"Yes, it is," Rick replied.

"If I'm suffering out here in this heat, how do you think he is doing?" I inquired.

"It's hot for sure, but the doctor cleared him to wrestle," he said.

"Well, I think it's stupid for him to work in these conditions. We're going home right now," I insisted.

At that moment I turned my attention back to Mike. I walked right over to him and I scooped his body off the canvas and placed him on my shoulder. I immediately slammed him to the mat; I attempted to go for the pin, but I quickly shifted my weight, and I pulled Mike on top of me. Rick dropped to the surface of the ring, he counted to three and the match was over. The match was supposed to end with Mike pinning me while applying the Iron Claw to my head as I lay on the mat. The three of us stood up and in the middle of the ring, Rick declared Mike the winner by raising his arm in the air. Rick walked over to talk to me before I exited the ring.

"That wasn't the finish that we were supposed to do," Rick confirmed.

"He's a Von Erich, right?" He was supposed to win, right?" I shot back.

"Yes," he returned.

"Then what's the problem?" I continued. "He won, didn't he?"

"I'm going to tell Fritz about this," Rick assured.

"I'm sure you will, Rick," I said with a grin.

I left the ring and I didn't hear another word about

my match with Mike for the rest of the night. Later that week when I arrived at the Sportatorium in Dallas, I ran into Fritz. I hadn't spoken with him since before I wrestled his son in Louisiana. Fritz had a reputation for being a bit difficult because he had a strong personality. He was the boss, and he wanted the wrestlers on his roster to abide by his decisions. So, I imagined that he was going to let me have it. I was fully prepared for a good ass chewing. Fritz noticed me and when he did, he walked in my direction and he approached me.

"Bart, I want to talk to you," Fritz said.

"Sure, Fritz," I answered.

"Thank you for taking care of my boy," he shared with sincerity.

"No problem Fritz. That's what the boys are supposed to do," I affirmed.

"Thank you," he told me as he patted me on the shoulder before he walked away.

Some of the boys had issues with Fritz and I think a lot of them were afraid of him. Fritz was a bit intimidating due to the loud, strong tone of his voice and his no-nonsense demeanor. I didn't have a problem with him at all. I liked him. I understood that he was the boss, it was that simple. When it came to the business of wrestling, I was a professional through and through. Everyone who worked with me knew it. Sometimes Fritz barked at me and sometimes I barked back. If a wrestler didn't draw the line with him like that when it was necessary, he lost all respect for them. If someone wanted to be a part of wrestling, they had to be tough. That's the bottom line!

At that time George Scott was the booker for World Class Championship Wrestling. George had already spent several decades in pro wrestling. By that time in his career, George had a rather good pulse of the in-ring sport. In his career, he had worked with some of the heavy hitters in wrestling, the Crocketts, Vince McMahon, and Jim Barnett just to name a few. I first met him when Ivan sent me to the Carolinas in 1981.

At the time, Chris Adams was holding that belt. Chris was from England and he had been wrestling for Fritz since 1983. He took his turns of playing the babyface and the heel. I think when Chris held the World Class belt, he was wrestling as a good guy. On a flight taking off from Puerto Rico, he had an altercation on an airplane while he was intoxicated. Chris had a reputation for being mean when he was drunk, and as a result, he head-butted the co-pilot when they wouldn't serve him any more alcohol while in the air. I assume the office looked at him as a liability. Some people thought he was going to get deported for his actions, but he only served jail time. My first night of wrestling at the Will Rogers Coliseum on this trip came with a surprise. I was in the dressing room, and I was putting on my gear while my bag was sitting on the floor. George walked by me and dropped the promotion's World belt onto my bag.

"You're the new Champion, Bart," he said with a smile.

"I am? Are you playing a joke on me?" I asked.

"No. You're the hottest heel in this territory right now and we need to have a heel champion," George continued.

"You beat Chris in El Paso and won the World Title."

"I did?" I asked with a puzzled look on my face.

"We are going to let the people know tonight," he said.

"George, I wasn't planning on staying here. I'm on vacation and I came out here to just visit my family," I explained.

"Now you have a reason to stay longer," George grinned.

"George, I live in Atlanta, I work for the Crocketts," I replied.

"How long have you wanted to work here in Dallas?"

he inquired.

"Ever since I started in this business," I told him.

"Okay. Here is your opportunity. Take a couple of weeks to finish up for the Crocketts, pack up your stuff and we'll see you back here," George said as he walked off.

I stood there for a moment as I tried to take in what just happened. I looked down at my duffle bag and I stared at the belt. George made a good point; I always wanted to work for Fritz. I might not have "won" the belt in a match, but George could have handed the belt to any one of the wrestlers on the roster. It made me feel good that he felt that I was capable of upholding that role. I bent down and grabbed the title. I lifted it closer to my face so I could get a better look at it. It was a nice-looking championship belt; I noticed my reflection on the shiny title when I felt someone standing beside me. I looked up and it was Kevin Von Erich.

"You do know that is my belt, right?" Kevin asked.

"You are going to have to take it from me," I promised.

"I plan on it, Bart," he said.

"I hope you try, buddy," I returned.

"I won't have to try too hard," Kevin said.

"You'll have to try harder than you think," I shot back.

Kevin is Fritz's oldest son. At one time, he had held the World Title for his father's company. I knew at that moment I was going to be stepping into the ring with Kevin quite often. A wrestler in Dallas at that time knew that the Von Erich boys were the superstars of that territory. If a babyface wrestler came into the territory, they needed to quickly understand that they were playing second fiddle to the Von Erichs. If you were a heel wrestler at World Class, you could make good money. That was because the top heel wrestlers fought the Von Erichs.

From the time that George put the belt on me, I had two weeks before I began wrestling with Fritz full time, I finished up my obligations with the Crocketts and moved all of my and Bonnie's belongings from Atlanta to Dallas. George suggested that I get a branding iron made. Not only would it now be my trademark, but I could also use it to draw more heat to my character. The fans never liked it when the bad guy had the advantage over their hero, and this gave me one because I could also use the branding iron as a weapon too. I went to the trailer company in Fort Worth where my Daddy, myself, and my brothers all worked at one time or another. I talked with the foreman, Ed who worked there for many years and I told him what I wanted. He grabbed his cutting torch, three-quarter-inch smooth pig iron, and proceeded to work at his welding station. When I returned to see the finished product, I was blown away. The brand itself consisted of two letters Bs next to each other. Since that day my branding iron has always been referred to as BB. I was immensely proud and appreciative of my friend's craftsmanship. I tried to pay him, but he wouldn't take my money.

"How much do I owe you, Ed?" I wanted to know.

"You don't owe me a dime, Bart," Ed said.

"I have to pay you. You have to let me pay you," I insisted.

"Bart, I just want you to go out there and be a success," he smiled.

"Thank you, Ed. It's a beautiful piece of work," I responded.

To me, it felt as if my title run with Fritz's World belt lasted a long time, but sites on the internet claim that my reign was only a couple of months. When I dropped the title back to Kevin at the Cotton Bowl, it was 45 degrees outside, and the match took place in drizzling rain. Fritz and Kevin, along with his younger brothers Mike, Chris met with me and Akbar at the stadium before noon to discuss the ending of our match. We didn't stop talking about it until we went to the ring when it was nearly sundown. It was only a six-minute match and Kevin was getting the title back! Akbar had offered several suggestions for the finale, but Kevin and Fritz didn't like any of the ideas that were shared. Fritz had final say, and the entire process was exhausting. I don't think I ever had to do discuss a finish to a match like that with any other wrestler or promoter in my 30-year career in pro wrestling! I found it frustrating!

Another time that I had to endure the absurdity of the Von Erichs lack of wrestling psychology was at the Sportatorium in November 1986. It was Kevin, Mike, and Lance Von Erich against myself, Brian Adias, and Crusher Yurkoff, who later became known as Bam Bam Bigelow. The way that Kevin wanted the contest to end went like this. Me and my partners would beat up and throw Lance and Mike out of the ring. Lance and Mike would be hurt so badly that they wouldn't be able to return to the inside of the ring. Kevin would then put the claw on Brian's head with his left hand and then put the claw on Crusher with his right hand. At that point, I was to run in to attack Kevin, and attempt to save my partners, then Kevin was to put the claw on my stomach with his foot and then beat me with a pin. This is how I remember that conversation in Fritz's office along with Kevin and Skandor Akbar.

"You want me to do what?" I asked.

"I'm going to put the claw on your stomach, but it's going to be with my foot," he said with excitement in his voice.

"Akbar, are you listening to this stupid shit?" I questioned.

"Kevin, can you run this by us one more time so I can make sure that I'm understanding all of this?" Akbar asked.

"Do you really need to hear that stupid nonsense one more time, Akbar?" I continued. "I'm not doing it!"

I looked at Fritz and his mouth was so wide that he could catch flies with it. Before he said anything, I spoke again.

"I will quit before I do that stupid finish! Tell me how

that is believable! The fans will laugh us out of this building!" I exclaimed.

The match didn't end the way that Kevin wanted it to, but he and his team still won. It was that sort of stuff that happened with the Von Erichs that drove us all nuts. They were all so concerned with looking superior to the other wrestlers on the roster that they let the wrestling product suffer. Whenever a wrestler held a belt for a territory or was in a long-standing feud with someone, the money was always better. I have always heard stories that Fritz never paid very well, that was not the case with me. I thought Fritz was very fair. Plus, I was home every night, so I liked that part of it. I made good money when I wrestled against the Von Erich boys.

Anytime I worked for one of Fritz's kids, I always had to fight for my life. That was one piece of advice that Terry Gordy passed on to me. He knew what it was like to wrestle Kevin and Kerry because he had done it for years during the Von Erich's and Freebird's feud. If I ever wrestled anyone in Dallas, without the Von Erich name, it was just like having a night off. Wrestling against a Von Erich meant extra work for me. The reason was, that I had to lead them by their nose and walk them step by step through the entire match. I had to tell them exactly what they needed to do while we wrestled. Sometimes, I had to put their holds on me myself! I had nothing but respect for Fritz and the Von Erichs boys until I had to work with them!

The problem a lot of wrestlers had with the Von Erichs, was that they didn't like showing their fans that they were taking punishment. They didn't want to sell anything! It was a constant battle for them to show any form of weakness at all! EVER! There was one night I was wrestling against Kevin in Fort Worth at the Will Rogers Coliseum. In our match that night, I was supposed to hit him with my branding iron, and he was to go down. I'm sure the finish called in that contest was supposed to be a disqualification. It would have been fitting for such a situation. However, since I was in the ring with Kevin, he had to make things difficult. I hit Kevin in the head with my branding iron.

"That didn't hurt, Bart," Kevin said.

"You're supposed to sell it, Dummy!" I hissed as I hit him again.

"You don't have enough strength to hit me with that thing and hurt me with it," he whispered into my ear.

"You can tell me about my last swing tomorrow," I vowed as I connected the iron with his skull as hard as I could.

Kevin dropped to the canvas like a sack of potatoes. There was no doubt that he was out. I looked at BB and I could see that I bent the iron slightly when I hit Kevin with it. As I turned around, Rick Hazzard stared at me intently.

"What the hell did you do, Bart?" Rick asked.

"I hit him with my branding iron. Wasn't that what I was supposed to do?" I questioned.

"You weren't supposed to kill him," Rick growled.

"He'll be alright," I replied.

"I will have to tell Fritz about this," Rick promised.

"I'm sure you will, Rick," I told him as I stepped out of the ring.

I went back to the dressing room, and I changed into my street clothes. I didn't see Kevin for the rest of the night. I left the building, and it might have taken me about an hour to get home that night. I remember as I walked in the front door of my house, I heard the telephone ring. I walked over to where it sat, and I answered it. It was Fritz on the other end.

"Hello," I said.

"Are you trying to kill my boy, Bart!" Fritz yelled!

"No," I replied.

“What the hell were you doing then?” he wanted to know.

“Fritz, if you would have whooped his ass when he was younger, he’d be a lot better off than he is right now!” I shouted right before I hung up the phone.

Moments after I ended my conversation with Fritz, I suspected that he was going to fire me. However, when I saw him the week after that incident, he didn’t say anything at all about me hitting his son with my iron or the tone I used with him in our phone conversation. I think that was because he knew that I spoke the truth. Kevin and Kerry were two of the toughest wrestlers I have ever worked with. I could hit them with everything I had, and they kept coming at me with all their might. The Von Erichs had no quit in them. I think a lot of that was because their father owned the company, and the bar was set high for them. Everyone who worked for Fritz knew how difficult he could be. I’m sure it was double the trouble for Kevin, Kerry, and Mike.

CHAPTER 21 – SCOTT CASEY

On October 12th, 1986, I dropped the World belt back to Kevin Von Erich at the 3rd Annual Cotton Bowl Extravaganza. In professional wrestling when a storyline with a wrestler ends another one usually begins with someone else. After Kevin took the World belt from me, our paths went in other directions. Kevin had a lot of matches with Brian Adias and Al Madril and I was put into a series of matches with Cowboy Scott Casey. I believe that this idea came from George Scott. Scott Casey was a babyface in Dallas when I arrived. He had started wrestling a few years before I had. Due to the way that wrestling ran back then, we both wrestled in some of the same territories, but at different times. Places such as the Carolinas, Florida, Texas, the World Wrestling Federation, and Japan, were familiar wrestling locations for both of us throughout our careers. The good cowboy against the bad cowboy is about what it boiled down to. This type of angle was perfect for Texas wrestling fans. Our little run didn't last as long as it could have, but I thought we got some good stories and matches that came out of it.

The thing that I liked about working with Scott is I thought he could tell a good story. He could talk and adlib, and he was belivable. If there was ever one thing that I thought I did very well, it was talking on the microphone. It just came easy for me. I think it was that for Scott too, but by this time in our careers we both had been doing it for a while.

My sister Linda loved Scott. He was her favorite wrestler. Every time that she knew that I was going to wrestle against him, she told me not to hurt him. Scott and I always slugged it out. We both laid in the punches hard, and it seemed as if we were both trying to hit each other harder than the last guy did. No one had to tell us to make it look real because it was. Looking back on it, working stiff was common practice for a lot of the boys in my era. We wanted our fights to look real without actually hurting each other, but there were always some wrestlers who didn't understand that.

If you are going to have two cowboys fight in Texas, there must be some kind of Western element added to it. Casey and I had a lot of gimmick matches. We faced each other in a bull rope contest that took place in Fort Worth. The stipulation in this contest was that we were tied at the wrist with a rope that had a cowbell attached to it. We were allowed to use the rope and the bell against one another, and the two of us did that the entire match! The winner was declared if he was able to drag his opponent to all four corners consecutively. Only minutes into the match, Scott went to work on my head with the bell. Before long, I bled, but I returned the favor and Scott soon sported a crimson mask also.

The match was moving along, and I thought it was going pretty well. In no time our fight left the ring and went out onto the floor. Wrestling comes down to trusting your opponent and that happens naturally when you take care of them, and vice versa. In this match, that isn't what Scott did. We were taking turns dishing out the punishment when he walked me over to a corner where the wooden steps led up to the ring. Scott was on the offense, and he moved the steps away from the ring and he placed my hand in between the two items. I had no idea what was going through his mind, but I trusted him. That was my mistake! Without any warning, Scott picked up his leg and thrust it into the steps which smashed my hand against the side of the ring which is comprised of metal! Instantly, I knew my hand was broken. The excruciating pain shot through my body immediately! I was pissed! After the match ended, I headed into the dressing room, and I arrived there before Scott did. Once inside, I inspected my hand and I could see that it was in bad shape. I knew alcohol was going to help. So, I chugged a beer, and then I waited for Scott to come back to where I was waiting. The door swung open, and Scott walked over to a bench and proceeded to sit down.

"What the hell were you thinking, Casey?" I shouted.

"What are you crying about? You won, didn't you?" Scott asked.

"Look what you did to my hand," I demanded.

"Don't be wussy, Bart," he shot back.

"Listen here, Dummy. When a wrestler gives you a body part, you are supposed to protect that body part," I insisted.

"What? You can't take a little pain, Bart?" He asked with a stupid look on his face.

"If you ever break another bone in my body, I will break your neck!" I promised as I walked away.

Trying to talk some sense into Scott at that moment was pointless. I could have spoken to him for another hour, and I don't think my point would have sunk in, some people are just so hard-headed. The next day I had a match with Kevin Von Erich. My hand was swollen and in a great deal of pain, but I had to wrestle. Back then, the boys pushed through the pain and injuries the best we could. We all had our ways of masking the pain. The way that I did it was by drinking beer, and I drank a lot of it. I know that I consumed a great deal of beer that day. Plus, I had heavily wrapped my hand with an ACE bandage. Since Texas has an athletic commission, we had to get checked by a doctor before we wrestled. I was reluctant about seeing the doctor this particular night. I was concerned that he wasn't going to let me work. With the way that I had it wrapped up, there was no way of hiding that something was seriously wrong with my hand. So, I figured that I'd get it over with and find out what the doctor's decision was ultimately going to be.

"So, what's wrong with your hand?" The doctor asked as he stared at my bandage.

"I'm not sure," I responded.

"Can you take that off for me so I can get a better look at what you have going on there?" He inquired.

"Sure. It will take a moment," I said as I went to work to reveal my hand to him.

"Oh my, have you had an x-ray done on this yet?" The doctor questioned.

"No. Do you think it might be broken?" I asked him.

"It looks like it could be, but how bad is it broken is the real question," he stated.

The doctor eyeballed my hand for another minute and then I attempted to make a fist. It hurt too bad, so, I refrained from moving my fingers at all. The doctor helped me wrap my hand back up and then he said that I could wrestle. I was relieved in one sense because I didn't want to miss my match with Kevin. However, now my attention turned to how I was planning to protect it once that I was in the ring. A little time passed, and I ran into Kevin in the dressing room before we wrestled that night.

"Hey Bart, how are you?" Kevin asked where I found a place to rest before my match.

"I'm good. And you?" I inquired.

"I'm doing well," he replied. "How is your hand? Do you think it's going to be alright?"

"I have it wrapped up pretty well, so it should help me," I spoke.

Instantly, Kevin's face lit up with a smile. I looked at him strangely because he had such a goofy look on his face.

"Do you want to tell me what seems to be so funny, Kevin?" I asked.

"The doctor told me that I should attack your hand because he thinks it could be broken," he grinned.

"That's nice," I answered with sarcasm. "He must be the Von Erich family doctor," I mumbled.

I give Kevin a lot of credit because he did not touch my injured hand at all. He actually took care of it. Kevin did that for me the entire time I wrestled him during that period. If he noticed that I was protecting it with the extra wrapping, he didn't mess with my hand. The boys did that for each other so, we could remain working to continue supporting our families. Scott never apologized for breaking my hand. He never said it was an accident either, so, I chalked it up as it being intentional. I was always leery of him every time we wrestled each other after that. Moving forward, I made it a point to try and knock him out when I hit him with every punch.

Another memorable match that I had with Scott was at Reunion Arena in downtown Dallas on Christmas Night in 1986. The loser had to ride a mule around the ring after the match. We dressed in our street clothes for this contest instead of wearing traditional wrestling gear. This match had more hype behind it than the bull rope match did. If you go on the internet and look it up on a certain wrestling database, it says that Scott Casey lost. Scott Casey didn't lose because while we were in the dressing room, he refused to ride the mule. I guess he thought that riding the mule would be too humiliating for him. So, the finish of this particular match was changed. I took the loss. I didn't care if I won or not. Winning and losing didn't affect my ego one way or the other. My concern was the possibility of the mule freaking out with being around all those people in the building whooping and hollering. Animals can be unpredictable at times, even the ones that have been trained properly. Can you imagine if the mule got spooked in a crowded arena? It could have easily run into the crowd and hurt some people! I remember that I had a stern conversation with the guy whose job it was of handling the mule.

"Are you ready, Bart?" The man with the mule asked me.

"Look here! You better make sure that this Ass remains

inside this barrier around the ring," I barked.

"I will Bart. Don't you worry," he said.

"If this animal hurts anybody, it's on you, not me!" I snapped.

"Yes Sir, I understand. Everything will be fine, Bart," the man returned.

I got up on the mule and the guy held the reins and walked us around the ring. The fans got to see what they came for, me ride the mule! Nobody got hurt, thank the Lord! I will say this about the bull rope match and that one with the mule, I believe they were two of the best matches that I have ever been a part of. I don't think any other two men could have performed in them better than we had. I don't think the World Class Wrestling fans had seen a set of matches quite like that in a long time. Scott knew how to piss me off, but he was one hell of a wrestler!

In almost every big match that Scott and I wrestled each other in, we bled. There always seemed to be a good amount of blood especially during our gimmick matches. I really don't know why that was, but that's the main thing that comes to my mind when I think about the matches I had with Scott Casey. The two of us bled buckets of blood that night I had to ride the mule! If the booker wanted to keep us working together longer while we wrestled in Dallas, I really think that we could have carried that feud over a long period of time. We had some very good traditional wrestling matches together, but when it came to the grand stage, I think that is really where the two of us shined.

It's hard for me to speak of Scott Casey and not mention an unforgettable story involving Steve Casey. Steve's real last name was Sasser, but he also wrestled under the name of Steve Dane. Steve was trained by Scott Casey so; he took on his last name and they were kayfabe brothers. I believe that it was in the summer of 1987. I was wrestling Steve at the

Sportatorium in a televised match. I was in the dressing room, and he arrived at the event with a brand-new pair of Austin Hall wrestling boots. The main difference between the Austin Hall wrestling boots and the traditional lace-up boots is the lack of ankle support that they provide. I wore the Austin Hall boots for most of my career, and so did wrestlers such as Dusty Rhodes, Blackjack Mulligan, Barry Windham, Sam Houston, and Magnum T.A. I remember having to get used to this style of boot when I started wearing it, so, I have to admit I was apprehensive when Steve suggested a certain spot that he wanted to have in the match that night while sporting his new footwear.

"Bart, I have a particular move I want to perform tonight," Steve explained with excitement.

"Hold on Cowboy. First off, those are brand new boots that you have there. Second, they have no ankle support, and your legs are going to be wobbling all over the place. That type of boot takes some time to adjust to," I insisted.

"I will be okay, I'm not worried about that," Steve said with confidence.

"I think you need to be worry, Steve. Do you want to break your damn leg?" I asked hoping make him hear what I was trying to say.

"Can we please talk about the match, Bart?" He questioned me.

"Sure, let's talk about the match," I replied.

Steve proceeded to tell me the idea of the move that he wanted to perform. He wanted me to throw him into the ropes and then set him up to backdrop him. Instead of him landing on his back on the mat, in mid-air he planned to escape from my grasp and land on his feet. As Steve was explaining this to me, Scott Casey came into the dressing room and he heard what we were talking about.

"Steve, I'm telling you. It's a bad idea," I told him.

"What's a bad idea? Scott chimed in with his question.

"The genius here wants to wear this brand-new pair of Austin Hall boots in our match tonight. He's never worn a pair of boots like that before, Scott," I explained.

"Those are a nice pair of boots, but Bart's right, it's not a good idea to wear them if you are not used to that type of a boot," Scott said.

"Plus, he wants to do a crazy ass spot where I toss him up off my back and he plans to land on his feet," I stated.

"That's a terrible idea. Don't do it, Steve," Scott pleaded.

"Well, I'm going to do it anyway. I don't care what you both say," Steve declared as he walked away.

"Okay Steve, I'm not responsible if you want to call that stupid move in the ring," I shouted. "It's on you!"

"Some people have to learn the hard way," Scott said as we looked at each other while shaking our heads.

Inside the ring, our match had been going on for a little while and Steve called the spot that he insisted that we do. I threw Steve into the ropes, and I bent down, he came toward me and I shot him off my back, he went into the air and as he landed, both feet planted onto the mat, I heard his leg snap.

"Oh shit!" Steve screamed as he fell and rolled around on the mat as he grabbed at his leg.

"I tried telling you that it was a bad idea," I affirmed.

"Let's take it home, Bart," he whined. "End the match!"

"We'll go home after I drop you on your ass with the compactor," I grumbled as I picked him up and proceeded to finish our match.

I did my finishing move on Steve and after he made an impact on the canvas, I covered him for the pin. Steve was out for several months until his leg finally healed. That incident happened near the time I was feuding with Scott. The possibilities of the angles that we could have had were endless if Steve stayed healthy. We could have prolonged the feud with the Casey brothers with me teaming up with someone like Wild Bill Irwin. I know the four of us could have carried on a lengthy program that the fans would have enjoyed. The untold stories and missed opportunities in pro wrestling were often created by unfortunate circumstances. In Steve's case, his unfortunate situation could have been easily avoided had he just listened to me and Scott!

CHAPTER 22 – MIKE & KEVIN VON ERICH

My second trip to Japan was in January 1987. This time I went to wrestle for Antonio Inoki, who owned New Japan Pro Wrestling. The boys had a nickname for Antonio because of his facial features. We called him Big Jaw. He was the boss over there, so, I knew that was the guy I didn't want to piss off. The only thing that I liked about wrestling in Japan was how much money I was paid when I worked there. However, as an American, I never felt welcomed in that country. Getting through customs was always a hassle too. I felt as if the country took advantage by overtaxing us on items we bought over there to bring back home to our families. On this trip, I was there for four weeks. To get through it, I drank a lot of alcohol and I pretty much stayed intoxicated the entire time I was there. Some of the American-based wrestlers that were on that same tour with me were Chris Benoit, The Cuban Assassin, Buzz and Bret Sawyer, Konga the Barbarian, and Darryl Peterson. The Barbarian and I were good friends. Some may remember him wrestling in Dallas for World Class in the latter part of 1983 under the name of Tonga John.

Probably one of the most significant memories of this wrestling tour was that Mike Von Erich went over there with us. I didn't know Mike on a personal level. I think the main reason was that he was pretty quiet and he kept to himself. We were both cordial with each other, but I never hung out with him. Mike was in Japan for only two weeks. This was Mike's first trip to Japan and his older brother Kevin didn't go with him. Kerry couldn't go because he was still hadn't returned from after having his motorcycle accident.

While in Japan, Mike wrestled a lot of the athletes who we considered to be the underneath guys. This class of wrestlers usually worked in the opening matches against someone who had very little or equivalent ring experience.

One of the main differences when wrestling in Japan, or especially back then was that the Japanese wrestlers had two or three people escort them to the ring similar to what one would see in the sport of boxing. They too were usually young upcoming wrestlers. On the second night of wrestling, Mike's opponent was Shiro Koshinaka. As the match was taking place, I was in the dressing room sitting on a bench. Buzz Sawyer was standing several feet away from me, watching Mike's contest through the curtain.

"Bart, you should come over here and watch this," Buzz informed me.

"I'm good," I continued. "I'm fine sitting here all by myself. I'm relaxing before it's time for me to wrestle."

"You should come over here and see what's happening," he said.

"I don't want to. Give me the play-by-play, Buzz," I insisted.

"Koshinaka and his crew are whipping the tar out of Mike on the outside of the ring," Buzz conveyed.

"Whippings are good sometimes," I returned.

"It isn't this time. Fritz asked me to keep a watchful eye over Mike," he informed.

"He did? What did he say to you, Buzz?" I wanted to know.

"He said take care of my boy," Buzz answered as he took off running to the ring.

At that moment, I got off my ass and ran to the curtain. As I peered through the hanging fabric, I could see Mike was taking some punishment and becoming a bit overwhelmed. Next, I watched Buzz arrive at ringside and he put an ass whooping to Mike's adversaries. The actions that Buzz took were of his own free will. Meaning, the booker for NJPW wasn't expecting Buzz to run out of the dressing and fight with their wrestlers. To mine and Buzz's knowledge what was happening to Mike wasn't supposed to happen either. To us, it seemed as if Mike's opponent was taking advantage of him. Since Fritz spoke to Buzz and asked him to take care of his boy, I'm sure that he felt obligated to protect Mike no matter what. Later that evening inside the dressing room, I looked over and noticed Mike sitting on a bench with his head down. Buzz and I walked over to him to see how he was doing.

"Hey Mike, are you alright?" I asked.

"Yeah," Mike replied quietly without looking up.

"You can't let those guys pull that kind of crap on you!" Buzz insisted.

"You have to draw the line in the sand with these wrestlers over here!" I interjected.

"They will do that to you every night if you let them get away with that stuff," Buzz added.

"Mike, whatever the Japanese wrestlers do to you, you have to give them double for it in return," I spoke.

"Do you understand what we're saying to you?" Buzz asked.

Suddenly, Mike lifted his head and looked straight at the two of us, and out of his mouth, we heard this.

"I don't want to be here!" Mike shouted.

Buzz and I stood there quietly for a moment. The two of us turned our heads and we stared at each other. It didn't take long for us to walk back to our lockers and finish getting dressed. The bus was waiting for us so that we all could return to our hotel. Mike sat there a little longer before exiting the dressing room. The bus rides in Japan seemed long most of the time when I was wrestling there. It all depended on how far the shows were from where we were staying. The beer helped with the long rides. However, on this bus ride I mainly thought about Mike and what he said in the dressing room to Buzz and I. I didn't have much interaction with Mike after that night or for the rest of the time he was on that tour. I would see him when we ate our meals and at the events, but we didn't speak to each other. I know Mike fought in every match after Buzz went to his aide. Mike had no other choice and he knew it. Japan wasn't for the faint of heart. I don't know if anyone from the Japanese office said anything to Buzz about the actions that he took to defend Mike. Since Buzz was pretty high-strung and a bit unpredictable, I highly doubt it. However, I felt as if I received some of the repercussions from the Japan office during that trip just because I was employed by Fritz.

About a week later, the Barbarian and I were in a tag team match against Antonio and Seiji Sakaguchi. My partner carried a heavy chain to the ring. It was part of the Barbarian's gimmick because he was portrayed a bit of a wild man. At some point in the match when things got a bit out of control, Antonio got his hands on my friend's metal links. As the four of us along with the referee were all running around the ring, I was struck very hard in the head with the chain. Since I was standing near the side of the ring, I fell and my head hit hard on the ring apron knocking me out. The ring apron is the side of the ring and it's all metal, so, that part of the ring is unforgiving. I understand that accidents can happen, but minutes before that occurred, Antonio nearly put his hand through my chest as he chopped me when I was in the corner of the ring. The look in his eyes said payback.

The boys and I returned back to the States beaten and bruised, but nothing could prepare us for the beating are hearts were about to take! Just three months later in April, panic struck the Von Erich family when Mike couldn't be found after a suicide note was discovered. Days after Mike went missing, his body was found in a sleeping bag at his favorite fishing spot at Lake Lewisville in Lake Dallas, Texas. He had consumed alcohol and overdosed on Placidly, a strong medicine used to help with sleeping. I was at the Sportatorium the next day when I found out about Mike's death. It was sad, but not shocking. The words that Mike shared with Buzz and me in Japan resurfaced in my memory. Maybe the statement that he made had nothing to do with that wrestling tour, and it had a much deeper meaning for him. One will never know. None of the boys discussed the situation surrounding Mike and the rest of his family at that time. I don't know why it was that way, maybe because the expressions on everybody's face said it all. I do know the fans were heartbroken because of what happened with Mike and I wasn't the only person who witnessed people in the crowd that night who had tears in their eyes. I didn't go to the funeral. I don't like going to funerals. The attendance at the shows took a huge nose dive and it was obvious that the fans couldn't take another tragic incident.

This was apparent just a few weeks later at Texas Stadium after Mike's death. In 1984, at the David Von Erich Memorial, the temperature was said to be over 100 degrees and that event drew over 43,000 people. At the 3rd Annual David and Mike Von Erich Memorial in 1987, the temperature was in the '80s and only 6,000 people came out to watch that show. I don't think anybody expected such a low turnout, but that pretty much told me that the fans were suffering from broken hearts. As time passed, people still attended the wrestling shows, but the sold-out venues were few and far between.

We went from the death of one brother, to the near death of another. November 5th, 1987 marks a day for me that I will never forget. I participated in an Eight Man Tag Team match at the Will Rogers Coliseum in Fort Worth. The contest was the main event of the evening and it was being recorded for television. It seemed like a normal night of wrestling on a Monday night. The building wasn't sold out, but there was a good crowd there watching the event. I had teamed up with Al Madril, Brian Adias, and Al Perez to go up against Kevin Von Erich, Bruiser Brody, and The Fantastics. The Fantastics consisted of Tommy Rogers and Bobby Fulton. A match like that, during this specific time in wrestling, was a good contest. Every wrestler involved was a good draw. Plus, there was so much tension among us all that fireworks could be expected to go off at any moment. The fans were full of excitement as I walked to the ring with the rest of my team. I knew this match was going to be one for the record books.

I can't remember who the wrestlers were that started off the match, but when Kevin and I entered the ring, the fans went nuts! Kevin and I had so many encounters in which we tore each other to shreds, and the fans hoped for that every time that we fought. Stepping into the ring with Fritz's son, I expected to get my ass beaten to a pulp. So, getting my whooping out of the way was what I liked to do whenever I could. However, this evening Kevin was not his normal self. I knew it the minute I locked up with him in the middle of the ring. Kevin didn't use any force against me at all. It was as if he had no strength whatsoever. Believe me, when Kevin was in his prime, he was a strong kid. From the center of the ring, I pushed him into the corner. Instantly his body became limp and his skin tone changed colors, as I watched him collapse in the ring corner. Kevin's body slid down each turnbuckle before he sat on his butt on the canvas. Kevin didn't wear any boots and he wore tiny trucks that resembled a slingshot. Because of his lack of in-ring apparel, a lot of his skin was exposed, and I could see that he was turning purple rather quickly. Since I'm not a doctor, I won't try to guess what was physically happening to Kevin, besides the fact that I knew he was dying. He wasn't getting enough oxygen and that was obvious. I instantly knew that this was a serious medical emergency. As I began to lock eyes with the other men in the match, they knew it was serious too. I thought fast and I grabbed Kevin to take him to the middle of the ring. I threw his body on the mat and I quickly went to throw a series of punches at him, in hopes my actions would mask what was going on. I stared at Bruiser and without either of us saying a word, we had a conversation with our eyes.

"Bruiser, he is going to die," I communicated.

"What happened?" Bruiser conveyed.

"I no clue, but I'm about to break kayfabe and give him mouth-to-mouth resuscitation," I informed.

"This photographer on the outside of the ring is taking a lot of pictures of Kevin," he transmitted.

"Take care of the picture guy and I will take care of Kevin," I eyeballed back to Bruiser.

Bruiser jumped off the ring apron to talk to the photographer. I decided to bend down and help Kevin. Back then, we protected the business and we never broke kayfabe. I was about to do it because I wasn't about to watch him die. I was concerned about Kevin's life, and I knew something had to be done immediately. It was at that moment Tommy jumped into the ring. He ran over to me and started punching me in the head. He made it look as if he was trying to keep me from pinning, his teammate, but he was trying to keep Kevin alive!

"I think he is going to die, Tommy," I warned.

"Stay in character. I will take care of him," Tommy returned.

I rolled out of the ring and Tommy assisted Kevin by giving him mouth-to-mouth resuscitation. Bobby had his hands full with my other partners. I looked to see what Bruiser was doing. On the outside of the ring, he was causing a bunch of commotion as he tried to get the guy to stop taking pictures of Kevin. The photographer was a regular at the shows there in Fort Worth. He was an acquaintance of the boys and the rest of the crew. He was always on the floor kneeling by the side of the ring. Wearing knee pads made it easy for us to notice him. Other than the boys, I think he was the only person who might have known that Kevin was in real danger. With him being so close to the ring, I have no idea how he couldn't have suspected something was seriously as wrong. As this was all happening, the other wrestlers in the match were doing everything they could to keep the fan's attention off the center of the ring where Tommy and Kevin were. I made eye contact with Bruiser once again.

"This guy won't stop!" Bruiser glared.

"Do something!" I suggested.

"I'm about to break his camera!" he got across.

"Do what you have to do, brother," I relayed.

Without another thought, Bruiser grabbed the guy's camera from him. The man tried to put up a fight, but Bruiser wasn't going to have any of that. The 300-pound wrestler pushed the shutterbug with one hand and threw the camera he snatched onto the concrete with the other one. Instantly, the camera broke into several pieces. Pieces of camera parts scattered all over the floor. Fans who had seen the camera destroyed right in front of them might have wondered why Bruiser had done something like that. So many things were happening on the outside of the ring to distract from what was taking place on the inside. Tommy continued to revive Kevin and at some point, he was successful. The match was ruled as no contest. I don't know what the fans thought was happening that night. I do believe that me and the other wrestlers in that match pulled off what we were trying to achieve, 100 percent distraction!

I know it was hard night for every wrestler in that contest to see Kevin in the shape that he was in. We all trusted Tommy to do all he could to help him. It wasn't easy keeping the match going knowing that there was something seriously wrong taking place, but we were trying to protect the business at any cost. I know that sounds foolish when someone's life is in danger, but that was the stuff we did back then. When the ring was finally cleared, Kevin was put inside an ambulance, and he was taken to the hospital to get checked out. That same night inside the dressing room was very strange. I think all of us involved in that match were in shock. There was a lot of silence inside the changing room and several of us just looked at each other with nothing to say. I was near Al Perez when he nudged me in my side with his elbow.

"What the hell happened in there, Bart?" Perez asked.

"I have no clue," I responded.

"Did Kevin tell you that he wasn't feeling well?" He wondered.

"He didn't say anything, Al," I stated.

"That was a close one. I hope he is going to be alright," Al returned.

"Me too Al," I replied.

That was on a Monday, and we did spot shows in small towns throughout the rest of the week. I didn't run into Kevin until Friday night at the Sportatorium. Nobody said anything about what happened in Fort Worth just a few days prior. It was just like nothing had ever occurred. It was business as usual and typical World Class behavior, mind your own business! I often wonder what would have happened if Tommy wasn't there to help save Kevin's life. Things at World Class would have been tragic, even more tragic than it already was...

CHAPTER 23 - THE WORLD CLASS STORIES

Despite the differences and uncertainties, we all experienced at World Class Championship Wrestling at that time, I still have plenty of fond memories. One of them involves my dear friend Mike Davis. Throughout our careers, one of us always showed up unexpectedly to work at a promotion where the other one was wrestling. When it came to Dallas, Mike made the decision to move there, not based on a position that Fritz had offered him, but because of the friendship that we shared. At the tail end of 1986 and the beginning of 1987, Mike was wrestling in Tennessee in a tag team with Tommy Lane called The Rock n' Roll RPMs. In February, the two men came to wrestle for Fritz and shortly thereafter they were in a feud with The Fantastics. It was nice to travel in a car with Mike again going from one show to the next. One night, it was late, and we had been drinking. We were driving near the Sportatorium and Mike had a suggestion.

"We should get off the road for a while," he said.

"What do you have in mind?" I asked.

"We're near the Sportatorium, let's just go there. I have a key to the backdoor," Mike informed.

"That doesn't sound like too bad of an idea," I responded.

"Anything beats taking a risk on the road in our condition," he mentioned.

It only took us a couple of minutes to get to the Sportatorium from where we were. Taking a chance of getting pulled over by the law was never a good idea. As I pulled into the parking lot, I drove to the back of the building where the door was located. I had never been to the Sportatorium after hours when I wasn't scheduled to wrestle, so this was a first for me. I had no idea what to expect and I don't think Mike did either. We proceeded to go inside. The Sportatorium was an old building that was in need of much repair. Being inside the facility when it was empty of all the people, allowed me to see it for what it was. The place was a dump! I think I always knew that it was, but that night I became convinced. Mike and I walked into the dressing room and so we could both lay down on the benches to get some rest. It didn't take us long to find out that we were not alone.

"Look at that!" Mike exclaimed as he pointed to a corner in the room that we were in.

"It's huge!" I gasped as my eyes focused on a rat.

"I've seen rats before, but that one can pass for a beaver," he blurted.

"Holy crap, I will never eat another hot dog from here ever again," I confirmed.

"We better hope it doesn't eat us!" Mike fretted.

"Where there is one rat, there are more," I spoke.

"How do you expect me to get any sleep now, Bart?" he questioned.

"That's a good question," I responded.

It took the two of us several minutes to get comfortable after that. We both began to settle down as time passed, but we had no intentions of turning off the lights. I was tired, but soon as Mike and I stopped talking about the rat, he dozed off. I knew he was sleeping because he started to snore. As my body relaxed, I heard somebody say something. It sounded like mumbling or if someone was talking on the other side of the wall. The voice was faint, almost like a volume dial of a radio was being turned up and then turned back down. I could make out a word or two every once in a while, but I couldn't make any sense out of it all. At first, I thought it was Mike messing with me.

"What did you say?" I asked as I looked over where my friend was. "Mike, are you screwing with me?" I asked trying to get his attention."

I told myself that it was just my mind playing tricks on me, and a minute or two later I was at peace again. Just when I closed my eyes, I heard the voice again. This time I couldn't tell if it was the same voice that I heard moments ago. It truly was odd. I could tell that they were male voices, but I couldn't make out what was being said. I lifted my head and turned my attention back to Mike. Mike was sleeping, and I listened to him snore and I heard the barely audible voices at the same time. I was convinced that somebody was in the building with us!

"Mike, wake your ass up!" I demanded.

"What is it, Bart?" he said groggily.

"Are you hearing what I am hearing?" I questioned.

"I'm hearing you waking me up," Mike hissed.

"I hear somebody talking," I stressed.

"I think you've been hit in the head too many times" he snapped.

Suddenly the sound of the voices came back. This time they appeared to be louder. The tone seemed to be muffled, but it didn't stop me from trying to make any sense of the speech. At that moment, Mike sat up on his bench and he turned his body toward my direction. He had a shocked look on his face.

"I hear that," Mike yawned.

"I knew that I wasn't making it up," I insisted.

"Who would be in here at this time of night?" Mike wondered.

"A ghost and a couple of his ghost buddies," I replied.

"Maybe it's one of the other wrestlers doing the same thing that we are doing," Mike suggested.

"Don't you think we would have seen a real person by now if someone else was in here?" I questioned.

"I think this place might be haunted. I think we are good to drive home now," Mike returned.

"I think you're right, Mike. Let's get the hell out of here," I spoke as the two of us stood up and we left the building through the same door that we entered into earlier.

I have no clue what Mike and I heard that night. It could have been a ghost or a spirit of some kind, or it could have been the pipes in that old place. A lot of sad and terrible things had happened within that wrestling company. Let's not forget the history of the fire that happened in 1953. The Sportatorium had a series of negative stories attached to it. If someone was to ask me if I thought that building was haunted, I would say yes!

When we weren't being spooked by ghosts, we were back at the matches. Professional wrestling has a reputation for doing things in a big way. Promoters want people to come out to the events and it is the booker's job to create shows that could do just that. So, when the office at World Class told me that they wanted me to come to the ring while riding on a horse, it didn't surprise me at all. I was willing to do it under one condition, and that was if I was able to ride my horse, Smokey. Horses can easily become frightened, so bringing them into an environment where there are a lot of people, is never a great idea. I only brought Smokey to a few events. I had to stop using him with my gimmick because people had no respect for Smokey and they mistreated him. The fans put lit cigarettes out on his legs and his ass. Most of the burns happened when I was not around to protect him, but there was one incident that happened at an event held at the rodeo grounds that I will never forget. I had ridden Smokey to the ring and I was supposed to get off and hand him over to my wife Bonnie. From there she was going to take him back to his trailer. Then I was supposed to be interviewed by Bill Mercer. As soon as I made my move to get down from my horse, a man in the front row pressed the hot end of his cigarette into Smokey's rear end and he flinched hard. For a moment I thought I was going to fall to the ground and land on my back. Before that happened, I corrected Smokey and calmed him down. I immediately got off my horse, but instead of meeting Bill, I walked straight over to the irresponsible fan.

"What the hell do you think you're doing?" I growled as I grabbed the man by his shirt.

"I didn't do anything!" he exclaimed.

"I saw what you did! You burned my horse with your cigarette!" I hissed.

"What are you going to do, Bart?" the man continued. "Are you going to hit me?"

"There is no way that you can afford the lawsuit," I said.

"What lawsuit is that?" he inquired.

"The one you will be responsible for when this horse tramples and kills an innocent bystander because of your stupidity!" I affirmed.

The man stood there speechless because, at that moment, he realized the damage that he could have caused. I eventually let the fan go and I handed Smokey over to my wife. I then walked over to where Bill was waiting to talk to me. I didn't have to get fired up for my interview because I already was!

There was one other incident with Smokey that sealed the deal for me not to bring him to any more wrestling events. The show was at the Sportatorium and I was told to arrive early. I showed up around one o'clock in the afternoon, but I wasn't going to ride Smokey until 8:30 P.M. that evening. I had planned to take my horse out of the trailer and walk him so he could get some fresh air and eat some grass, but someone in the office said I couldn't do that. I then suggested that I just take Smokey back to the farm, but it was made clear that I had to ride the horse to the ring for that event. As a result of being in the carrier for too long of time, Smokey tore up the inside of that horse trailer. A horse trailer like that is made for transporting an animal, not for housing one. It wasn't uncommon to battle with the office over creative and logical decisions. I wasn't being too smart when I decided to ride the horse through the crowd to get to the ring, but I did it anyway. I knew Smokey was in a mood, and when an animal is in that sort of condition all bets are off! Thank God Smokey kept his cool, and nothing happened to any of the fans inside the venue. The Sportatorium isn't a place that is safe to bring a horse in anyway, but I just did what the office asked me to do. I never agreed to do that again!

While working in Dallas, I had the pleasure of working with my friend The Grappler once again. He and I hadn't seen each other since our Mid-South days. Since The Grappler and I were both heels, we rode together often. I enjoyed making trips with him because we had a lot in common and we both enjoyed having a good time. Being around The Grappler was always fun, even when we got into trouble. One night, we were driving back from Greenville, Texas. Of course, we were drinking and we had two cases of beer in the front of my truck. I wasn't paying attention to my speed and because of that, I suddenly noticed police lights in the rearview mirror.

"Oh, you did it now, Bart," The Grappler stated.

"Dadgum!" I grunted.

"Not good, Bart," he said.

"I know that it isn't good. I'm no dummy," I spoke.

"Well Bart, you're drinking and driving and you are driving way too fast, that's pretty dumb," The Grappler chimed in with a grin.

As soon as I found a safe place to park on the side of the highway, I pulled over. I looked back in my rear-view mirror again, and all I could see was the red and blue lights rapidly flashing. I knew the officer was coming to our vehicle because as he got closer to us, I heard the sound of gravel underneath the soles of his shoes as he walked toward me.

A flashlight was shined into my face and I flinched due to the glare. I shielded my eyes with my hands.

"Hello officer," I greeted.

"Black Bart, is that you?" he asked.

"Yes. It is me," I said as he shined his light into the cab of my truck. The brightness of his flashlight revealed our supply of alcohol plus the several empty cans that were on the seat and floorboard around The Grappler's feet.

"Bart, what are you guys doing?" the officer wondered.

"We just got done wrestling and we are trying to get home," I responded.

"Do you have any idea how fast you were going, Bart?" he asked.

"I don't know, Sir," I replied.

"You were going 15 miles over the speed limit," he informed.

"I will slow it down," I promised.

For a moment the policeman got quiet and shined his light back to where the beer cans were located in the vehicle. He then shined a light on The Grappler and stared at him for a moment. Before he lowered his light and turned his attention back to me.

"Do you know who my favorite wrestler of all time is?" he questioned.

"I hope it's Black Bart," I said with a smile.

"No, it's The Grappler," he told the two of us.

"You don't say?" I asked.

"I like his wrestling style and his attitude. He's fun to watch," the policeman continued. "Do you know him?"

"Of course, I know The Grappler. By the way, I have someone you might like to meet," I grinned as my passenger nudged me with his elbow. Of course, since the person next to me wasn't wearing a mask, the officer did not realize who I was with.

"No, no. Don't do it, Bart," The Grappler whispered.

"Do you want to go to jail," I asked my friend quietly so I wouldn't draw any attention to us. It was then that The Grappler spoke up.

"Officer, may I step out of the vehicle so I can show you something? I have something that you might want to see. It's in the black duffle bag that is in the bed of the truck," The Grappler said.

The policeman obliged. The Grappler stepped out of the truck and he walked to the bed of it. As the officer shined his flashlight in the back of my truck, The Grappler reached over and unzipped his bag. Right on top was his wrestling mask, he pulled it out of the bag and lifted it up to show the policeman.

"Would you look at that!" the officer exclaimed.

"I'm the Grappler," my friend admitted.

"Wow!" the officer said.

"You can have that," The Grappler said as he handed the mask to our new friend.

"Are you sure?" he asked.

"I'm positive, I want you to have it," The Grappler continued.

"I have other masks at my house. I'll even sign a photo for you if you'd like me to."

"That would be awesome Grappler," the officer grinned.

"Call me Len," he returned.

The Grappler made that policeman's night. We were fortunate that we didn't receive a ticket of any kind. I was always surprised to find out who our fans were. Back then, we stuck out like sore thumbs and that was solely due to the power of television. A lot of times the people that we ran into in public acted like they knew us. That might have had something to do with being on the T.V. in their living room every week. Since I was a heel, I felt like I always had to uphold a certain persona. However, it was important to be respectful to everyone we met, because I never knew if I was interacting with a paying customer or not.

Another story that I remember vividly that occurred while I wrestled in the Dallas Territory was with The Great Kabuki. Kabuki was from Japan and he started wrestling professionally in the mid-60s. He first came to wrestle in the States near the end of 1970. After wrestling for nearly two years here, he returned home to Japan. In 1978, at some point he returned to the United States and eventually he found his way to Dallas, Texas in 1981. Throughout his career, he wrestled under several different names, until settling on The Great Kabuki after accepting a job with Fritz Von Erich. Kabuki had long black hair, and he covered his face with white, red, and green costume paint. Walking to the ring he wore an ancient-looking mask and a kimono. He also swung num chucks around his head while standing inside the ring in an attempt to intimidate his opponent. Right before the match started, Kabuki spayed a green mist onto his hands and into the air. The Great Kabuki was an ominous character!

One night I was in the dressing room waiting for my match to start. I was sitting on the bench like I normally do and I was sharpening my knives. Kabuki was in there with me. The two of us got along pretty well. He is one of the boys that I considered a friend. Though I don't think he ever spoke on television, his English was pretty good. However, to keep the mystery about Kabuki's character a secret he had a manager speak for him. In Dallas, his manager was mainly Gary Hart.

This particular night as I was trying to get my knife razor-sharp, Kabuki walked over to where I was sitting and he stood right in front of me. He wore a very loose-fitting black pair of pants that resembled what one would wear in mixed martial arts. As Kabuki stood within my space he spoke up, but he had no intention of talking about mix martial arts or my ability to sharpen a knife.

"Bart, can you look at my dick?" Kabuki asked.

"What?" I asked with a surprised look on my face.

"I need you to look at something," he pleaded.

"Kabuki, I like you, but I don't want to see your pecker," I returned sharply.

Without saying another word, Kabuki pulled at the waist string on his pants and he exposed his manhood to me. The tip of his penis was swelled up like a tennis ball and the whole thing was red, and it was seeping a thick yellow pus. In his foreskin, he had a pearl sewn into it. My eyes widened and I was in a state of shock!

"Kabuki, what the hell am I looking at?" I questioned.

"My dick," he replied.

"I know that dummy! What happened to it?" I wanted to know.

"I was in Japan and I did a traditional ritual," Kabuki explained.

"Buddy if you do not go to the hospital right now, your dick is going to fall off!" I demanded.

"I have to wrestle this evening," he replied.

"Dag gum it! Your pecker is infected and you need to go to the hospital right now and get some antibiotics!" I insisted.

"Do you think it's that bad?" he inquired.

"Get out of here before I kick you out of here!" I exclaimed.

Kabuki followed my directive and left the show to get medical care. I didn't see him for a couple of days. Upon his return he looked to be in a better mood, I'm sure his infection had caused him a lot of pain.

"Kabuki, it's good to see you back. How are you feeling?" I asked.

"A lot better, Bart. Thank you for insisting that I go see a doctor. I feel so much better." He spoke.

"I'm glad to hear that," I told him.

"Do you want to see my dick?" he continued. "It's healing!

"No! I don't want to see your dick; I didn't want to see it the first time you showed it to me, Dummy!" I shouted.

CHAPTER 24 - WRESTLING IN SOUTH AFRICA

Life can be weird, but when life is combined with pro wrestling that is when it can get really strange. In 1988, Wild Bill Irwin and I traveled to South Africa for a five-week tour to battle against Steve and Shaun Simpson. Steve and Shaun were from Johannesburg and their father, Sammy Cohen was a promoter for his wrestling company there. The Simpsons offered Bill and me a chance to take the feud that we were doing with them in Texas, to their country as well. Here is the strange part! If it wasn't for Fritz sending Lance Von Erich up to Portland, Oregon in 1985, Lance would have never met Steve who was wrestling for Don Owen at the time. Don owned Pacific Northwest Wrestling in Portland. Lance was instrumental in bringing Steve to World Class. So, if it wasn't for the "fake" Von Erich, I might not have ever stepped foot on the continent of Africa.

Sometime in the Summer of 1987, Lance made his escape from Fritz's promotion. The Simpsons stayed in Dallas and that's when Bill and I started a series of matches with them. I guess Steve thought it would be a good idea for us to take our feud overseas, so that's what we did. I already traveled outside of the country to wrestle in Japan twice. I didn't know much about South Africa before I went there. The contrast between Japan and South Africa is huge! There is no comparison between those two countries. I learned about the Apartheid. The way it was explained to me, it was racial segregation under the law. If you know a little bit about world history, in 1994 a democratic government was formed and that was when Nelson Mandela came into office over there. However, Bill and I went over there several years before all of that. When I went there it seemed as if there was a strong sense of civil unrest. The non-white people were treated like second-class citizens and I got to witness many of them living inside cardboard boxes on the side of the road. I found it disturbing to see human beings treated like that, but over there everyone seemed to be quite used to it. By the late 80s, several American companies stopped doing business in South Africa due to the Apartheid. Traveling from the United States to South Africa was not very easy or convenient. Since we couldn't fly to South Africa directly, we had to fly into Europe and switch to a flight that flew into the country. The Simpsons informed Bill and me that there was hostility over there, but they reassured us that we were going to be safe.

The plan for Bill and I was to go over there and wrestle the Simpson brothers in several cities throughout the country. On the schedule were all the big metropolitan areas and several municipalities in between. In my opinion, Sammy had it planned out correctly. Our first stop was a television station in which Steve and Shaun were guests on a highly watched T.V. program. The show reminded me of a nighttime talk show like we have in the States. Our visit to the television studio was for one reason: to promote the wrestling events. The announcer was talking to the hometown heroes about the series of upcoming matches they were going to have with us when this occurred.

"So, tell us a little bit about your opponents from Texas," the announcer inquired.

"Well, they some rough and tough mates with a bit of an attitude problem," Steve described.

"I see," the talk show host replied.

"They are worthy competitors, but I have no doubt when it is all said and done, we will still be holding onto these belts," Shaun explained as Bill and I walked out onto the television set.

"What did I hear you say, boy?" I shouted as I walked in their direction.

"Now wait, we don't want any trouble!" the host

exclaimed.

"Trouble is already here!" Bill informed.

Without hesitation, Bill and I attacked the Simpsons right there on the set. We punched, kicked, and we even used furniture on the two brothers. We even beat up the T.V. personality and he was left in a puddle of blood just like our opponents were. That staged introduction to the South African people set the tone for our entire visit. We quickly found out how much the Simpsons were adored by the people in their homeland. In certain places where Bill and I went, it was necessary to have guards with us for our protection. We had heat, but that was the whole point. When heat is present in pro wrestling, it attracts people and they spend money. Wrestling in cities like Cape Town, Johannesburg, Pretoria, and Durban was always exciting because the crowds were so huge. The wrestling events took place in large indoor arenas or outside in very large Cricket stadiums. Some of those venues held more than 10,000 people. No non-white people could watch the wrestling matches; however, they sold the food and cleaned the facilities. That was another indication to me that they looked down on people of color there.

The cities that were smaller than the higher populated areas usually drew crowds of about 2,000 people. Either way, the turnouts were good. However, every once in a while, we could find ourselves between two cities on the outskirts of town. Traveling did come with some risks, but Bill and I never did that by ourselves. Sammy always had one of his wrestlers or crew members escort us from one place to another. Driving in a desolate area one night was quite the reality check. We had been driving for some time, and it was very dark outside. I stared out the window, but because there were no street lights, I couldn't see anything at all. There were no gas stations, no electric signs, no marquees, nothing at all. All of a sudden, off into the distance, Bill spotted a light when he looked out of his window.

"Look at that," Bill informed. "It appears to be some kind of light out there.

"That's a campfire," the driver said.

"A campfire?" I asked surprisingly.

"Yes, I suppose someone is camping out there," he let us know.

"Wow!" Who would be out here in the middle of nowhere?" Bill questioned.

"It could be someone who is traveling and they decided to camp for the night," he stated.

I'm not sure why Bill and I thought that was so out of the ordinary, but that wasn't the only thing on that trip that struck us as odd. Later that night, we suddenly came upon a roadblock. My first impression was that we were about to get robbed, but as we pulled up closer to the barricade, we saw what appeared to be military soldiers.

"Hello mates, where are you headed?" the soldier asked.

"We are on our way to Durbin," our driver replied.

"That's quite the drive from here," he said.

"Yes, we make it quite often, but it can be a long drive," the man sitting behind the steering wheel mentioned.

"What business do you have there?" the officer asked.

"We are with a wrestling company and we have a show there tomorrow," our crew member explained.

"Do you mates have any guns?" he asked as he shined his flashlight into and throughout our van.

"We do not have any guns," the driver relayed.

"Okay then, carry on," he told us.

The one thing that sticks out to me the most is that a lot of the white people in South Africa carried guns. Of course, today in the United States you can see that is more common in certain states, but back then, only law enforcement had that ability in our country. So, seeing people carry guns out in the public was very new to me. I found this fact out the first night we wrestled the Simpsons on that tour. I was on the outside of the ring with Steve laying on a table as I was beating the ever-loving piss out of him! My opponent and I were covered with blood. For some reason, my attention gravitated to a guy in the front row. He was wearing an orange jacket. It was thin, loose-fitting, similar to a windbreaker. The moment I made eye contact with this spectator, he pulled his jacket back from his waist and he revealed a handgun resting in a holster. I continued my assault until another fellow a couple of seats away from the first person showed me his pistol also. I watched the second man stand up and lean toward the railing to speak to me.

"If you don't stop, I will blow your brains out," the man promised.

"Okay," I replied as I decided to get off the floor and return to the ring. I threw Steve inside the ring and I went to the corner to meet Bill.

"They have guns," I stated.

"Who has guns?" Bill asked.

"The people do," I returned.

"What people?" he inquired.

"These people in the crowd. They have guns, Bill!" I exclaimed.

"You expect me to believe that. That can't be possible," he said as he tagged my hand to take his place on center stage.

By this time Steve traded places with his brother Shaun, and he and Bill went at each other like there was no tomorrow. The two men slugged it out and eventually, they wound up on the outside of the ring. As they fought each other on the floor, I was now standing in the corner of the ring, and a bit elevated so I had a better view of the crowd. I was already on high alert and since Bill was busy kicking Shaun's butt, he was not aware of the harm that was waiting for him from the audience. I had given him a fair warning, but he chose to dismiss it. It didn't take long for Bill to find out what I learned a few minutes earlier. I saw a man yelling at Bill and he finally got my friend's attention.

"I think our boys had enough," the fan told Bill as he lifted his shirt to expose the weapon that he had hidden on his body.

"Okay," Bill said right before he walked to the ring to meet me in the corner.

"You're right Bart. They have guns," Bill fretted.

"I told you, Dummy!" I shouted.

"Okay, fine. Let's go home and finish this match," he said.

I returned to the action inside the ring and the Simpsons got their comeback and they won the battle. I started to rethink the entire trip. I didn't want to put up with that same scenario every night for the next five weeks. When Bill and I made our way back to the dressing room, I made it a point to let one of the crew members know that I wanted to speak with Sammy. A few minutes later, Sammy entered our room and he walked over to where I was sitting.

"Hello Bart, did you want to talk with me?" Sammy asked.

"I did. Thank you for coming back here," I returned.

"What can I do for you Bart?" he continued. "Is everything alright?"

"Look here Sammy, we can't be getting any more heat like this," I said sternly. "We will have to turn it down a few notches or we are going to have to go back home."

"What's wrong? I thought everything was going so well," Sammy wondered.

"It appears that everyone in the crowd is packing a gun!" I exclaimed.

"A lot of people carry guns here," he said.

"That is a problem for us! We are out there killing your boys and the fans want to kill us for doing it!" I shouted.

"It's going to be okay, Bart," Sammy assured.

"Don't get me killed Sammy!" I insisted.

The next night was a different day and another new experience. This time we were inside the dressing room as the referees for the event were getting dressed in their uniforms. One by one, Bill and I watched the three men take their guns from their waists and place them inside their duffle bags. It became quite clear to Bill and me that this was a common practice in South Africa. One of the referees noticed the two of us looking in their direction and it was then that he spoke up.

"Hello mates," one of the men said.

"Hello," I returned.

"How are you doing?" he asked.

"What is up with all the guns? Does everybody carry guns here?" I wanted to know.

"Just the white people. Almost all white people do. We do for sure," he explained.

Sometime while we were there, Bill and I were able to form our opinion about the country's gun laws. This happened when we wanted to go into a grocery store to buy some food one afternoon. The store was close to where we stayed and it was easy for us to walk there to buy what we needed. The difference between the grocery stores there and the ones in the States was the entrances. In the States, we have glass doors that slide open. Over there, the front of the building is wide open and the door is similar to one of a garage that rolls up into the ceiling. This day, as we got closer to the building, we noticed something wasn't right. We saw a police vehicle and some officers, but the severity of the situation hadn't hit us quite yet. It wasn't until we began to enter the store was when we were stopped by the authorities.

"Mates, you can't go in there," a policeman ordered.

"What going on?" I wondered.

"There has been a situation, step back from the building," he demanded.

Just then Bill nudged me in the arm and he pointed to an area in the store. It took me a second to focus, but I eventually made out what he was trying to show me. I noticed part of a leg to a body that was on the floor sticking out of a grocery aisle. The body was still. It was apparent somebody had been shot and they were now dead!

"That's why you don't let everyone have a gun," Bill said.

"It is kind of stupid," I returned.

"It's like the damn wild west over here!" Bill exclaimed.

At the very beginning of our trip, Bill and I went to the local bars a couple of times. We didn't think much of it at all. Of course, this was before we found out that the country was so gun-happy. Somehow Sammy caught wind of our nightly visits to the watering hole and made it clear that we shouldn't be doing that. So, instead of going to the cantinas, we drank in the room. A lot of times, we did that until three in the morning. Some of those nights as we sat in our room, we could hear all kinds of commotion outside. Mainly it was gunshots, but at some point, I think we became numb to the sound of gunfire during the rest of that stay. When it was time for us to return home, I couldn't have been happier!

CHAPTER 25 - BRUISER BRODY & OTTO WANZ

I first met Frank Goodish in Dallas when I was training with Ivan back in the mid-70s. I called him Frank, but inside the world of professional wrestling, he was known as Bruiser Brody. He wrestled with Fritz from time to time and he was as wild as could be. Frank stood six feet eight inches tall. He weighed 300 pounds, or at least that was the weight he was billed at. Frank had long, black, curly hair, with a beard to match. His wrestling boots were unique in the sense that they were covered with rabbit fur.

In those days, Frank spent some time at Doug's Gym, which was right next door to Ivan's facility. It was there at the gym that I first saw and learned about Frank's particular eating habits. It was common for Frank to reach into his duffle bag and pull out a can of food when he wanted something to eat. Of all the wrestlers I have known, I have only known Frank to eat this way. Everyone else ate out at restaurants when they were on the road or we grabbed something from a fast-food drive-thru. I don't think I ever witnessed him eating at a restaurant.
However, I have watched him eat a lot of sardines, tuna, beans, potted meat, and Vienna Sausages right from the cans.

"Frank, what are you doing?" I asked.

"I'm eating. What does it look like I'm doing, Dummy?" Frank shot back.

"I know that you're eating. But you shouldn't eat out of a can like that," I stated.

"How am I supposed to eat it?" He questioned me.

"You should take that food out of the can and put it on a plate or put it into a bowl," I said.

"I don't have a plate or a bowl," he replied.

"If I were you, I wouldn't eat it like that Frank," I pleaded.

"Well, you aren't me. So be quiet!" He barked.

Frank knew how to stop me from badgering him. I never asked him why he ate that way again. If I had, I don't know if he would have given me a straight answer anyway. Maybe he did it to save money, or he did it because of the convenience. Whatever the reason, it was just what Frank did.

In 1987, I worked with Frank quite a bit. Instead of me taking him on as Bruiser Brody, I wrestled him as Red River Jack. Red River Jack was Frank under a mask, and he wore jeans and a pair of cowboy boots. I believe the storyline was that he lost a Loser Leaves Town match as Brody, and this was his way of sticking around. I think everyone knew it was Frank. His hair and bread came out from the bottom of the hood, and it gave his identity away. From time to time, he lifted the mask so the fans could see that it was him. Every time that we wrestled against each other, it was like we were trying to knock each other out. We used chairs, tables, and even the timekeeper's bell as weapons. Nothing was off-limits for us! It didn't take us more than 10 minutes to start seeing stars and tweedy birds. We never knocked each other unconscious, but we tried. Frank didn't believe in pulling a punch and I don't think he could have even if had tried. He pounded the hell out of everyone he got into the ring with. His opponents knew what was coming. Frank was a bad dude, and he was respected by most. If he didn't get the respect that he thought he deserved, he just took it.

In the dressing room after we wrestled each other was always the same scenario. Both of us were usually covered in blood and sweat, and the two of us were usually smiling.

"What are you looking at big Dummy?" Frank asked as he put his head back to rest it against the wall.

"I'm looking at the big Dummy sitting across from me," I answered back.

"Bart, have you started lifting weights? He inquired.

"No! Why do you ask?" I responded as I picked up a towel

to wipe the blood that was running down my face.

"I could feel you punching me tonight," Frank grinned.

"I can always feel you punching me, Frank!" I snapped.

"Bart, that was a hell of a match, brother." He shared.

"I know it was, and the fans know it too," I responded.

When it came to professional wrestling Frank was all business. He took it very seriously and he understood it so well. He knew how to get the crowd behind everything that he did. Frank was just like a puppet master; he pulled the strings and puppets went out and danced. He was one of the nicest guys that I have ever met, but he would whoop someone's ass in a minute if he wanted to. Frank was a bleeder. I don't know if he bled in every match, but he did get color often. He was just like me in that sense, If I was going to bleed, I was going to bleed a lot. We didn't believe in a little trickle; we believed in making a puddle of blood. If you are going to do it, do it right! I will never forget the time that Frank came back from a match he had in California. I was in the dressing room at the Sportatorium when he walked in to get ready for his match. I was pulling on my boots when I got distracted by something on Frank's face. At first, I wasn't quite sure what I was looking at, but when he got closer to me, I noticed that something wasn't right. Frank had a razor blade cut from the top of his brow that went down over the top of his eyelid, and it continued down to the side of his cheek. I was in shock!

"Frank, what the hell did you do?" I asked.

"What do you think I did? I cut myself," he snapped back.

"Frank? Why would you do something like that? Why would you cut your eyelid like that?" I asked with a puzzled look on my face.

"I wanted to see what it would feel like," he answered.

"What? I bet it hurts like hell, big Dummy!" I blasted.

"Are you going to shut up now, Bart?" He wondered.

"I will shut up. I will before you decide to cut my eyelid," as I shook my head in disbelief.

I turned my attention back to putting my boots on. The thought of him doing something like that seemed a bit insane. I think his unpredictable nature about things made him special. Inside of the ring or outside of it, Frank could dish it out and he could take it. Unfortunately, he appeared to be fearless almost every time I was around him. A lack of fear isn't always a good thing. Sometimes fear can get you into trouble and sometimes it just might save your life! Let's just say, Frank was a little different than most people I wrestled with back then.

It was in July of 1988. I was in bed sleeping when the phone rang. I had no idea what time it was, but it was a Saturday morning because I had wrestled Skip Young the night before at the Sportatorium. Skip was also known in the ring as Sweet Brown Sugar, and the fans loved him. Of course, none of the babyface wrestlers got over like the Von Erichs had, but he was popular in his own right. I was not fully awake when I rolled over in the direction where the phone was resting on my nightstand. I grabbed the receiver and put the handpiece to the side of my head.

"Hello," I said in a faint and quiet tone.

"Bart, are you awake?" The caller asked.

"No," I replied.

"Bart, I need you to listen to me. It's Frank. Wake up, Dummy!" Frank snapped.

"I'm awake Frank, what's going on?" I asked as I sat up in bed.

"I need you to go to Austria and wrestle for me in my match with Otto Wanz. I am going to be here in Puerto Rico longer than I had anticipated," he explained.

"Sure Frank, but have you talked to Fritz about this yet?" I inquired.

"Don't you worry about Fritz; I will take care of that conversation. Are you able to write a number down?" Frank asked.

"Yes, I have something to write with, go ahead," I responded as I reached for a pen and a small piece of paper that sat next to the phone to which I proceeded to write. Frank finished giving me the information I needed and I hung up the phone.

I reached out to the wrestling office in Austria. It was my understanding that Frank had already been in contact with Otto. When I made the call, it seemed as if the person on the end had been expecting to hear from me. That was when I found out that my flight had been scheduled and paid for. It was my understanding that Otto took care of that for me. From the way Frank had explained it to me, the match against Otto was important. In all my years of knowing Frank, I can't remember there being a time when he was a no-show when I worked with him. I was honored that Frank trusted me enough to go to Europe and represent him. That was the main reason why I wanted to go over there and give Otto and the fans in that country a spectacular match!

Otto Wanz was a big dude! He stood a couple of inches over six feet tall and weighed around 375 pounds. He looked like a tree trunk with a pair of legs, and he had some strength to him. I had heard along with being a wrestler, he was also a boxer. It wouldn't surprise me if he was a powerlifter too, he had the body for it. Otto wrestled around the world. In 1982 and 1983, Vern Gagne brought him into his American Wrestling Association based out of Minneapolis, Minnesota. Otto even held the AWA World Title when he defeated Nick Bockwinkle in the Fall of 82, only to lose it back to Nick 41 days later. Otto was the promoter for the Catch Wrestling Association which ran shows in Austria and Germany.

When I arrived in Austria at the airport, I was met

by a young man who told me that he was there to pick me up for Otto. However, I didn't know who he was. If he had mentioned his name, it didn't stick with me at that moment. We left the airport, and he escorted me to our vehicle. It was a black pickup truck that had a roll bar on it. It was quite impressive. I learned that they had rented that for me, so I had transportation the entire time I visited their country. I was mesmerized by the scenery over there. With every head turn, it was like looking at a beautiful postcard. The mountains and rolling hills were covered with bright green grass. The entire place reminded me of the movie, "The Sound of Music." It was quite nice, and I was expecting Julie Andrews to show up from out of nowhere and sing to me. Most of the buildings looked like little cottages and it was not uncommon to see small wineries when I traveled. Let me not forget to mention the beer that I discovered while I was there. The people in Austria like their beer, and so did I!

From the airport, my chauffeur took me to a press conference that was in what looked like a banquet room of a hotel. I guess they had rented the space to drum up some publicity for our upcoming event. It looked like a legit press conference. There was a long table set up on one side of the room that had a cluster of about 20 reporters and photographers set up in front of it. There were photographers taking pictures with their cameras and there were also television photographers who had video cameras resting on their tripods. The media crews were ready to cover the action that was about to take place. The scene reminded me of a weigh-in that is held for big-time boxing events. I took my seat at one end of the main table and Otto was already sitting down in his chair a few feet away from me. There were several microphones on the table. Most of them were sitting right in the middle of the two of us in hopes of hearing what we both had to say. The object that caught my attention that day was

Otto's CWA Championship Title. It was propped right in front of him where he sat. The belt was big and the gold metal emblems on it shined bright. On each side of the black leather strap were three engraved gold plates. It was pretty!

The press conference began, and the reporters asked two or three questions before I decided the need to let the "Black Bart" gimmick out! So, without any warning, I jumped out of my seat and flipped the table over with a good bit of force. Everyone in the room was caught off guard and they all took a step backward. Their faces looked as if they had just seen a ghost! I immediately confronted Otto and started yelling at him. I stood right in front of him, face to face, and nose to nose. I pushed a few of the people away who had tried to hold me back. My intention wasn't to put my hands on Otto, but I sure made it look that way. When I broke free from Otto's protectors, I grabbed a chair and threw it in his direction. Suddenly, I heard someone say that the press conference was over. My chauffeur and a dozen other men surrounded me and ran me out to where my rented truck was parked. There was a buzz of confusion and disarray in the place when I fled. Once my chauffeur and I were safely inside the truck we drove away. I let out a burst of laughter.

"Did you see the looks on those people's faces?" I asked my driver.

"I did and I imagine that my face looked like everybody else's," the chauffeur replied.

"That press conference turned out a lot better than I had expected," I said.

"I think you even surprised my father," he mentioned.

"Who is your father?" I inquired.

"My father is Otto Wanz, the man you will be wrestling against in a couple of days," the chauffeur answered.

"That's too funny," I chuckled.

"I think we are off to a good start Black Bart," he smiled as he drove the truck to the hotel where I would be staying. "The fans will be shocked when they watch what happened today!"

Back then, when I was actively wrestling, I wrestled almost every night. So, I was surprised when I found out that I only had to wrestle in one match, during my entire stay while I was in Austria. I was scheduled to wrestle Otto in the main event on the fourth evening after my arrival. I was paid the equivalent of $3,000 (U.S. dollars) in advance. I felt good about how the press conference went because the wrestling fans were expecting Bruiser Brody and now, they were getting Black Bart. Being a replacement for Bruiser Brody isn't an easy thing to do, he is one of a kind. However, I was determined that everyone in Austria was going to remember my name by the time I left. I had time before the event to go out and see some of the sites the country had to offer.

"When the hell am I ever going to be in this part of the world again?" I thought to myself.

When I was out doing my sightseeing, I went by the arena where I would be wrestling Otto. Most of the time, I would see the wrestling building when arrived on the evening of the event. Then again, I usually didn't have the luxury of extra time like I did on this trip. The event where I was to wrestle was called Eishalle Liebenau Located in Graz, Austria. Today, I believe it may be called something else, but as far as I know, it still stands. The arena was a regular venue for hockey. The seats throughout the inside of the structure hold around 4,000. I imagine when chairs were set up on the floor around the ring, several hundred more people could attend easily. Otto's son told me that the Catch Wrestling Association rented that building every night for 6 months straight. He also mentioned that it is almost always a sold-out show. Honestly, I find that a little hard to believe knowing how the wrestling business can be. Maybe the sport is different over there, or maybe it was different back then. I just had trouble wrapping my head around that one.

Otto's son was a true promoter. I say this because anytime we were out in public, he talked about me and told everyone about the upcoming match between his father and me. Since I was a cowboy, I stuck out in that country like a sore thumb. The people there stared at my hat and my boots, but the whip attached to my waist was a whole other story. I could tell that they were terrified of it. I'm sure that they wondered why I was carrying it around town.

"Look at this man. This man will fight my father," Otto's son blasted.

"He looks mean," a young boy stated.

"He is meaner than a rattlesnake," my handler insisted.

"What is that rope for?" The boy asked.

"It's not a rope, it's a bullwhip!" He exclaimed. "Bart, show us your whip.

At that moment, I took the whip from my waist and stretched it out with a single turn of my wrist. I snapped my leather whip with such strength, that it sounded like a loud pop when it connected with the sidewalk. Some of my spectators jumped and some even backed away in fear. It was quite humorous.

When it came time for Otto and me to step into the ring, I was ready. Word of our press conference spread like wildfire! The fans let me know their dislike for me the moment that I walked from the back of the building onto the arena floor. The people there hated me. That was what I wanted. I knew it was going to be a great night. I could feel it. When the crowd is that hot, it always fueled me to be that much more of a heel! It was like taking candy from a baby. Otto's fans were so loud and their energy was so intense, it felt as if I was having an out-of-body experience as I walked to the ring through a sea of people. It was wild!

The wrestling matches in Austria were remarkably

similar to boxing matches. Instead of wrestling continuously as we do here in the States, the matches were broken into three-minute rounds. Sine I wasn't used to this, I became winded and I had troubles catching my breath. As the match progressed, I could tell that this stipulation was causing me a lot of problems. By the third round, I could tell that Otto was getting tired as well. I assumed that he would be used to this kind of a match, but the sound of his loud, agonizing gasps for air disputed that thought. I tried not to think about it too much, I knew that it wouldn't last forever, and besides, I was having fun. It was during the sixth round of the contest when I decided that I was going to get some color. In other words, it was time for me to bleed! I always tried to cut myself high near the hairline, so my forehead didn't end up looking like a road map. However, on that night, I was concerned that I might have hit an artery. I cannot remember a time when I had ever bled that badly. I was a bloody mess! I could tell by the horrified look on Otto's face that he was concerned for my well-being.

"Are you okay?" Otto whispered into my ear as we wrestled.

"Yes, I'm fine," I returned with a punch.

"There is a lot of blood," he mentioned standing closely as we choked one another.

"Keep on going Otto," I spoke into his ear as I grabbed him into a headlock.

He was right, there was a lot of blood. So much that it was running into my eyes and impairing my vision. I tried wiping it away the best I could, however, I didn't accidentally want to find out what Frank felt when he cut his eyelid. I had a piece of the blade taped inside my right index finger and with everything that was happening at that moment, I had to be careful. Plus, if I had cut my damn eyelid, I would expect Frank to call me a Dummy. I couldn't stand myself if that were to happen. So, I continued the best that I could. I wasn't hurt,

I just couldn't see all that well. I knew that Otto was right in front of me because I felt him punching me with great force. The pounding that I took was a bit jarring, I instinctively ran my tongue across my teeth on the inside of my mouth to make sure that they were all still in place. My teeth were intact and that made me happy. So, the fight continued. At some point, I managed to use the shoulder strap from my singlet to remove some of the blood from one of my eyes. It helped a little and now I was able to see Otto when he swung at me.

I believe it was the ninth or tenth round of our match when we found ourselves on the outside of the ring. It was a wild night, and I could tell that the fans were in awe just by the looks on their faces. Being on the outside of the ring at this point in the match was perfect. It was time to take this contest home and get my ass into the shower. I grabbed a chair and used it on him. Bang! Then he grabbed a chair and used it on me. Bang! Star light, star bright! Do you know what I'm saying? When I first came out for the match, the fans were loud and quite vocal, but now they were silent. Then Otto grabbed a nearby table and he put me through it. Since I knew I wasn't taking his belt, we both decided to keep our fight on the floor. In doing so, the referee counted us out when he got to 10, we were both disqualified. The crowd erupted in a roar of chants to celebrate their champion, Otto.

Sitting in my dressing room after the match was somewhat euphoric. I was enjoying the adrenaline rush that had carried me through the night. I reflected on the match that I just had, and I was replaying some of the night's highlights in my head. I bent over to pull my boots off when I heard a knock at the door as it opened. One of Otto's office workers poked his head in.

"Hello Sir, are you doing, okay?" He asked.

"Yes. I am fine, thank you," I returned.

"Sir, are you hurt?" He questioned.

"No. I'm not hurt. I'm doing well," I said.

He left and that was when I noticed a mirror inside my room. I stood up to get a better look at myself.

"Oh my, what a mess?" I thought.

It was now so obvious the reason for all the concern. The blood covered my entire face and chest. It was like a dark red blanket that covered my upper body and arms. The features on my face were unrecognizable. Only the whites of my eyes could be seen, and just barely. Again, I was interrupted by a knock on the door. This time it was Otto. He spoke in a strong Western European accent.

"May I come in Bart?" Otto asked.

"Yes, come in," I replied.

"Bart, are you okay?" He inquired.

"Yes. I'm fine," I told Otto.

"Do you need to go to the hospital, Bart?" He wondered.

"No, no, no," I returned.

"Are you sure?" Otto questioned.

"I assure you, nothing is wrong with me," I said with laughter.

Otto stuck out his hand to shake mine. I quickly grabbed a towel to wipe off any sweat and blood that was left on it. I reached out with my right hand, and we shook. I could feel that he had something inside his grasp. It was paper I knew that much. I accepted it in our exchange, but I didn't look at it. I thanked Otto one more time and he left my room. I picked up my hand to see what he had given me. It was more money. It was approximately $2,000. I assumed that was a bonus because he had given me three grand when I arrived. I was blown away by the payday that I had earned! $5,000 and a trip to Austria in exchange for an ass whooping; is a deal in my book!

I returned to Dallas, and I wrestled Bill Irwin at the Sportatorium on July 15th. I was anxious to speak with Frank to tell him about my trip to Austria. Sadly, only two days after my match with Bill, Frank was stabbed in the shower area of the dressing room in Puerto Rico. Jose Gonzalez claimed self-defense. Frank died shortly after the incident. When I heard of what happened to Frank, I was in shock. Thoughts of the good times that I had with Frank ran through my mind, only to be interrupted by the agonizing dull pain that engulfed my entire body, especially my broken heart. The best way that I could describe how I felt at that moment was an overwhelming emptiness. I've been hit hard in all of my years of wrestling, but nothing like that. I couldn't put two words together. Jose was a wrestler and a booker over there in Puerto Rico. He and Frank had heat. They had real heat; those two men couldn't stand each other. Much has been said about Bruiser Brody's death, some of it makes sense to me and some of it doesn't. I believe that Frank died because he was about to gain 51 percent of the Puerto Rico wrestling office. Frank was a very vocal person and he spoke his mind. He had said many times and made it known to Jose if that was to happen, Jose would be the first person fired from that territory. The world may never know the entire story of that tragic day, but all I know is that I lost a good friend. The sport of professional wrestling has never been the same!

*On July 17, 1988, Bruiser Brody was stabbed in the shower area of the dressing room before a wrestling event in Puerto Rico. Jose Gonzalez was arrested for his involvement in the incident, but acquitted of all charges.

CHAPTER 26 - THE UWF & THE WWF

By June of 1987, my first run with World Class Championship Wrestling came to an end. It took me almost no time at all to start working for Bill Watts again. However, this time that I worked with Bill his wrestling promotion had a new name. In 1986, Bill rolled the dice and rebranded his regional Mid-South promotion and transformed it into a national organization called the Universal Wrestling Federation. I didn't feel like I was getting a huge push from Bill while being at his company during this period. However, most of the time I wrestled at the mid-card status, and the work was steady. Wrestling in the UWF was like a homecoming for me because I reconnected with some familiar faces that I worked with before. Guys like Terry Gordy, Dick Murdoch, Terry Taylor, Steve Williams, Arn Anderson, Barry Windham, and Big Bubba were all very good friends to me over the years. I respected their in-ring work and I got along with them. Many others were in the mix as well. Wrestlers like Sting, Shaska Whatley, Shane Douglas, and the Steiner Brothers were all grinding it out in the ring for Bill. Shaska also wrestled under the name Pistol Pez and I consider him to be a very good friend of mine. It was hard not to be in a good mood when I was around Pez, he was always very nice and easygoing.

In my opinion, Shane Douglas is another underrated and underutilized wrestler just like I thought Brad Armstrong was. These two men could work in any position on the card, would do anything that was asked of them, and they were hardworking and loyal to the business. On top of that, they were good people and fun to be around. Don't ask me why promoters and bookers never saw what I saw in Shane or in Brad.

At times, the traveling was grueling, and the work schedule was a bit tough. However, the time that I spent with the boys was probably the best part of it all. The one thing that I will always be able to say about the Steiner Brothers, was that they could out-wrestle anyone! I'm not talking about a street fight, though, I'm sure they could take care of themselves like that too. On the mat, those two dudes were unstoppable, and they could tie your ass up like a pretzel in no time. Rick and Scott both wrestled collegiately for the University of Michigan and those boys were no joke!

Most of us arrived early to work for Bill because he still enforced strict rules. Knowing we had some time to kill, we always found something to keep ourselves occupied. In the dressing room, the guys moved everything out of the way so there was a big enough place on the floor so they could wrestle amateur style. Everyone threw their travel bags on the floor beside the walls, so they were out of the way. Let me make this clear right now! There were no mats, only concrete, and the Steiners took this type of competition quite seriously!

One day we are at an event in Oklahoma City. We all had been on the road driving, and I had a good bit of beer in me. I'm sure that I had already guzzled a 12-pack before arriving at the venue. So, I was feeling good, and I was quite ballsy. I walked into the dressing room, and I started watching Steve Williams and Rick wrestle on the floor. The two of them were going at it! Steve had a strong amateur background in wrestling too, so, I know that bragging rights were on the line between those two that day. Steve and Rick weren't playing. Wrestling with intensity on a mat is one thing, but wrestling on a hard, cold, concrete slab is a whole different story. I'm not sure if it was all of the beer that I drank or if I just got lost in watching them battle it out for supremacy, but I started to get some ideas that I could do that too. I didn't want to wrestle Steve, because I knew he could whoop my ass easier than butter melting in a hot pan. I wanted Rick. I had all the courage I needed to call him out. When Rick and Steve finished their contest I spoke up.

"Steiner, it's you and me, buddy! Let's go!" I shouted.

Everybody in the dressing room looked at each other and then their eyes came back onto me as if I had lost my mind.

"Do you want some of this Bart?" Rick asked with a questionable look on his face.

"I don't think I stutter. The real question for you Steiner is, do YOU want some of this?" I bragged as I showed off strutting in his direction.

"You better get your ass over here, right now!" He snapped back at me. "I'm not playing. You better hope that you change your mind in one second."

At this time, I bent down and proceeded to get on my hands and knees on the floor right in front of him.

"Steiner if I was to tie a bologna sandwich to my back, you couldn't take a bite out of it before this match is over," I stated.

"We'll see about that Cowboy," Rick growled as he made his way down to the floor beside me. "Is somebody going to say go?"

"Go!" Steve yelled out as he wore a smile on his face from ear to ear.

Rick flipped me over and dropped me on my back. It only took him a couple of seconds to tie up both my arms and place his knee into my groin.

"Uncle!" I groaned. "Uncle, Uncle!

"I'm still looking for that bologna sandwich, Bart," he growled.

"I'm sorry. I'm sorry. If you let me go Rick I won't say another word," I pleaded.

Rick let me go and then he stood up. He stretched out his hand and I grabbed it and pulled me up and off of the floor. I stood to my feet, and he looked me dead in the eye.

"Bart, you are either crazier than a lunatic or you have guts in your guts. It might take me a little more time to try and figure that out," he said as he shook his head.

"Thank you for the kind words, Rick," I grinned and walked over to pick up my bag from the pile that accumulated on the side of the wall. I then sat on the bench in the dressing room and I kept my mouth shut.

Rick and I became good friends after that. There was mutual respect between the two of us. I love that dude. I am so glad that he didn't kill me that day on the dressing room floor, because he easily could have.

In the Summer of 1987, The Crocketts bought the UWF from Bill, and I was back and solely wrestling for them. They were running shows all across the United States and I made a lot of those shots. By this time The Crocketts were stretching their travel and I even went as far a California for them. In January of 1988, I wrestled on the same circuit that I worked with the Crocketts in 1981. I was back on some familiar roads and I returned to some memorable venues. I felt as if the fans in Georgia, Virginia, and the Carolinas still hated me and that made me feel like I was at home! In the Springtime of that year, I got a call from J.J Dillion. He, Ron Bass, and Blackjack Mulligan were wrestling with Vince McMahon in his World Wrestling Federation. I was interested in what J.J. had to say.

"Hello Bart, It's J.J.," he greeted.

"Hello J.J.," I replied.

"How are things going?" he asked.

"Things are good," I said.

"How are the Crocketts treating you," J.J. inquired.

"They treat me alright, J.J.," I continued. "What's going on J.J.?" I wanted to know.

"We want to bring you up for a three-day tryout," he explained.

"A three-day tryout? Is Vince offering me a job?" I questioned.

"We want to bring you up for a three-day tryout," he

spoke straight to the point.

"Are you joking with me right now, J.J.?" I grilled him.

"No, not at all," he responded.

"Do I have the job or what?" I asked with intensity in my voice.

"We want to bring you up for a three-day tryout," he repeated himself for a third time.

"I will have to talk about this with Bonnie and I will get back to you," I affirmed.

"Sounds good," J.J. spoke before he hung up the phone.

I will have to admit the idea of going to Connecticut on J. J.'s offer didn't appeal to me at all. I had worked with J.J. for years, and he knew how talented I was. The fact he was offering me a tryout without any promise of a job, really bruised my ego. On one hand I had an invite from the biggest wrestling company in the world. On the other hand, I was making more money than I ever had working for the Crocketts. I just couldn't see myself taking a risk without a guarantee of a spot, knowing the Crocketts would fire me if it didn't work out. I talked about the idea of wrestling for the WWF with Bonnie.

"So, they want to bring you in for a tryout?" Bonnie asked.

"Yes. That's what J.J. told me," I explained to my wife.

"You and J.J. worked together for some time, he knows what you bring to the table," she stated.

"That's the same thing that I thought. Why would I waste my time for a tryout and risk the chance of the Crocketts cutting me?" I wondered.

"I don't think it sounds like a good idea," Bonnie insisted.

"I don't either," I replied.

After Bonnie and I discussed J.J.'s proposal, I wasn't comfortable about going to Connecticut at the specific time. I never thought about it again. Shortly after that, I ended up leaving the Carolinas and I traveled back to Texas, Florida, and Tennessee. In Tennessee, I worked for the United States Wrestling Association owned by Jerry and Jeff Jarret. Some of the wrestlers that were on the roster then were Jerry Lawler, Dustin Rhodes, Cousin Junior, Iceman King Parsons, Bam Bam Bigelow, The Rock & Roll Express, and The Master of Pain. The stability that I once felt that I had in wrestling was no longer there. That was a hectic two years for Bonnie and me and our young daughter. Bonnie didn't like moving as often as we did and she wanted to stay in Florida because she had family there. Though the uprooting of my family was a strain on my marriage, Bonnie put up with it the best she could. I knew a lot of the boys who didn't marry for that specific reason and I knew a lot of guys that had gotten divorced over it too.

Near the end of 1989, I received another call from J.J. He came at me again with an offer to wrestle in the WWF, and this time I took it. The territories were pretty much gone or going to be very soon. By this time, I was in Hillsboro, Texas working on a job outside of wrestling. I was only making minimum wage; it was a vast difference from what I was used to being paid as a wrestler. This time nothing was said about me having to go through a tryout, but I probably would have if it was requested of me. When I agreed to work for Vince McMahon, I was pleased that the dollar amount of the contract it was the best money than I had ever been offered. I knew my figures were equivalent to some of the top name wrestlers. However, I guessed I overlooked the fine print when I realized that there was no intention of using me as a top-tier performer. I was getting squashed by all of the stars on their roster and I found it humiliating. New guys breaking into the business can expect that, but by this time in my career, I had been working for 15 years. I thought that my body of work had proved my worth. However, with the direction that pro wrestling was going in, it didn't leave me too many other choices. The WWF had become the biggest stage in wrestling and little did we know at the time it was about to be the only stage!

Some of my very first matches with the WWF were with Koko B. Ware. Our lead-off contest took place at Madison Square Garden. Koko was getting a lot of television time, and he beat a lot of people, but when it came to facing the top wrestlers, he lost those matchups. Koko was nicknamed the Birdman, and because of that he always had a bird with him. Most of the time he was spotted with his parrot named Frankie, who sat on his shoulder while he did promos or when he walked to the ring. Koko had a move called the Birdbuster. When performing this maneuver, he lifted his opponent in the air as if he was going to execute a Suplex, but instead, he dropped to the canvas driving the person's head into the mat kind of like a piledriver or a DDT. This was Koko's finishing move and it was what he was known for. However, before our first match together, I told him what I thought about him doing the Birdbuster on me.

"Koko, due to my size I don't think it's a good idea," I said.

"Bart, I've done this move a hundred times! What can you possibly be worried about?" he asked.

"I'm worried about you breaking my neck. I weigh 300 pounds. That is a lot of weight coming down on the upper area of my back and around my neck," I explained.

"Nothing bad is going to happen," Koko assured.

"I don't want to take that bump. I don't think that you're big enough to protect me," I insisted.

"It's my finishing move, so we are going to do it," he demanded as he walked away from where I was standing in the dressing room.

Koko and I were in the ring for only a few minutes, when he set me up to catch me in the Birdbuster. He picked me up and my feet left the mat, I knew the landing was going to be hard, and it was. When I hit the canvas, I heard my back make a popping sound. I didn't feel any pain right away and I believe that was because of the adrenaline that was racing through my body during the match. Unfortunately, when my adrenaline rush wore off, the pain shot through my body and I became very uncomfortable. It took me quite some time to get out of bed the following day. Even though I knew the injury in my back was serious, it didn't stop me from wrestling. A lot of insurance companies back then didn't cover any kind of injuries that occurred in the ring. Coverage for what they considered an act of war didn't fall under their responsibility. So, I never had a doctor look at my back.

Years later, when my in-ring career slowed significantly, I was working for a private business outside of pro wrestling. I was in charge of the maintenance department. The company was moving from one building to another. It was my job to make sure that the inside and outside were going to be ready when the business took over at the new location. One day, I was helping in the yard and I was on a riding lawn mower. Suddenly, I felt a twinge in my back and then it felt as if a firecracker went off inside my ass. I stopped the lawn mower immediately. My nephew who was working with me was using a weed eater in the same area that I was mowing. I asked him to trade jobs with me and he did. As I operated the weed eater by moving my arms back and forth from side to side, it only took a matter of minutes before my entire body shut down and I could no longer move. The guys at work took me to the emergency room. They had to pull the truck up as close as they could to the entrance, so they could carry me inside. The doctor ordered X-rays and when he reviewed them with me, he shared something very interesting when we looked at the images together.

"Whatever happened to you, happened a long time ago," the doctor revealed.

"Why do say that, Doc?" I wanted to know.

"Do you see these dark areas around your L4 and L5?" he asked as he pointed to the images.

"I do. What does that mean?" I wondered.

"The discolor makes me believe that you suffered a broken back about 12 years ago." The doctor explained.

"Wow! You don't say?" I was in shock.

"Did something happen to you 12 years ago?" he pried.

I couldn't believe what the doctor told me. I knew that something happened to my back, but I have to admit that I just dismissed it. Being a pro wrestler comes with aches and pains, so over the years I became accustomed to hurting. Back then, being sidelined meant not working, and not working meant no money. I traced back to where I was 12 years ago from my visit to the emergency room. My estimation put me back to when I started wrestling for the WWF against Koko B. Ware. I ended up having surgery. The doctors inserted a metal rod, along with screws to repair the damage in my back. They also fused my L4 and my L5 disks. I never said anything to Koko about that. As a wrestler, I did all kinds of things that put my body at risk. However, I know the doctor got this one right with my broken back. I knew the moment that Koko dropped me to the canvas something serious happened to my spine.

Dealing with strong personalities in wrestling has gone on since the game first started. I had to learn how to cope inside a very ego-driven locker room. When you have that many muscleheads and that much testosterone on one roster, there is going to be a struggle for dominance. It's hard to think of one guy who didn't walk around with his chest puffed out. I saw guys on the bottom of the roster have chips on their shoulders. As soon as I walked into the building to wrestle in the WWF for the first time, I felt the tension. The surprising thing about it all was that I had worked with most of those guys at different places throughout my career. I knew a lot of them. The dressing room was very cliquish. Take my word for it, money, power, and prestige can and will change a man! Pro wrestling is full of egos. I know this because I have one too!

Some guys acted like they were the rooster, but in reality, they were just a bunch of cocks! Speaking of cocks, the WWF was the first company where I witnessed wrestlers who were openly free with their sexuality. Never before have I ever seen two men make out with each other and even try to take it further than that in the dressing room. I was asked certain personal questions and if I wanted to go somewhere and party with wrestlers that participated in such behavior. I immediately realized that I was being propositioned. It made me feel a little uncomfortable, but I was there to do a job and I wasn't there to do anything else. It didn't take me long to realize I needed my own private dressing room. The company wasn't going to give my own space, so I created one for myself. I always made it a point to pick an area away from a lot of foot traffic. With tables, chairs, partitions, tablecloths, and anything that I could get my hands on, I made an enclosed space for myself. I sat in there and sharpened my knives or took naps. I found it easier to remove myself from the environment that was already established, instead of trying to change it. At some point, other wrestlers came in there too to get away from any kind of dressing room drama they wanted to escape from. The Road Warriors, Animal and Hawk, Dusty, Rick Steiner, and Demolition (Bill Eadie and Barry Darsaw) came to visit me often. The guys who hung out with me in the makeshift room seemed to like it too. My friends all thought it was innovative, but some thought that it lacked décor and certain amenities.

"This is a cool little spot you have here, Bart," Animal continued. "However, you need something on the walls."

"If you bring a Road Warriors poster, I will hang it up, just for you," I shot back.

"I will do it," he replied.

"Don't forget. I will hold you to it," I joked.

"Okay, I promise," Animal laughed.

"Bart, you need to put a restroom in here," Hawk suggested.

"That's a good idea and when I do, we can use your poster for the toilet paper," I laughed.

On every show I worked on for the WWF, I made myself a dressing room no matter where we wrestled. As time passed during my employment there, if anyone was ever looking for me, they knew where to find me. The guys in management didn't seem to mind and the running joke was that I could always be found in my office. That is what I call making lemonade out lemons!

CHAPTER 27 – THE UNDERTAKER GIMMICK

I traveled quite a bit with the World Wrestling Federation. I wrestled with Vince for a total of 13 months, and in that time, I wrestled all over the United States for him. Wrestling in New York, at the Garden, was always a challenge. That was due to the difficulty of getting to and from the airport, along with getting to and from the venue itself. Trying to get a car to rent there was never easy. I hated to resort to taking a taxi anywhere because I always felt as if I was flushing my money down the drain. So, I usually got frustrated with the whole situation. Trying to find a parking spot close to the venue was another task that had to be factored in. Some of the boys learned the way by leaving their cars several blocks away from the arena. In New York especially, the vehicles didn't always look the same way they had left them. I heard stories about cars that were driven by the heels. Some were flipped over by fans that left them resting on the roof, and the tires were left staring up at the sky! Crazy stuff!

The television tapings were not what I considered fun. I don't know what it was like for everyone else, but I do know what it was like for me. On a typical day of production, I'd arrive around 11 in the morning and I could be there well after midnight. Another downside to all that was how I got paid for those days. Instead of getting a set rate of $50 a match, I was paid $250 per day. Looking back at it now, maybe the company looked at it like it was a bonus. Who knows? My contract with the WWF guaranteed that I wouldn't make less than a certain amount, and I never did. For whatever reason, I couldn't help feeling like I was being screwed over on the days that the WWF recorded for T.V. or, maybe I just didn't like my role in Vince's company. I was getting beat by just about everyone on McMahon's roster. Especially by the wrestlers who had a name.

I find the term "jobber" somewhat offensive. Maybe

because I worked in that position for the first seven years of my career. At that time, most of the jobbers or enhancement talent didn't have a recognizable name. If it wasn't for Dusty who gave me a push in Florida and the Mid-Atlantic territories, I might not have had any notoriety either. Despite my disappointing situation, I never stopped interacting with the crowd and I still took their emotions on a roller coaster ride every night that I worked. I gave the fans in the WWF a reason to want to hate me even if they didn't think they needed one. I never stopped calling the matches and I never stopped controlling the crowd. Those two elements were instilled into me in my early days of pro wrestling and I would never be able to change that.

During my time in the WWF, some of the guys working with me were Andre the Giant, Roddy Piper, Jimmy Snuka, Dusty Rhodes, Terry Taylor, The Big Bossman, Ted Dibiase, Kerry Von Erich, The Barbarian, The One-Man Gang, and so many others were all there. It was also at this time when the gimmicks were catering to kids. Wrestling during this era felt very cartoonish. Vince turned the Gang into Akeem the African Dream. In my opinion, The One-Man Gang gimmick was a homerun. I understand this probably had a lot to do with trademarks and naming rights. Back then, if a wrestler had a long-standing gimmick, he wanted to keep it. It had to be a really good idea for a wrestler to change their name and switch characters midway through their career. Since my early days in the business, I had seen some ideas that worked in wrestling and ones that didn't. At times it seemed as if the creative team just threw spaghetti at the wall to see what would stick. Some of the ideas like The Million Dollar Man worked very well. Pro wrestling, just like anything else can be a game of hits or misses. Do I have to mention the Gobbledy Gooker, or the Ding Dongs?

Everyone that I worked with during this period, including myself wondered why anyone would wear black tights with yellow polka dots, but Dusty Rhodes pulled it off. The yellow dots weren't Dusty's idea, but he embraced the change. He and Randy Savage had some epic matches during their feud that they had with each other for several months in 1990. Lumberjack matches and Steel Cage matches were scheduled to settle the score between the two men. However, the matches that seemed to grab the attention of the fans, were the contests that included Dusty's and Randy's female managers, Sapphire and Sherri Martel.

The next story that I am about to share even had my co-author Vinny Berry a bit credulous. I know that he believes that I am telling him the truth, but because of his training as a writer, he did everything he could in trying to track down Dustin Rhodes for confirmation. I know that Vinny sent emails to his last known agent, tried reaching out to him on social media, and even sent letters to a post office box address that is registered to his training school. At the time when this book went to print, Vinny still hadn't heard from Dustin. However, I was there and I know what happened. Many may not believe me, but I'm telling the truth! In the Fall of 1990, after wrapping up a wrestling show at a building in Connecticut, Dusty, his oldest son Dustin, and I left together to drive to our hotel room. We planned to stay there for one night and drive to the next city the following day. Stopping for our supply of beer before we arrived at the hotel was a priority for us. I usually always made sure that I had a case of beer for myself. Most of the boys did it that way too.

The hotel wasn't fancy, but it was nice. The rooms were located inside the building and I always preferred that style of lodging. I was relaxing inside my room and drinking when I heard a knock at the door. While on the road it was common for one of the boys to stop by and visit if it wasn't too late. I got off my bed and I drank the rest of the beer that was left in the can I was enjoying. Upon finishing my beer, I tossed the can into a nearby waste basket and I answered the door. It was Dustin. Dustin had bleached blonde hair just like his father; however, he stood about six and a half feet tall. He was just a few inches taller than his dad and not as chubby. Dustin debuted in 1988, so at the time, he might have been about 21 years old. In Dustin's early days of wrestling, I had stepped inside the ring and wrestled him quite often. I felt as if I helped him a lot in the beginning. It was a pleasure for me to do that since his Daddy had done so much for my career.

"Hey there Dustin. What can I do for you? Did you want to come inside?" I asked.

"No. Thank you, Bart. My dad wanted me to tell you that he'd like you to come by the room. He wants to talk to you about something," Dustin mentioned.

"Okay. Is he up there right now?" I questioned.

"Yes, he is. He said for you to come right up," he explained.

"Okay then. I will grab some beer and head that way," I informed.

"Okay, Bart. See you later," he said.

"Okay Dustin, thank you," I returned.

"No problem. Good night," Dustin replied.

Dustin walked away from my door and went down the hall. In no time he was out of my sight. Inside my room, I put on my shoes and grabbed some cans of beer. I made sure that I had the key to my room before I headed off to see Dusty. I had no clue what Dusty wanted to talk to me about, I assumed he wanted to shoot the breeze or talk shop. Anytime I had a chance to talk about wrestling with Dusty was a good day in my book. When I arrived at Dusty's room, I knocked on his door. As I stood in the hallway for a couple of seconds, I heard the lock to the door from the other side being turned. The door opened and, in the doorway, Dusty stood there in his normal fashion. He was wearing only a T-shirt. I thought nothing of

Dusty being half-naked. I had known him for nearly seven years by then and I had seen Dusty like that at least a hundred times. It was common practice. Things might have been strange; had he been wearing pants. I proceeded to enter his quarters as he greeted me.

"Bart, how are you, Baby?" Dusty asked as he motioned me to come in.

"Hello Dusty," I returned.

"Come in here, Bart if you will," he continued. "I see you brought some beer, that's good."

"Dustin said that you wanted to talk to me," I replied.

"Yeah Baby, come have a seat, Bart. I have something I want to show you," he explained.

I walked over to a small table that was in a corner of the room. The table was round and it had two wooden chairs that were sitting next to it. Dusty had what looked like a folder similar to what a student might use while attending school. Dusty opened it up and inside were a few pieces of paper that had sketches on them.

"Take a look at this, Bart," Dusty said with a smile on his face.

"What is this?" I wanted to know.

"It's the idea that I have for a wrestling gimmick, Baby," he returned.

"Do you have a name for this character?" I questioned.

"Bart, I call it The Undertaker," Dusty explained.

"The Undertaker?" I replied. "I like that."

"I think you can become this gimmick and run with it," he assured.

"I believe I can too," I said with confidence.

As I looked over the drawings that Dusty had in front of me, I was impressed. I wasn't sure if Dusty drew up the sketches himself or if he had someone else do them, but I liked what I saw. The character on paper that I was staring at looked like The Undertaker in his early days. The drawings showed a flat-brimmed hat, a long black coat, and there were purple gloves on his hands. Knowing that this idea was coming from Dusty himself, and with the success he has had with other creative ideas, I was all in on his plan! Heck, he altered my life when he turned me into Black Bart, so, changing my name was a no-brainer for me! I knew that Dusty's idea was going to give me the push that I so desperately wanted while I was wrestling in the WWF. However, that was the last time that The Undertaker gimmick was ever discussed with me. Nearly two weeks later in November, Mark Callaway debuted as the ominous character. The Undertaker had been introduced to the world of pro wrestling and its fans. I first met Mark a year before in Tennessee when he wrestled as The Master of Pain when I worked there. It was there that I struck up a friendship with Mark. I didn't get The Undertaker gimmick, but that didn't change my feelings toward him. He was still my friend and I cared about him very much. Some wrestlers can become like brothers in this business and I would put Mark in that category. Business is business, and I'd like to think I know and understand the wrestling business very well. With all that being said, Mark Callaway was, is, and always will be The Undertaker. No one could have done what Mark had done with that character for the 30-plus years that he did it. I know I couldn't have done what he did with that role. He was born to wrestle as The Undertaker! Period!

Dusty and I never discussed the gimmick ever again. However, right after Mark started wrestling as The Undertaker, I saw Dusty, and though he and I never shared any words about what happened with all of that, I think the looks that we shared and our faces said everything. I know that Dusty believed in me and I know he wanted me to be a success in the WWF. My thoughts took me back to the conversations that I had with Ivan in my early days of pro wrestling. His warnings of how the business could be cutthroat were apparent. Politics existed in wrestling and I was watching it from a front-row seat. My only guess was that Vince McMahon didn't want to put the gimmick on me. I couldn't help but wonder why Vince wasn't giving me a push in his company. Several of the road agents who worked for the WWF at the time were baffled that I wasn't being used differently on the roster. Guys like Jay Strongbow, Earl Hebner, Tony Garea, and Blackjack Lanza couldn't understand why my Black Bart character wasn't getting more media attention. Especially, after all the success that I had gained with the name in Florida and the Mid-Atlantic territories. Those four men know wrestling inside and out. In the middle of writing this book, I woke up one night and I couldn't go back to sleep. I turned on the television and I came across a wrestling show and the panel of experts was talking about The Undertaker's career. On that particular program, I recall Vince Russo and Bruce Pritchard taking credit for the idea. Of course, since it's Vince McMahon's company, he may say that it was his idea, however, I know that it came from Dusty. Dusty Rhodes came up with the creation of The Undertaker character and he intended it for me!

My run with the WWF ended in March of 1991. I was released on a day that approximately 16 other wrestlers were let go and one day away from Desert Storm, the conflict between The United States and the country of Iraq. We all heard the swirling rumors of budget cuts. However, there one other incident that happened right before my firing that probably didn't help my case. It was my refusal to do a job. In layman's terms, I was asked to wrestle in a match at Madison Square Garden at a television taping and I didn't do it. This incident occurred with Dave Hebner when I was about to leave the building for the day. The conversation I had with Dave also happened after I had already wrestled and lost eight times that same day. This is my recollection of what was said between the two of us.

"Bart, where are you going?" Dave asked as I was about to make my way out of the building.

"I'm leaving," I continued. "I was scheduled to wrestle in eight matches and that's what I did. I'm done, Dave."

"We need you for one more match," he insisted.

"Dave, if I lose one more time in this building tonight, these people won't believe that I can kill a fly," I grunted.

"What do you want me to tell Vince?" Dave wanted to know.

"Tell him whatever you are going to tell him, Dave," I replied.

I knew the office wasn't going to like that decision. Since I fulfilled my obligations of wrestling in the eight matches, I felt justified in not wrestling in another one. I had more than one meeting with Vince on the day that I was fired. In one of the meetings, I think he was trying to feel me out to see what kind of mood I was in. I was hoping I could piss him off, so he would take a swing at me and I could hit him back. However, I'm sure I wasn't the first wrestler that wanted to punch him. So, I imagine that he knew exactly how to handle tense situations like that. Of course, we talked about my contract or the fact that I no longer had one. At the end of my third and last meeting, I still didn't have a job wrestling for his company, so it didn't matter. I knew that it was time for me to leave his office. When the two of us finished talking, I stood up from my chair, turned around, and I walked over to the door. As I reached for the door handle, I heard Vince speak up.

"You should have come here when we called you the first time," he said in an arrogant tone.

I paused for just a moment and I wanted to turn back around and give him a piece of my mind. Instead, I acted as if I didn't hear him at all. I placed my hand on the doorknob and I turned it, I opened the door, and I walked out of his office without looking back. When I told my wife that I was fired, she cried. Bonnie didn't cry because she was upset, but she cried because felt relieved from the pressure we had felt from me working with the WWF. The money was good, the schedule was awful, and my position on the roster SUCKED!

Sometime later, I found out that the office talked about putting Ron Bass and me back together as the Long Riders. This was around the time I didn't come up for the tryout that J.J. invited me to. In the Summer of 1987, Blackjack Mulligan used the name, Sarah Jo Puckett in several of his promos on a regular basis. Supposedly, the Sarah Jo Puckett character was to be Blackjack's girlfriend. In the storyline, instead of partnering up with him, she was going to work with Ron and I as our manager. What I was told, my wife Bonnie was considered to play the role of Sarah Jo. Since I never went up there for my three-day tryout, all that never happened. The wrestling world never got to meet the Sarah Jo Puckett that Blackjack was talking about during his interviews on television.

In 1993 or 1994, after my time had ended with the World Wrestling Federation came to Dallas for a show at Reunion Arena. My two kids, Jessalynn and Joshua were very young at the time, but they wanted to go to the event. They both wanted to see The Undertaker. Mark had met my children already, so they were comfortable being around him and they felt like they knew him. When my kids had visited with him in the past, they all played together and got along very well. Mark made my kids feel special and important. Wrestling to me had always felt like one big family, since we had spent so much time with each other and our immediate families. Arriving to show that particular evening, I parked in the back just like the boys did. I then walked to the back door where they entered. I knew my kids wanted to see The Undertaker, but I was hoping to see several of my other friends there too that I had worked with over the years. Being stopped at the back door was not what I had expected. The security guard on duty and I had some words.

"Name, please. What is your name?" the security guard asked.

"It's Black Bart," I said. As he flipped a couple of pages on a clipboard that he had in his hands.

"I don't see it on here," he returned.

"I'm a wrestler too," I told him.

"I know who you are Bart, but your name isn't on the list," he said sharply.

It was about that time; my friend Ray Traylor noticed me. Ray was formerly Big Bubba in Mid-South, but now he went by the name Big Boss Man. He overheard the conversation I was having with the guy at the door.

"Bart, it's good to see you. What are you doing?" Big Boss Man asked.

"I'm trying to get in here to visit with the boys, but I'm getting pushback," I told him.

"Look here," Boss Man said to the security guard. "You better put this man's name on as my guest right now!"

"Yes Sir," the man replied.

"Give this man a little more respect than that!" Boss Man demanded. "He has done more for wrestling than your ass ever will!"

And just like that, what was taking me several minutes, took Big Boss Man a few seconds. It was great to see Ray and a bunch of the other guys. I briefly visited with Mark Henry and John Cena in the catering room. John and Mark were very kind and showed me nothing but love and respect. They made me feel appreciated. I have to admit it was nice. Talking to the guys brought back some good memories. I hadn't seen some of the boys for several years, but it didn't feel like that at all. With a few of them, it was like we picked right up where we left off on our last visit. It was especially that way with Brett Hart and

Jim Neidhart. I introduced them to my children along with the guys from Demolition. My visit backstage that day felt similar to a family reunion. Sharing smiles, laughter, and stories reminded me of the bond that we all shared when I was working with them.

Some of the guys that we had visited with could only stay a few minutes. Everyone had to get ready or record promos for their upcoming matches. It was now time to see The Undertaker, the man that Jessalynn and Joshua were looking forward to seeing again. I wanted to see Mark too, it had been a while since I had been around him. I knocked on the door.

"Come in," I heard a voice say through the other side of the door.

"Is everyone decent?" I asked as I poked my head inside the door.

"Yes," I heard Mark say as he was sitting down with his back turned to me.

"Hey Mark, my kids wanted to meet The Undertaker," I said cheerfully.

If Mark said anything at all, I don't remember it. He wasn't welcoming at all. I could tell that my kids felt his unenthused attitude as well. My daughter's face went from wearing a smile to a blank stare in seconds. My little boy was so intimidated that he stood between my two legs. He held on to one of my legs so tight that I could feel his little hands press into my thigh. When I realized that Mark's disposition wasn't going to change in the short time that we were with him, I knew it was time to go. I said goodbye, we turned around and the three of us walked out of his dressing room. From there, we left the building and we headed to where I parked my vehicle. I didn't go to the show as a fan; I wanted my children to see Mark as The Undertaker. How many people can say that they worked with one of the biggest stars in pro wrestling history?

After getting into my truck and situating my children in their seats, I sat in the parking lot for several minutes. I couldn't wrap my head around Mark's behavior. Some parts of the night were enjoyable, but my visit with Mark was a disappointment. It was a long ride home back to Fort Worth. I have to admit that my encounter with Mark at Reunion Arena bothered me. He was one of the guys who I felt I had a close friendship with. We spent time in the business and we spent time at each other's homes. My kids loved Mark and when he was around them, they always had a good time, he made them laugh, and they just thought the world of him.

I may never be able to completely put into words how Mark made me feel on my last visit with him. However, that feeling doesn't change of how much I appreciate what Mark has done for pro wrestling. The Undertaker is a legendary figure in our sport and he will never be forgotten!

CHAPTER 28 – JAMES BEARD & JOHNNY HAWK

After my run in the World Wrestling Federation came to an end, I was able to jump back into the mix of working for World Championship Wrestling in the Spring of 1991. As far as large wrestling companies that were in operation at the time, WWF and WCW were about it. There were other places for wrestlers to work in the United States, but those promotions were not thriving as they once had and many of them couldn't stay afloat. A lot of the guys that I knew stopped going to Puerto Rico after Bruiser Brody was killed there. A lot of the wrestlers from the States were disgusted with how that incident was handled. Many of the boys didn't feel safe there and I neither did I. I had only gone there one time after that happened.

My stay this time in WCW only lasted five months. The work was steady and I was grateful for that, but I would be lying if I said I liked how I was being used as a talent there. Again, just as it was in the WWF, I was wrestling against guys that I had known since I had started in this business. I had a lot of matches regularly with guys like Sam Houston, Dustin Rhodes, Michael Hayes, and Jimmy Garvin, and once again I was a job guy. When it came to my role in the sport, it wasn't always consistent. Sometimes I was on top and then other times I was on the bottom. Even though, it bothered me that my skills as a wrestler were not being utilized to my potential, I played it off the best I could. It truly was a roller coaster ride at times for me. One of the main differences between being at the top of the roster and being on the bottom of it is the pay. The times that I was wrestling on the mid-card or in the main event, I was making great money. The challenge came in the way of finances when that next wrestling opportunity didn't want to give me a push.

When I wrestled for WCW this time, Dusty Rhodes was the booker. At some point he had put me in a team with Dutch Mantel and Randy Colley called The Desperados. The working chemistry the three of us had with each other was apparent to Dusty. Dusty thought we could take our characters further than the ring. That was when he presented us with an idea to do a television show of the same name as our tag team. I didn't have to think twice about the opportunity. It was being produced by the Turner Broadcasting Station and the intention was for Fox Television to pick it up. I thought the sitcom was going to be entertaining and since it came from Dusty, I had high hopes for the project to be a success. Soon after the idea was pitched, we started shooting the pilot in a ghost town near the Carolina mountains. The genre of the show was a western comedy and our characters were loosely based on The Three Stooges. Randy was to play the protégé and it was up to me and Dutch to teach him how to be a real cowboy!

However, not everyone at WCW was excited about the proposal. It was disappointing to find out that The Nature Boy Ric Flair was making the most noise. At this time, the television program on TBS was 90 minutes long, and Ric was the biggest star on the show. He was getting 30 minutes of air-time. I couldn't understand why it bothered him so much that Dutch, Randy, and I were getting a television show outside of the wrestling program. This is how I was told the scene played out when Ric went to Ted Turner's office.

"What can I do for you, Ric?" Ted asked.

"Are you kidding me?" Ric asked.

"Am I kidding you about what?" Ted continued. "I'm not sure what you are talking about. Can you please explain why you are so upset?"

"Are you going to give a TV show to those three jabronis?" Ric asked angrily.

"Who are the three jabronis that you are referring to,

Ric?" Ted questioned.

"Mantel, Bart and Cooley. Those three jabronis!" Ric stated.

For some time, I thought that everything was going as planned. We had several days of filming and I was under the impression the first show was being produced. So, when I received a phone call from the producer of the show one day when I was at home, I was a bit surprised.

"Hello," I answered.

"Hello Bart, it's John from The Desperados production team," he said.

"Hey, John. What's happening?" I wanted to know.

"Bart, I have some bad news," he mentioned.

"What kind of bad news?" I questioned.

"The show has been canceled," John sighed.

"Why?" I asked.

"Ric Flair wasn't happy about the show. He spoke to Ted," he explained.

"Ric wasn't happy about it. What does he have to do with anything?" I inquired.

"I'm sorry, Bart," he replied.

As I hung up the phone, I felt a sinking feeling in my stomach. I was upset because I believed that the sitcom that we were putting together had merit and could have set us up for life. I have to admit that I was counting on it to be the break that I most desperately needed. Especially, since my last couple of runs in wrestling didn't go as I had planned. For years I resented Ric for doing that. I had begged Dusty to put me in a match with him just so I could kick his ass, but he wouldn't do it. The resentment I had toward Ric lasted for years. I give all the credit to my Lord and Savior Jesus Christ for helping me with that one. I was able to forgive Ric and when I did, it felt like the weight of the world was lifted off my shoulders. Just a few years ago, I ran into him at a wrestling convention and I was able to visit with him and hug him. I haven't thought about that show and what Ric did to stop it until I started working on this book. I was truly blessed with a peace and forgiveness that I couldn't have achieved on my own doing. Thank you, Jesus!

In August of 1991, I returned to Texas once again. Dallas was still running shows and doing a television program, but attendance had dropped off. The company working out of the Sportatorium at that time was called Global Wrestling Federation. As for the Von Erich brothers, Kevin didn't come around that much at all that year. At that time, the youngest brother Chris had already started his wrestling career. Chris didn't have the height or the body size to be a pro wrestler. I never wrestled against him. I heard that the asthma medicine that he took while growing up, stunted his growth and it made his bones brittle. Unlike Mike, Chris wanted to wrestle, but he physically couldn't do it. I didn't know Chris at all. When I first started working for Fritz in 1986, he was a teenager. Chris might have been about 15 or 16 years old then. He was always pretty quiet when he was around. When it came time for Chris to wrestle, the fans were curious to see what he could do inside the ring. Unfortunately, Chris was compared to his brothers and he couldn't come close to what they were able to do. I did hear that the boys who competed against him, took it extra easy on him. Sadly, just a few weeks after I had been back in Texas, Chris Von Erich, died from an apparent self-inflected gunshot wound to his head. Once again, the fans and the wrestlers were left wondering about the latest Von Erich tragedy, "How much more can this family take?"

Coming home also meant seeing familiar faces. Working with Skandor Akbar, Bil Irwin, Steve Simpson, Steve Casey, Johnny Mantell, John Tatum, Iceman King Parsons, and referee James Beard made my return to Dallas wrestling feel complete. I met James in 1986 and we had become good friends over the years and we are still close to this very day.

James is one of the nicest guys that I have ever met. His personality is so kind and warm, the first time that I met him, I felt like I had known him all my life. James may not be a wrestler, but he is one of the boys! By far, James Beard is the best referee to officiate a wrestling match!

There are several reasons why I say this about James. When he was inside the ring, he was always where he needed to be, and he was never in the way of the wrestlers. Having the opportunity to work with an array of referees over the years, this can be a challenge knowing two grapplers can be going in any direction at any given time. Another thing I respected about James, was how he handled the finish of the match. If Black Bart was slated to win, but my shoulders were on the mat and James counted to three, I lost the match. That didn't always go so well when James had to face the booker in the back of the building. I remember Gary Hart saying something to James as I walked past the two men.

"What happened out there, James?" Gary wanted to know.

"Bart had his shoulders on the mat for the three counts, so he lost the match," James replied.

"I see that, but Bart was supposed to win the match," Gary snarled.

"I'm well aware of that Gary. Do you expect me just to stop counting at two even though Bart is still lying on his back?" James asked.

"Yes! That's exactly what I want you to do," Gary returned.

"Well, I'm not going to do that! If Bart is supposed to win the match, he needs to get his shoulders off the mat before I count to three!" James insisted.

"Don't be difficult with me," Gary stated.

"I'm not being difficult Gary, I'm being realistic," James informed.

Another task that James did very well while working as a referee was communicating the finish of the match correctly. This was done from one dressing room to the other. I can't tell you how many times in my career when it came time to end the match, either me or my opponent zigged when one of us was supposed to zag. That comes down to the man in the striped shirt communicating the same message to all the people competing in the contest. James always got it right. Every time that he gave me instructions, they were clear and precise. He never bogged the conversation down with extra details which often confused some of the boys. James' finishes were always clean and believable.

I don't know exactly when James and I started acting like we had heat with each other. When we yelled at each other, the fans thought we were going to tear the house down at any moment. I guess one night I started arguing with James to see what he would do. In return, he yelled back. If I yelled at him again, he didn't stop either. We both found out that we had good working chemistry with each other inside the ring. Our confrontations at times were so intense that they didn't end until we were staring at each other with our noses touching.

"Bart, when I tell you to break, I need you to let go of your opponent and walk away," James insisted.

"Don't you have anything better to do, I'm trying to work!" I shouted.

"Don't make me tell you one more time!" he yelled back.

"What do you think you can do about it?" I wanted to know.

"Keep up your antics and you find yourself disqualified!" James screamed.

The two of us could do that a couple of times a night, night after night, over a long period. The audience expected James and I to banter and they all waited for one of us to throw a punch at each other. I think they may still be waiting! That simple action helped build heat between me and the fans, and for a heel wrestler, that was what I wanted. I never carried on like that with any other referee, it just worked with James and the fans ate it up! James was always a very good sport about it too.

When the wrestling territories were thriving, the wrestlers who worked in those areas were the top stars of the industry. As Vince McMahon and Eric Bischoff were competing for the top in-ring talent of the day, the smaller television markets struggled to keep permanent talent. To me, even though Global was a good product and it had the potential to grow, it didn't quite compare to Fritz Von Erich's World Class Championship Wrestling in the early to mid-80s. At this time, new or a lot of lesser-known wrestlers were getting the opportunity to showcase their skills on television. That was how I met John Bradshaw Layfield. However, when I met him, he wrestled as Johnny Hawk. In the beginning, he was greener than grass, but he had the willingness, work ethic, and the essential skills to make it in pro wrestling. As this book was being written, John's nearly three decades of working with World Wrestling Entertainment prove that. Not to mention the many different championships that he has held in that company including the WWE Title itself! One doesn't work for Vince that long by being lucky, a person works for Vince for that long by being the best, and that is what JBL is!

In October of 1992, after being trained by Brad Rheingans in Minnesota, John came to Dallas looking for a job. Verne Gagne's American Wrestling Association had already folded. With Verne closing up shop said only one thing: Vince was taking over pro wrestling and doing it in a very big way! Though Brad had a more decorated amateur career than he ever had professionally, his name goes a long way among the boys! Brad could wrestle! A wrestler doesn't make the U.S. Olympic team if he can't. When Brad turned pro, it was Verne and Billy Robinson who showed him the ropes. Having Brad's name on Johnny's resume, meant that Johnny probably knew a thing about wrestling. Johnny comes from a good wrestling pedigree, no doubt about it!

On the day that Johnny came to the Sportatorium, it was a Friday, and it just so happened that Lou Perez wasn't able to make the show that night. Lou was said to be Al Perez's younger brother, but they were actually cousins. Lou was supposed to wrestle against the then-current Champion Rod Price. Inside the old tin building, James and Akbar were working on reshuffling the card to cover for Lou's absence. There was a knock on the door and from the inside James opened it.

"Hello, how can I help you?" James asked.

"Hi there, I'm looking for a job," Johnny said.

"Come on in. My name is James," he said.

"My name is Johnny," he returned.

"That's Akbar over there," James said as he pointed to where he was sitting at a desk.

"We are just going over tonight's card and it appears that we might have an open spot," James explained.

"I'm ready and willing to work in any position you need me to fill," Johnny assured.

After talking to Johnny for several minutes, it didn't take James or Akbar very long to find out that the six-and-a-half-foot tall, 285-pound, former offensive lineman knew a thing or two about wrestling. So, the decision was made to put him inside the ring against Rod that same evening. James was going to officiate the bout, and if it became apparent that Johnny was in over his head by facing Rod, James could stop the match early. However, it didn't happen that way. John held his own against the Global Wrestling Federation Champion, and he was hired right there on the spot!

In the months leading up to Johnny Hawk arriving in Dallas, I was wrestling quite a bit with Johnny Mantell in the team we named The Rough Riders. Like me, Mantell is a journeyman wrestler who could do anything in the business of pro wrestling. At that time the two of us had been wrestling for nearly 20 years. When World Class Championship Wrestling was in its heyday, Mantell had a significant role for Fritz. When the incoming heel talent was hired by Fritz, they had to go through Mantell first to get to the Von Erich boys. Mantell and I complimented each other quite well, so, things were smooth and easy for us as a team. The North American Tag Team Titles was the prize that we had their eye on. Unfortunately, so did the Ebony Experience a team composed of Stevie Ray and Booker T. When our feud with the Ebony Experience came to an end, Mantell and I were left holding the belts. We were also ready for new challengers and that was when we were introduced to The Texas Mustangs: Johnny Hawk and Bobby Duncum Jr. I worked with Bobby's father in my beginning days while wrestling for the Crocketts. Bobby had a reputation for being tough as nails, and Junior inherited every drop of his daddy's fortitude!

I will never forget the very first time that Johnny and I stepped in the ring with The Texas Mustangs. I can't forget it if I wanted to. As things were progressing in our match and the momentum was building, I was struck by something, literally and figuratively. It came in the form of Johnny Hawk's fist! As I called the match, Hawk followed my instructions, but every time before he took his bump, he punched me in the face with sufficient force. In wrestling, we call that getting tattered. When I could get near the corner where my partner Johnny Mantell was standing, I filled him in on what had just happened.

"That little piss ant, Hawk just tried to punch my lights out," I said as I tried to get my wits about me.

"Come on, Bart it can't be that bad," Mantell said with a grin.

"I'm telling you the truth. They are really me hitting out there," I assured.

"In all the years you've been doing this Bart, you can't handle a stiff wrestler?" he asked while laughing.

I returned to the center of the ring and I tangled with Hawk a little longer. I ate a couple more of his knuckle sandwiches before he tagged out to Bobby. I have to admit it, I was relieved when Bobby entered the contest until he gave me some of the same medicine that Hawk had. At first, Bobby and I were going through the motions and performing basic moves. It was when I started calling for some takedowns was when I started to see stars again. Trust me! These were not the stars in the sky! After I performed a shoulder tackle and before Bobby hit the mat, he hit me so hard that my head rattled! I returned to my corner to speak with Mantell about the punches I had received once again.

"He's doing it too!" I exclaimed.

"He's doing what?" Mantell questioned me with a sarcastic tone.

"Bobby is punching me too," I shouted.

"What's wrong Bart? Have you forgotten how to handle a greenhorn?" He asked sounding arrogant.

"Okay Mantell, you get your ass in here!" I insisted.

Mantell took my place and shortly thereafter Hawk traded places with Bobby. Mantell and Hawk squared off and I watched my partner set up a move by grabbing Hawk's arm and tossed him into the ring ropes. As Hawk returned from the ropes, he hit Mantell so hard with a shoulder tackle that it sent him sailing over the top rope! My partner ended up landing on top of a table on the outside of the ring. I looked at Mantell as I smiled from ear to ear.

"I told you. Didn't I say that they were stiff?" I asked

sarcastically.

"Yes, you did," Mantell returned.

"It's not so funny anymore, is it?" I wondered.

"These guys have a lot to learn," he said.

"They need to be smartened up!" I insisted.

Mantell and I worked with Bobby and Hawk quite a bit back then. In wrestling, we called it "putting on the polish." The two men knew how to wrestle, they just needed to be fine-tuned. Bobby and John were destined to be superstars. It is no accident that Johnny Hawk (John Bradshaw Layfield) has had the career that he has had in pro wrestling. JBL is truly ONE-OF-A-KIND! Unfortunately, Bobby died in the year 2000 at the age of 34 from an accidental overdose. Just like his daddy; Bobby Sr. I believe that Junior could have had a long and successful career in wrestling as well. Sadly, with Bobby Junior dying so young, the world will never know what he could have become in the sport. I truly believe that he was headed for greatness as well!

CHAPTER 29 - KERRY VON ERICH

What can I say about Kerry Von Erich? He looked like a million bucks, and he was a nice guy! When I started working for his father in 1986, Kerry already had his motorcycle accident. For the next eight months, Kerry recovered from a severe foot injury that he suffered in that collision. It was years later when I found out the extent of damage that he endured. The doctors did everything they could to save his right foot, but when Kerry reinjured it while going down some stairs during the recovery process, the medical staff had no other choice other than to amputate it. While Kerry recovered, he made television appearances and did some commentary for the televised matches, but his absence from competing hurt ticket sales. Fritz did everything he could to keep the loss of Kerry's foot a secret, but eventually, that information got out to the boys and to the public. After my run in the World Wrestling Federation, I started to work with Kerry a lot more and I gained an enormous amount of respect for him and his ability to overcome his challenges. Kerry was always known to be a very gifted athlete, but I think all those who were around him after the real truth came out about his injury, found out how truly gifted Kerry was.

Kerry and I crossed paths in the WWF. His run with Vince McMahon lasted longer than mine did, plus he had a much better spot on the roster than I had. While working for Vince, Kerry wrestled as The Texas Tornado. I would have liked for him to keep the Kerry Von Erich name since it was so recognizable then. He was all over the wrestling magazines, so, Kerry was a much bigger star than just in the state of Texas. However, I'm sure he didn't have much of a say in that. He started wearing what looked like tassels from the tops of his boots. They were kind of stylish, but since Kerry had a bit of a stiff limp after he lost his foot, he used the tassels to distract from that. While Kerry was there in the WWF, he had a couple of good series with some big-name opponents. I think the angle between him and Curt Hennig is the one that fans may remember the most. They had some classic battles for the Intercontinental Title. The WWF put that belt on Kerry and he held it for two months before losing back to Curt in November of 1990. For the next six weeks, he and Curt went at it in some heated matches until the company switched gears. Curt was put into an angle with the British Bulldog and Bret Hart, and Kerry went into a series of matches with The Million Dollar Man Ted DiBiase.

Ted was another opponent that Kerry worked with for a good bit of time. They had some spots on television, but for nearly two months they traveled North America and entertained spectators in every venue where they wrestled each other at. However, when Kerry and Ted were finished with their storyline, Kerry bounced around the United States and wrestled an array of talent. He wasn't getting squashed, but he wasn't on the top of the card either. Kerry didn't hold another title with the company, and his role with Vince McMahon played its course in the summer of 1992. I don't know all the particular details that led to Kerry parting ways with the WWF, but there were plenty of stories floating around to keep enough of the boys wondering.

When Kerry returned to Dallas a couple of months later, he seemed a bit embarrassed about being released by the WWF. By this time, I had known Kerry for a while and he seemed different to me. He had a certain degree of humility that I had never seen in him before. I imagine that his world was turned upside down when he worked with the WWF. Having to pay the bill, plan for travel and lodging can be taxing. When I had to do that, I realized if it wasn't for how the boys helped each other, I never would have survived. Kerry might have come to that same conclusion. Before working for Vince, he worked in a safe bubble that his father created for him with preferential treatment. He finally got to see what the wrestling world was really like. I don't know who smartened him up to the business, but someone surely did. It was like Kerry finally understood storytelling and wrestling psychology. He finally realized that it wasn't about kicking everyone's ass and making himself look good. His entire attitude was completely different. Kerry was one of the most charismatic wrestlers of his time. He was friendly to the fans, to the boys, and everybody seemed to like him. Kerry changed his wrestling style after he lost his foot and he adapted more of a ground game. Sometimes it was easy to forget that he was missing part of his foot because of what he was still able to do during a match.

Kerry might have tried to keep a good appearance on the outside, but those who knew him well could see that he wasn't himself. Being fired by the WWF weighed on him heavily and it was no secret that he and his wife Cathy were separated. Kerry feared that his marriage was ending. We all knew that situation was affecting him deeply. There was also talk of Kerry having legal issues. Ultimately, he thought that he would pay a stiff penalty if and when he went to court. Some of his friends thought he blew a lot of that trouble out of proportion, but for Kerry it was what he thought he might be facing. So, it was obvious that he was dealing with some stressors. Let's not forget that three of Kerry's brothers died since 1984. The grief and depression that comes from losing a loved one can derail anyone. Despite everything that Kerry had to deal with, he went on the best that he could.

Kerry and I started working against each other in a feud while wrestling for the Global Wrestling Federation. Before our in-ring battles started we drew the fans into our story emotionally by using some simple wrestling psychology tactics. Every time either of us was doing an interview, we attacked one another. Our altercations were so intense that the other guys wrestling on those shows had to rush out and try to pull us apart. These segments were always so physical and since we wanted them to look realistic, they were. Some problems occurred when newer wrestlers were coming out to stop us that were inexperienced in this type of a spot. There were many times that Kerry and myself took a punch to the face or a finger in the eye because the rookies didn't know what they were doing. Kerry and I didn't just attack each other on television, we did it at the small shows throughout the week as well. We fought and harassed each other for almost six weeks until we stepped into the ring together.

The fans were eating up what Kerry and I were dishing out, and slowly but surely, we all noticed that the crowds were increasing at the shows. This was a thrill for me because the excitement that once filled the Sportatorium, hadn't been present for such a long time. The matches that we attempted to have at the beginning of our series ended in double count outs and disqualifications. These kinds of finishes added to the fan's anticipation of wanting to see more matches with the two of us. In wrestling there is a formula that works well with feuds. Usually, a conflict in wrestling starts slow and it builds up to the extravagant gimmick matches, but we did it the opposite way. At this time, we were planning for the moment. The promotion was desperately trying to save the wrestling business in the North Texas area.

Our first matches started in the cage. The stipulation was that the winner would be the first person to exit through the cage door! In our first steel cage match, it looked like a battle to the death for the two of us. In the end, we were both covered in blood and beaten. Kerry was laid out in the middle of the ring and without much of a struggle, I escaped from the cage. My feet hit the floor first and I was awarded the victory. The fans went nuts for a couple of reasons. The first reason was that the match was damn good, and the second reason was because they were expecting their hero to win and he just got beat! I don't think the fans were expecting that. We planned to move toward lumberjack, bull rope, and whatever else we could come up with. The stuff that we did in that feud just kept drawing the fans into what we were selling! When Kerry and I returned to the dressing room we spoke.

"What did you think about that, Kerry?" I asked.

"The crowd was really into it," he replied.

"It's like taking candy from a baby. We made it look easy!" I exclaimed.

"Our matches lately have been great," he said.

"Kerry, we could have done this stuff years ago. We could have saved this territory if you and your brothers cooperated with us," I continued. "You guys were so concerned about being on top and looking good. There is a reason, why we bump, do spots, sell, and use phycology."

"I hear you, Bart. I do," Kerry conveyed.

"Hey, let's go out tomorrow night and do it again," I grinned.

"You got it, but tomorrow night I'm kicking your butt," he promised.

"You better bring a sack lunch," I laughed.

I was having a good time with Kerry in this angle. He had improved so much since the last time that we had worked together. I was glad to be in a feud with him. I could be in the ring with Kerry and he wasn't splitting my head into two pieces with the Iron Claw. Seeing stars was no longer a common practice after receiving his Discus Punch. He still struggled with his interviews a bit, but he was 80 percent of a better worker when he returned home after wrestling for the WWF. I was having a lot of fun working with Kerry, more than I ever had with Kevin. Finally, the familiar excitement that we all once knew was back in the air at the Sportatorium. Referee James Beard and I talked about the resurgence of pro wrestling in Dallas.

"Damn James! It's looking like the old days out there!" I exclaimed.

"It appears that way indeed," James replied.

"The people are coming to see the magic!" I shouted.

"Something is different," he grinned.

"And there is nothing wrong with that," I returned

"There is nothing wrong with that at all," James said.

There were several reasons why the embers were getting heated up in Dallas again. Kerry was back, he and I were having great matches, and the office had good talent and good booking. The marketing strategy being used at the Sportatorium at this time was different than in previous years. Fans paid for parking and the concessions, but the tickets to the shows were free. We were filling up that old venue for the first time in a long time. Despite the free tickets upon entry, the bills were getting paid. On the outside looking in, all appeared to be just fine. The boys were happy, and the fans were happy, however, Kerry was not. To me, it seemed as if he was drifting away from us a little by little. From time to time one us would ask him how he was doing, but he always told us what we wanted to hear. Kerry put on his best-looking poker face and we all fell for it. Like I mentioned, we knew Kerry was dealing with some personal problems, but maybe we didn't understand the severity of his pain.

In February of 1993, I went to the Sportatorium late one Friday afternoon. I remember walking into the building and thinking something wasn't right, but I couldn't put my finger on it. I did my normal routine and went to the dressing room. It didn't take too long for some of the other wrestlers to arrive as well. Wrestling on the card that night was Booker T, Stevie Ray, Tim Brooks, Steve Dane, Johnny Hawk, Bobby Duncum Jr., and several others. Mike Davis and I shared some words and visited with each other like we usually did. Within minutes after the boys said their hellos and began getting ready for the show, I noticed that Akbar had made his way into the room. Knowing Akbar for all the years that I had, I could tell right away that something was on his mind. He had an unsettling blank look on his face that said almost everything before he opened up his mouth. When Akbar finally spoke up, the dressing room was quieter than a church service.

"Hey guys, I need to tell you all some very sad news," Akbar continued as he tried to hold back the tears. "We lost Kerry. Kerry took his life yesterday," he sighed as his head dropped down.

Akbar liked the Von Erich boys, Kerry in particular. The news hit him and the boys hard. I closed my eyes and I said a prayer. The names and faces of his loved ones passed through my mind. I wasn't shocked, but at the same time I had trouble accepting the news. We were told that Kerry shot himself in the chest at his father's ranch. Three suicides! For a few moments no one said a word. As tough as I have known Akbar to be, he didn't show any signs of it that day. His face was covered with sadness and disbelief. I knew he was hurting. Other guys in the room had blank looks on their faces too. It was like the news hit us like a ton of bricks. I made my way out of the building and I retreated to my car. I sat in the driver's seat and I put my head back. I felt a huge sadness in my heart and the tears began to roll down my cheeks. I truly had a hard time wrapping my head around everything. Not just the news about Kerry, but all of the Von Erich family's tragedies. I don't know how long I sat in my vehicle, but when I started to hear the chatter of fans walking through the parking lot, I knew I had to regain my composer. I couldn't let the fans see a heel cry. I knew it was going to be a long night. As usual, the show went on as it always did. Wrestlers have always been good about taking care of the business at hand, and sorting through the mess and figuring it out later. When it was time for the matches to start, the bell rang, and we wrestled. Whether it was a good day or a bad day, we always wrestled. NO MATTER WHAT!

I was honored to know and to have wrestled against the Von Erichs. I still remember the times that I shared with my daddy watching Fritz when I was just a kid. It had always been a dream of mine to be a wrestler, but my career exceeded all of my expectations when I was hired by Fritz. Kerry was a great guy and I was proud of the work that we did in the ring together. I know that Kerry's death angered a lot of people because he chose a permanent solution for a temporary problem. There is no telling what he could have done had he lived longer. I truly believe that he could have been a positive inspiration for other amputees. Kerry's personality was so special and because of it he could connect with people in ways, that others just couldn't do. People are always asking me when World Class Championship Wrestling ended in Dallas. The promotion changed names and owners so many times, it clouded everyone's perspective. Many argue that it was 1986 or 1991, but World Class Championship Wrestling died on February 18th, 1993, and that's the God's honest truth!

CHAPTER 30 - NECRO BUTCHER

If the word wrestling is on the marquee outside at the venue, there needs to be wrestling inside the ring! Call me old-school, but if you want tacks, glass, ladders, barbed wire, and light tubes you better get your ass down to the hardware store! I understand that Death Match wrestling is extremely popular with this generation's fanbase, but it doesn't fly with me! I don't know what to call it, but it sure the hell isn't the pro wrestling that I grew up with. When a person has access to any kind of weapon that they want to use, it's not wrestling!

Back in my day, we had gimmick matches. There was a steel cage, bunkhouse, bull rope, taped fist, and barbed wire matches. The barbed wire was filed down. We weren't trying to kill our opponent; we were trying to bring people into the building. The style of matches I just mentioned was about as hardcore as I ever took wrestling. Cactus Jack and Terry Funk pushed the envelope with their style of wrestling, but I believe they did that to extend their careers. Who knows what the wrestlers are trying to do these days? To me, it looks like they are truly trying to kill each other and that isn't wrestling!

In the late 90s when my career in pro wrestling started to slow down, I got a full-time job working at a nuclear plant in Glen Rose, Texas. Along with wrestling in a few spot shows on the weekends, I also trained whoever wanted to become a wrestler. I ensured all my students that by the end of their training with me, they could wrestle anywhere, or anyone. I passed on the same teaching and training that Ivan the Terrible had passed onto me. During that time, I trained several young men. One of my students was Dylan Summers. Dylan was married and had three small children. He was in the Army and was stationed at Fort Hood located in Killeen, Texas. Killeen is about 55 miles southwest of Waco and about 150 miles from Fort Worth. All my students knew where I stood with my convictions about wrestling. I made it quite clear that I hated Death Match wrestling! So, to find out that I trained a wrestler that is synonymous with Death Match wrestling is beyond my conception! Dylan Summers is Necro Butcher!

Training several people at one time was common for me back then. My trainees arrived at my home in North Texas on a Friday, and they stayed with me until late Sunday evening or sometimes until Monday morning. Driving in from other states to learn from me was not out of the question. I even had a young man drive from Ohio to train with me in my backyard. Behind my house, I had a professional wrestling ring and a trampoline. During the training sessions, students traded time between the two so they all could get continuous practice. Sometimes on one weekend, I could have up to eight people go through my seminars. I had a couple of wrestlers that also helped me that went by the names of Canyon and The Grave Digger. They worked with the beginners inside the ring, and I gave them direction and advice from the outside of it. They acted for me the same way that Buddy and Jack had done for Ivan. From time to time, I got in there with the trainees if I felt like I needed to, but having Canyon and Grave Digger take most of the bumps saved my body from having to do it. My training was repetitious and long. There were times that we could stay on one move, hold, or counter for a couple of hours. Practicing a particular move multiple times only ensured my students that they would eventually become as natural with wrestling as if they were with walking down the street. There is so much to know about pro wrestling, and it takes time to ingest all of it. My students trained with me for a full year before they went out on their own.

At the end of a training day, when it came time to sleep, some of my students rested in their cars, while others slept underneath the stars. Some, especially Dylan and his family stayed inside my home. I had spare bedrooms to accommodate the whole family. Over the years, I have trained quite a few people. I have never felt as close to any of them, as I did with Dylan. His wife and my wife Bonnie got along so well too. When Dylan's wife was not taking care of their children, she was in the kitchen with Bonnie helping her prepare meals for the entire crew. When Dylan first came to train at my home, I didn't know him at all. However, in a short period, his family felt like my family. The way that he picked up on the attributes of wrestling was astonishing. He was able to put matches together and he understood the psychology of the in-ring sport. He knew wrestling as well or better than a lot of the pros that I have met throughout the years. I could not have been prouder of him!

The last day of Dylan's training is one for the memory books. His behavior that day was so out of character that I questioned if I knew him as well as I thought that I did. I was in my backyard running through some drills with some of my other pupils. I had expected Dylan to be with us already because it was a big day for him. Dylan was going to wrestle one last time before he officially turned pro. He couldn't be found anywhere, and my students told me they had no idea where he might have taken off to. After some more time passed, he finally arrived. I was on the outside of the ring with a couple of my students while a few of them were inside practicing with each other. I looked at Dylan and he had a strange smirk on his face as he walked my way as if had a pair of grapefruits in his pants. In one of his hands, he carried a bag. As Dylan made his way next to the ring, he looked in my direction and gave me a hard stare. At this time, he never spoke a word.

"What the hell is this guy doing?" I thought to myself.

Dylan climbed into the ring and stood there silently gazing at the other trainees. No one had a clue of what was about to happen. Suddenly, he lifted his arm that held the bag and he proceeded to pour its contents out onto my wrestling mat. Hundreds if not a thousand metal tacks that you can buy at an office supply store were lying in the ring. I quickly yelled out to him.

"Stop! Stop!" As my voice got louder.

"What should we do Bart?" One of my students leaned out of the ring and asked me.

"We aren't doing anything! Dylan, you will get every one of those tacks out of my ring right now!"

Dylan said something back to me, but I couldn't make any sense of what he mouthed. He didn't need to say anything else because his attitude and his disregard for my request said everything. I was determined to put an end to this. Since Dylan ignored my first command to clean up all the tacks, it was time to play hardball. My other trainees looked at me for direction and at the same time, they tried to keep their eyes on Dylan who was highly unpredictable at this moment. Still, my students stood in the ring with him waiting for his next move. I spoke up once again.

"Since you are so defiant and refuse to clean up the mess that you've made, I want all of my boys right now to show you what it's going to feel like to have all those tacks in your body!" I shouted. "Slam him into the tacks. I hope you like it, Idiot!"

My students cornered Dylan and one after another my young wrestlers picked him up and threw him onto the sharp metal tacks that were waiting to pierce his body. There was no way for him to create any offense since my guys outnumbered him significantly. When it seemed as if the punishment was sufficient, I told my students to stop. That was how Dylan's last day of training ended. It was not quite the way that I expected it to go. I went over to my utility room and I found a broom and a dustpan. I walked back to the ring where Dylan was crawling around on the mat, and I put the two items by his side. As I looked down at him, I could see he was in agony, I couldn't believe all of the tacks that were stuck into his body. To me, he looked like the Rhinestone Cowboy, but not as cool.

On top of the training that I was doing, I was also running small spot shows in towns outside of Fort Worth with a gentleman by the name of Rick Fowler. Wrestling in places like Weatherford, Granbury, and Mineral Wells was where a lot of my newbies got their start. We set the ring up in a small community center or even a gymnasium when we could. These opportunities were great for someone breaking into the business. Most of the time, our shows were put on for small crowds. Performing in a setting like that helped take the pressure off those who didn't have a great deal of experience wrestling in front of people. It was set up just like the way that I learned in my early days.

Some time passed and I put on a show in Plano, Texas. I cannot tell you what possessed me to book Dylan for that show, but I did. I guess I wanted to give him another chance. I did care about him, and I believed that he was one heck of a wrestler. I made it clear to him once again on how I felt about the Death Match wrestling style. Surely, he wouldn't try any of the same shenanigans he did previously. How wrong could I be? I didn't know this at the time, but after Dylan turned pro, he started wrestling with different independent companies doing more of a hardcore style of wrestling rather than the style that I had taught him. When Dylan arrived at the building for my show we spoke for a moment. I couldn't tell if he was upset about something or just having a bad day. His gear for the day wasn't your traditional wrestling attire either. Dylan showed up wearing cut-off jean shorts and a t-shirt along with sneakers instead of wrestling boots. Since his mood wasn't what I was used to, instead of putting him in a match with one of the boys, I changed things up at the last minute. The plan was for Dylan to run into the ring and interfere in my contest. At that point, he was to give me a chair shot to my stomach. The reason for attacking my stomach instead of targeting my head, was that I wasn't planning to bleed that day. If a wrestler's head meets a metal chair, a metal post, or a metal anything, blood is expected to appear. It's just part of the game.

After Dylan was to finish his assault on me, I was to make a comeback and I'd chase him out of the ring with my banding iron. However, he went off script again and our original plan was thrown out the window. Instead of attacking me in the stomach, he stood right in front of me and swung the chair as if it were a baseball bat. When the chair connected with my skull, it wasn't the flat side, it was the bottom side. The bottom side of the chair has all the hard edges and corners. After Dylan hit me, he dropped the chair at our feet, and he started to laugh. The sirens went off inside my heads. The pain was horrific! I went down on my knees. I guess he wanted to knock me out and add it to his resume. Instantly, blood started running down my face and as it dripped onto the mat. It started to form a small puddle. Immediately, my wife came to the side of the ring. Bonnie had seen me wrestle a thousand times and not one time did she ever come to the ring to check on me. I was physically and mentally out of it at this point, however, when I saw Bonnie come to my aid, I knew this was a bad situation.

"Are you okay?" She asked.

"I'm hurting pretty badly, Bonnie," I replied. "I think the S.O.B. tried to kill me."

"It did appear that way," She hissed.

Dylan's lack of regard for my well-being pissed me off! I had enough. As I got back to my feet, I grabbed the chair with one hand on my way back up. Dylan was standing nearby, so, I swung my weapon and hit him with it as hard as I could. Dylan started collapsing, but he didn't go all the way down to the mat, so, I hit him again. It was at that point he dropped to his knees, and I hit him again. When I did that, the chair wrapped around his head like a horseshoe. It was almost like I was in a dream state and there were moments I thought I was going to pass out. Bonnie was upset! She got on the apron of the ring, and she yelled at Dylan incessantly. As I was trying to pull myself together, at some point Dylan left the ring and went back to the dressing area. Within a few minutes, I made my way back there too. I wanted to talk to Dylan all by myself. Once inside, I found him in one of the corners of the room lying on the floor. I walked over to him and at first, I didn't know if he was passed out, asleep, or in outer space.

"Dylan, get your ass up," I shouted. Get up damn it."

"Huh? What?" He mumbled.

"Be glad I don't have my shotgun with me right now!" I yelled. Hello! Earth to Dylan!

"Uh," he babbled.

Bonnie met me inside the dressing room and insisted on me going to the hospital. I didn't argue with her. When I entered the emergency room, the staff didn't know if I had been in a car accident or I had been shot. I was a bloody mess! That day I received 16 staples in my head to seal up the wound that I suffered at the hands of Dylan.

The last time that I have ever saw Dylan was when he was lying on the floor of the dressing room. We never spoke again. I had a strong disdain for him. However, I didn't know how bad until 2008, when the movie, "The Wrestler," with Micky Rourke came out. Dylan had a role in the movie. I had no clue that he was going to be in it, but as he appeared on the screen the resentment that I had for him came back stronger than ever. Since then, and as my relationship with Jesus Christ has grown, I have come to forgive Dylan for what he did to me. I've learned in life that you don't stop loving people just because they disappoint you, you love them despite it. Thank you, to my Lord and Savior Jesus Christ for helping me do that!

CHAPTER 31- MY FINAL THOUGHTS

I have been going to church since I was a little kid. Attending weekly service and going to my bible classes was important to my parents, but more than anything else, they wanted me to have a relationship with God. The scriptures I share here have strengthened and guided me throughout my entire life!

John 3:16

"For God so loved the world that he gave his one and only Son, that whoever believes in him shall not perish but have eternal life".

Romans 5:8

"But God shows his love for us in that while we were still sinners, Christ died for us."

At the age of 16, I was baptized. It was a commitment that I felt strongly about and the decision brought great peace to my soul. A week after my purification, I shared my testimony with our parish. During my talk, the pastor at the Pentecostal church where my family attended leaned over toward me. While whispering he said that I couldn't play sports and serve my Lord and Savior at the same time. I had never heard that before. As I stared into the pastor's eyes, I turned my attention back to the people that were sitting in the pews. I pulled away from the pastor, stood up straight and I thanked everyone for coming. When I was done talking, I set the microphone down, and I walked out of the church. I was hurt. I knew that God loved me and I believed that he gifted me with my talents. My parents and I knew that there was a lot worse things that I could have been doing as a teenager. Sports wasn't one of them! That wasn't the last time that I stepped foot inside of a church, but it was the last one being of the Pentecostal denomination.

Luke 12:32

"Fear not, little flock, for it is your Father's good pleasure to give you the Kingdom."

My in-ring wrestling career continued up until 1999, but it seemed as if wrestling was over for me in 1994. I think that there was a part of me that thought it was going to last forever. When the Global Wrestling Federation in Dallas came to an end, my hope for pro wrestling to sustain in North Texas went away for me. Pro wrestling has been very good to me and I have been good to it. In my opinion, if I wanted anything from the sport, I had to put something into it. I did. I put a lot of blood, sweat, and time into professional wrestling. Trading in my football cleats for a pair of wrestling boots was the turning point for me. There was no other job that I wanted to seek out. I was willing to do whatever I needed to do to support my family, but I wanted to be able to do it pro wrestling. I achieved that.

My wife Bonnie did a fine job of taking care of our kids. She was a caring mother and she provided stability for our son and daughter when I wasn't there to do it myself. I know it must have been quite the burden for her to pull double-duty. I loved her with all my heart and we were very good for each other. Sadly, Bonnie passed away in March of 2005 due to complications of pneumonia. Me and my kids took her death extremely hard.

Psalm 34:18

"The Lord is near to the brokenhearted and saves the crushed in spirit."

Both of my children withdrew and they covered up their emotions with a lot of negative influences. It was difficult to communicate with them, and I was also mourning Bonnie's death. It really seemed as if our world was falling apart. The connection that my wife had with Jesselynn and Joshua was one that I never had with them. All the time that I was away from my home and all the traveling that I did for wrestling didn't help matters. Bonnie, was their rock and she was mine too. Bonnie was a great wife, mother, and friend, and she is missed by so many people to this very day.

Joshua 1:9

Have I not commanded you? Be strong and courageous. Do not be afraid; do not be discouraged, for the LORD your God will be with you wherever you go."

In October of 2005, I married my second wife Linda. Throughout my career, and especially after Bonnie's passing, my drinking got out of hand. Just when I thought it couldn't get any worse, it did. During my grief, if I was awake there is a good possibility that I was drunk. I don't think that I would have lived very long if it wasn't for me meeting Linda. She motivated me to make some major changes in my life. I finally let go of the alcohol and tobacco which has benefited my health. She is very good to me and for me! I know if Bonnie could have met Linda; she would give us her blessing.

Isaiah 41:10

"So do not fear, for I am with you; do not be dismayed, for I am your God. I will strengthen you and help you; I will uphold you with my righteous right hand."

Mike Davis was just like a brother to me. I loved him just as I did all of my siblings. He was more than a friend; he was my family. Mike was there for so many of the good times and so many of the bad times. His companionship on the road and throughout my career, sure did help when the bad days came my way. I hope I was the friend for him that he needed me to be. Mike died on Christmas Day in 2012, his passing was very difficult for me to deal with. He was a great person, friend, and wrestler. I was grateful to spend three decades of my life with him. I think of him often, and at certain moments I often imagine what Mike would say to me if he was still here.

I cannot express enough gratitude to God for blessing me with my friendship of Skandor Akbar. He was always so kind to me, and so giving of his time and advice. I swear a tear welled up in my eye the day he addressed me as a Ring General. It truly was one of the best compliments I have ever received! Akbar died in 2010, but I can still hear some of the truths that he shared with me while he was alive to this very day.

My friend Preacher was loyal. Never did I think that I would know him for as long as I did. The day that he and his biker friends walked into Ivan's gym. I am so glad that I didn't judge him by his appearance when I first met him. If I had done that, I would have missed out on a friendship that lasted the span of four decades. Our careers went in different directions, but we stayed in contact with each other from the first day that we met. Preacher was one tough dude! After suffering a stroke and a heart attack, he stepped into the ring to have a match at the age of 68. At 68, I could barely get my butt through the ropes. Preacher is in Heavan now, I will always remember him and I am glad that he was a part of my life. Preacher was a good example of loyalty for me.

Proverbs 17:17

"A friend loves at all times and a brother is born for adversity."

As I was in the middle of writing this book with Vinny, I was diagnosed with cancer. The initial news was quite the blow. I was overwhelmed with so many thoughts and concerns. After the shock wore off, I still had my faith and my love for my All-Mighty Father! I put my entire life in his care, and I know that he has me in the palm of his hand! My faith in Christ and the love for my family and friends drives me to never stop trudging!

Psalms 41:3

"The LORD sustains them on their sickbed and restores them from their bed of illness."

For my brothers and sisters in Christ, I know you understand everything that I am sharing on these pages. For those who want to have a relationship with God, and for whatever reason you feel that it's too late, IT'S NEVER TOO LATE! All you have to do is ask him, he loves more than you will ever know!

Psalm 107:10

"Oh, give thanks to the Lord, for he is good, for his steadfast love endures forever! Oh, that men would give thanks to the Lord for His goodness, and for His wonderful works to the children of men! For He satisfies the longing soul, and fills the hungry soul with goodness."

Thank you & God Bless You!

Photo by Peter Lederberg

Black Bart in Florida -1985

WORDS FROM VINNY BERRY

When the idea was brought to me about writing Bart's story, I was overwhelmed with other projects. I declined the offer, but when I got caught up, I asked if Bart was still looking for a writer. I obtained Bart's telephone number and I gave him a call. The first words out of his mouth were, "Vinny! I have been waiting for you to call me!" Come to find out, Bart had been wanting to work on a book for nearly a decade at that point, for many reasons, it never panned out. Before I ever agreed to do the project, I was already listening to his story and taking notes. The two of us started this book in March of 2022, and we present it to you now. We hope you find enjoyment from reading his stories as much as we enjoyed telling them! It has been a pleasure getting to learn about Bart's story. I knew who Bart was when he wrestled and I watched him as I was growing up. I would have never guessed then, that I would eventually write his book. I am grateful to call Bart my friend! THANK YOU, BART!

Photo courtesy of Vinny Berry

Vinny Berry & Black Bart in March of 2023

SPECIAL THANKS

A special thank you goes to my wife Sandy Berry. Your support and encouragement have been so appreciated through the entire time of this project. At one point in my life, I thought it was only my dream to become a writer, it is now clear to me that Sandy and I share the same dream for me! I LOVE YOU, HON!

Cover & Graphics – Alyssa Berry

Layouts – Wrestleville.com

Photography – Rick Harris, Jon-Paul Le Blanc & 4 Corners Photography, Mike Lano, M Roof Photography, Andrew Anderson, Duane Long, James Beard, Sam Houston, Greg Bowle, Mike Andrews, Peter Lederberg, Len Denton, Ric Davies, James Beard, Bill Irwin

Editor & Proof Reader – Cole Denckla

Special thanks *to Sam Houston, Denny Brown, Bill Irwin, John Bradshaw Layfield, Kevin Sullivan, Len Denton, Andrew Anderson, & James Beard*

Advice, Guidance & Support – Jeff Bonugli, John Cannon, Kenny Casanova, Scott Coyer, Rex Leach, Jenny Martinez, Gary Tomlin, & Keith Elliot Greenberg

Website: wrestleville.com

Dedicated to Philip, Carole, & Beth Berry

Lance by Chance
Wrestling as a Von Erich

Lance By Chance takes you back to the 1980's when World Class Championship Wrestling was at its best. Read about the Von Erich's, Gino Hernandez's death, Mike Von Erich's funeral, Kerry Von Erich's motorcycle accident, Chris Adams' troubles and why Fritz Von Erich thought it was necessary to create the Lance character. Find out about his time wrestling in Portland and in South African and what happened after he left Dallas. Read the story from the perspective of a man who never wanted to wrestle, but when he was offered the opportunity, he took the CHANCE!

ORDER YOUR BOOKS AT WRESTLEVILLE.COM
or on AMAZON

The Pro Wrestling Vault: Volume 1

This book contains 35 mini bios of wrestling veterans and stars on the rise. It is the first book in the two-volume series. Learn information about some of your favorite wrestlers plus many that you might not have even discovered yet. Read stories about Harley Race, Barrett Brown, Tim Storm, Tracy Smothers, Larry Hennig, Ricky Morton, CW Anderson, Shawn Hernandez, Bobby Fulton, Chazz Taylor, Chris Michaels, Bushwhacker Luke, and many others. All stories are told by the wrestlers themselves. The book also contains 400 photos from the independent wrestling scene and honors former champions from the National Wrestling Alliance!

ORDER YOUR BOOKS AT WRESTLEVILLE.COM

or on AMAZON

The Pro Wrestling Vault: Volume 2

The Pro Wrestling Vault: Volume 2, contains over 46 mini bios of wrestling veterans and stars on the rise. Stories include such wrestlers as Jazz, Kamala, Bobby Eaton, Thunder Rosa, Scott Casey, Kerry Morton, Justin Credible, Leilani Kai, PJ Black, Nikita Knight (aka Thea Hail from NXT) Mario Mancini, Blake Christian, Susan "Tex" Green, Dontae Smiley, The Northern Wrestling Federation, Madie Wrenkowski, and many others. Enjoy learning about your favorite stars. All the interviews were conducted and the stories were written by Vinny Berry, and told by the wrestlers themselves. A must read for everyone who loves pro wrestling!

ORDER YOUR BOOKS AT WRESTLEVILLE.COM
or on AMAZON

Printed in Great Britain
by Amazon

47210485R00188